POST-POSTMODERNISM

POST-POSTMODERNISM

or, The Cultural Logic of Just-in-Time Capitalism

Jeffrey T. Nealon

STANFORD UNIVERSITY PRESS

STANFORD, CALIFORNIA

Stanford University Press
Stanford, California

Printed in the United States of America on acid-free, archival-quality paper

Library of Congress Cataloging-in-Publication Data

Nealon, Jeffrey T. (Jeffrey Thomas), author.
  Post-postmodernism, or, The cultural logic of just-in-time capitalism / Jeffrey T. Nealon.
    pages cm
  Includes bibliographical references and index.
  ISBN 978-0-8047-8144-2 (alk. paper)
  ISBN 978-0-8047-8145-9 (pbk. : alk. paper)
    1. Culture—Economic aspects—United States. 2. Literature—History and criticism—Theory, etc. 3. Post-postmodernism—United States. I. Title. II. Title: The cultural logic of just-in-time capitalism.
  HM621.N427 2012
  149'.97—dc23
                                                              2011045584

Contents

Acknowledgments

As this book was written over an embarrassingly long time, it has incurred more debts than simple acknowledgments can hope to repay. First and foremost, Rich Doyle has helped me sort out, laugh off, and rethink all of this material in a way that makes me believe again in the productive politics of friendship. Gregg Lambert has likewise been there every step of the way, with just the right cocktail of encouragement and productive skepticism.

I'd also like especially to thank Fredric Jameson, who (at a crucial turning point in this writing) graciously came up to State College for a few days to hang out and talk to my graduate seminar. He greatly sharpened my sense of this material, as well as the stakes and directionalities where it might lead, even though I doubt he agrees unequivocally with where I've taken it.

Undoubtedly, many ideas populating these pages were stolen from the Penn State English Department theory reading group—Robert Caserio, Jonathan Eburne, Brian Lennon, and Janet Lyon. Indeed, the theft goes back to the earlier iteration of that group: Marco Abel, Tony Ceraso, Jeremiah Dyehouse, Elizabeth Mazzolini, John Muckelbauer, Dan Smith, and Evan Watkins. Who says it doesn't pay off to spend long hours at Zeno's?

Along the way, I got a lot of help thinking about these topics from Mona Ali, Bruce Andrews, Charles Bernstein, Michael Bérubé, Marc Bousquet, Pascale-Anne Brault, Claire Colebrook, Frank Donoghue, Grant Farred, Gregg Flaxman, Henry Giroux, Cecil Giscombe, Ann and David Gunkel, Doug Henwood, Shannon Hoff, Caren Irr, Jane Juffer, Amitava Kumar, John Leavey, Rick Lee, Todd May, John McGowan, Jennifer Mensch, Michael Naas, Chris Nealon, Cary Nelson, Johanna

Oksala, John Protevi, John Russon, Dennis Schmidt, Alan Schrift, Susan Searls-Giroux, and Cary Wolfe.

One of the great pleasures of the project was getting to know Emily-Jane Cohen from Stanford University Press. Thanks also to Tim Roberts and Cynthia Lindlof for the timely expertise they offered in getting the manuscript into print.

Prototypes of some of these chapters have appeared in the journals *Rethinking Marxism, Parallax, Symploke, jac, Postmodern Culture,* and *Theory & Event;* and a version of Chapter 1 appeared in Carsten Strathausen's edited collection, *A Leftist Ontology?* Thanks to those publications and their editors for so many helpful suggestions and so much encouragement along the way. Special thanks finally to Vitaly Komar for permission to use "Post-Art #1, Warhol" as cover art.

But in the end, this book owes itself to Leisha, Bram, and Dash—who are the inspiration for everything herein despite having had to withstand a decade of dinner conversations on its topics. Like Charles Olson's Maximus, "I have had to learn the simplest things / last. Which made for difficulties"; but I have finally learned what matters, and I have my family to thank for that. It all started with a dice throw in Vegas, and it's just intensified wild positivity from there. They prove every day that there's life in post-postmodernism.

Preface: Why Post-Postmodernism?

"Post-postmodernism" is an ugly word. And not in the sense that swear words or racial slurs are ugly, or even in the way that "rightsizing" or "outsourcing" are ugly words (which is to say, evasive spin-doctored words that try to paper over something foul). Post-postmodernism is, one might say, just plain ugly: it's infelicitous, difficult both to read and to say, as well as nonsensically redundant. What can the double prefix "post-post" possibly mean? Insofar as postmodernism was supposed to signal the end of modernism's fetish of the "new," strictly speaking, nothing can come after or "post-" postmodernism, which ushered in the never-ending end of everything (painting, philosophy, the novel, love, irony, whatever).

But at the same time, there are a number of things to recommend the title "Post- Postmodernism" over its undoubtedly more felicitous rivals—such as "After Postmodernism," "The End(s) of Postmodernism," "Postmodernism's Wake," "Postmodernism 2.0," "Overcoming Postmodernism," "Whatever Happened to Postmodernism?," and so on. For my purposes, the least mellifluous part of the word (the stammering "post-post") is the thing that most strongly recommends it, insofar as the conception of post-postmodernism that I'll be outlining here is hardly an outright overcoming of postmodernism. Rather, post-postmodernism marks an intensification and mutation within postmodernism (which in its turn was of course a historical mutation and intensification of certain tendencies within modernism).

So the initial "post" in the word is less a marker of postmodernism's having finally used up its shelf life at the theory store than it is a marker of postmodernism's having mutated, passed beyond a certain tipping point to become something recognizably different in its contours and workings; but in any case, it's not something that's absolutely foreign to whatever it was before. (Think of the way that a tropical storm passes a certain threshold and becomes a hurricane, for example: it's not a difference in *kind* as much as it is a difference in *intensity*—or, more precisely, any difference in kind is only locatable through a difference in intensity.) With its stammering inability to begin in any way other than intensifying the thing it's supposed to supersede, "post-postmodernism" is a preferred term for suggesting just such a super-postmodernism, hyper-postmodernism, or maybe a "late postmodernism," as opposed to the overcoming or rendering obsolete of postmodernism that would be implied by a phrase like "after postmodernism." Related and more pragmatic reasons to hang on to the moniker "post-postmodernism" might be that it has its own Wikipedia entry and that the term has been popping up everywhere from the *New York Times* to literary criticism journals, though it has been used in architectural circles for at least fifteen years.[1]

Indeed, postmodernism has seemingly been lingering at death's door, refusing to pass definitively, for quite some time: John McGowan, author of *Postmodernism and Its Critics* (1991), jokingly suggested to me in the early 1990s that my first book, *Double Reading: Postmodernism after Deconstruction* (1993), would be among the last suggesting that postmodernism was still an ongoing phenomenon. In 1997, John Frow made the fatal tense change official, asking "What Was Postmodernism?" in his *Time and Commodity Culture: Essays in Cultural Theory and Postmodernity*, though we should note that Brian McHale consciously repeated Frow's titling query in an essay a decade later in 2007, suggesting that there may be something about postmodernism that resists outright overcoming or obsolescence.

But for me the most compelling reason to hang on to the awkward "post-post" is that (as is clear from my title) I want to position this analysis squarely in the orbit of Fredric Jameson's authoritative work, *Postmodernism; or, The Cultural Logic of Late Capitalism*—which argues, among many other things, that postmodernism is best understood as a historical period of capitalist development rather than (or, really, as the prior ground of) understanding it as a style of artistic practice, a movement within various art and architecture discourses, or even a kind of zeitgeist. In short, I argue throughout that capitalism itself is the thing that's intensified most radically since Jameson began doing his work on postmodernism in the 1970s and '80s. The "late" capitalism of that era (the tail end of the cold war) has since intensified into the "just-in-time" (which is to say, all-the-time) capitalism of our neoliberal era.

Following out Jameson's core observation—postmodernism named a stage of capitalist development before it named anything else—I take this to be a book that travels very much in the orbit of his founding texts, but it's most certainly not a book "about" Jameson (after the introductory chapter, there's relatively little overt discussion of his texts); nor is it (Jah forbid) a tome that attempts to distill a critical template from Jameson's texts and then applies it willy-nilly to other material. Rather, this book takes its primary theoretical and methodological cues from the way that Jameson actually does his work. In short, this book both tries to intensify Jameson's understanding of postmodernism as a phenomenon (a field of relations born of mutations within capitalism) and, just as important for my purposes, simultaneously tries to redeploy what one might call the *style* of Jamesonian critique. (How that style of response works will become clearer in the opening chapter.)

Suffice it to insist here in the Preface: my aim is not to render obsolete either postmodernism or any particular analysis of it (as if either were possible) but to intensify, highlight, and redeploy certain strands within Jameson's analyses of postmodernism, and thereby to suggest some further structuring mutations in the relations among cultural production and economic production in the years since Jameson originally produced his magisterial analyses.

A word about the organization of this book: I begin with a methodological and historical introduction to the topic of "post-postmodernism" in Chapter 1, followed by three more chapters in Section 1 on culture and economics. Section 2 takes up the question of theory going forward, a topic I introduce through an interruptive Excursus on theory as style of engagement rather than mode of interpretation. I conclude with a Coda taking up the future of the humanities and/as theory. It may seem a little odd to dedicate so much space to the question of academic theory and its future in a book on the changing relations among cultural production and economic production, but I do so at least in part because in its heyday, postmodernism was often simply equated with theory. Or at least there was a sense that this mongrel hybrid called theory was an invaluable tool for diagnosing the postmodern condition: in a paradoxical, fragmented world, one needed theoretical tools that worked both *with* and *through* notions of chiasmus, undecidability, open-endedness, and so on.

So if I dedicate considerable space to the questions of theory yesterday, today, and tomorrow, I do so to argue that a changed cultural and economic situation (a changed sense of the "cultural dominant") likewise suggests that we need a new theoretical and methodological toolbox for responding to post-postmodern culture. I fear that if we can't engage robustly with the present, humanities disciplines that are invested in cultural production risk becoming wholly antiquarian archival exercises: Jameson's theory-era cri de coeur "always historicize" is a long distance from what seems to be developing as the new humanities research slogan, "shit happened." So I'm interested in revisiting a series of crucial postmodern concepts from the era of big theory (commodity, deconstruction, interpretation, literature, among others) to see what changes have been wrought in their critical effectiveness by the cultural and economic shifts that travel under the name post-postmodernism. Hence, each chapter also attaches to a postmodern keyword that it's trying to intensify, rethink, or redeploy.

Arguing against the contemporary "death of theory" hypothesis, I want to insist that just as postmodernism was a synonym for theory, so post-postmodernism needs to be as well. If we can say one thing for sure in our uncertain present, it's that the world hasn't gotten any *less* complex over the past few decades. Which, to my mind at least, suggests that in making post-postmodern sense (which is importantly different from postmodern "meaning") of our situation, it's a very bad time indeed to give up on the discourses of theory. I am following the suggestion of another, more sage Nealon (Christopher) in his reading of Jameson, when he argues that the project of theory in the present is less a continuation of the postmodern "hermeneutics of suspicion" than it is a toolkit for the construction of a "hermeneutics of situation," an intensification perhaps of Jameson's long-standing dream of producing a cognitive map of the present. As I'll suggest at more length when turning directly to the status of theoretical discourse in midbook, I see the questions of theory in the present as having little or nothing to do with academic professionalism or orthodoxy (finally getting theory "right" after all these years), and everything to do with responding to the post-postmodern present.

SECTION I

CULTURE AND ECONOMICS

CHAPTER I

Post-Postmodernism

Any political philosophy must turn on the analysis of capitalism and the ways it has developed. —GILLES DELEUZE, *Negotiations*

How Soon Is Now?

After the economic meltdown of fall 2008, it may have seemed for a moment like the era of unbridled faith in free-market or neoliberal capitalism was waning. When the US government orchestrated huge bailouts of the private sector, it might have seemed logical that the slick era of "small government and big business," born in the Reagan 1980s and intensified through the Clinton '90s, was definitively over and that we were on the verge of a retooled era of mid-twentieth-century Keynesianism. When Paul Krugman can wonder out loud in the *New York Times* magazine, "How Did Economists Get It So Wrong?," you'd almost have to conclude that, more than a decade into the new millennium, 1980s-style neoliberalism was soon to be a discredited thing of the past.

This of course turned out to be wishful thinking, or at least sadly mistaken—neoliberal capitalism was temporarily discredited, maybe, but is hardly a thing of the past. In the wake of the bailouts, the budget and debt battles in the US were fought and won not by liberal Keynesians offering a government-backed New Deal 2.0, but by free-market conservatives who take their neoliberal mantras directly from the 1980s book of Reagan: "Government is not the solution to our problems; government is the problem," as Reagan infamously put it in his 1981 inauguration speech. Likewise, what we saw in the financial meltdowns and the budget-cutting debates that followed were not really changes of course or swerves away from market dictates at all—quite the contrary. What you see when you see a government bailout of private industries is not so much the beginning of a brave, new socialism, but simply the other shoe dropping: with the privatization of wealth on a massive scale comes the socialization of risk on an almost unthinkable scale, $1.2 trillion of what amounts to "success insurance" loaned out to private companies in public, taxpayer funds.[1] Ultimately, these bailouts were not the abandonment of free-market ideology, but simply the other face of the privatized, free-market coin we've become so familiar with since the 1980s.

Indeed, it feels a lot like the 1980s both economically and culturally these days. Even the fashion and entertainment segments of CNN are '80s saturated: the hottest new radio format is "all '80s," with several stations having gone from the ratings cellar to number one in about the time it takes to play the extended dance remix of "Tainted Love." On the fashion front, the runways and malls are filled with '80s-style fashions—I recently saw a designer-ripped T-shirt that said, somewhat confusedly, "Kiss Me, I'm Punk," and the skinny tie has made its inevitable comeback. All kinds of diverse media (from Iron and Wine's post-postmodern cover of New Order's 1984 "Love Vigilantes" to Hollywood fare like *Hot Tub Time Machine* and *Wall Street 2*) stocks our collective iPad with reminders that we both have and haven't come a long way since the 1980s. But, as always, the real confirmation comes in the TV commercials: Joe Jackson urges us to Taco Bell "One More Time," while the Clash add rebellious street cred to the Nissan Rogue. I swear not long ago I heard the Smiths, whose myopic '80s anthems to frustration were perhaps second only to American Music Club for their sheer misery quotient, playing over an upbeat commercial for a sport utility vehicle.

While the return of the '80s is hardly surprising—how long could the nostalgia industry keep recycling '70s hip-huggers?—it remains a decade with something of a PR problem. Put most bluntly or economically, the '80s are haunted by the specter of Gordon Gekko's "Greed is good" speech in the 1987 film *Wall Street*. It's difficult for the '80s to shake its reputation as the decade in which self-interested capitalism went utterly mad; indeed, it's hard to imagine the '80s without conjuring up pictures of cocaine-addled yuppie scum with slicked-back hair and suspenders, floating worthless junk bonds to finance leveraged buyouts (LBOs) that callously ravaged what was left of "good jobs" in industrial America. Mary Harron's 2000 film version of Bret Easton Ellis's 1991 *American Psycho* cannily tries to replay some of the madness of the 1980s—the kind of madness thoroughly documented in Bryan Burrough and John Helyar's *Barbarians at the Gate*, on the mother of all LBOs, 1988's KKR hostile takeover of RJR Nabisco.

The '80s, in short, was the decade when the dictates of the market became a kind of secular monotheism in the US, thereby opening the door to the now-ubiquitous "corporatization" of large sectors of American life: welfare, media, public works, prisons, and education. In fact, such a market dictatorship, honed in the many palace coups that were '80s LBOs, has become the dominant logic not only of the US economy, but of the fast-moving phenomenon known as "globalization." Downsize, outsource, keep the stock price high—those are the dictates of the new global version of corporate *Survivor*.

Indeed, it seems clear that the American TV hit *Survivor* and its clone shows can be dubbed "reality" television only if we're willing to admit that reality has become nothing other than a series of outtakes from an endless corporate training exercise—with the dictates of '80s management theory (individualism, excellence, downsizing) having somehow become "the real." In fact, the exotic, "primitive" physical locations of *Survivor* argue none too subtly for the naturalization and universalization of these corporate strategies. Watching *Survivor*, it seems as if GE's corporate template for the '80s—"eliminating 104,000 of its 402,000-person workforce (through layoffs or sales of divisions) in the period 1980–90" (Jensen 2000, 38)—had somehow become the way of nature. In the end, *Survivor*'s "tribal council" functions simply as a corporate board, demanding regular trimming of the workforce, until finally the board gets to award a tidy executive bonus of $1 million—with all decisions along the way having been made according to an economist's notion of subjectivity, what Michael Jensen has dubbed the "resourceful, evaluative, maximizing models of human behavior" (194).

On further reflection, then, maybe it's not so much that the '80s are back *culturally*, but that they never went anywhere *economically*: the downsizing and layoff mania of the '80s—designed to drive up stock prices and impose market discipline on corporate managers—has now simply become business and cultural orthodoxy, standard operating procedure. Following *Survivor*'s lead, one might call it "reality," a rock of the real as tailor-made for the boom cycles as it is explanatory of the bust cycles that inevitably follow them. Less dramatically, one could say that the economic truisms of the '80s remain a kind of sound track for today, the relentless beat playing behind the eye candy of our new corporate world—a world that's been shocked by recent downturns, but one that has hardly abandoned the monotheistic faith that markets are the baseline of freedom, justice, and all things good in the world, for so-called liberals and conservatives alike. For a concise version of this mantra, one need look no further than Barack Obama's remarks in the summer of 2008: "I am a pro-growth, free market guy. I love the market. I think it is the best invention to allocate resources and produce enormous prosperity for America or the world that's ever been designed."

This across-the-board and continuing acceptance of '80s-style market principles is, it seems to me, one of the primary reasons why one might want to "periodize" the '80s, to steal a phrase from Fredric Jameson. Because to periodize the recent past is, of course, simultaneously to periodize the present: to begin figuring out how the cultural, political, and economic axioms of today (mandates only beginning to take shadowy shape) are related to the axioms of yesterday (mandates on which we should presumably have a better theoretical handle).

At this point, the reader might wonder how, why, or even if Jameson's work offers us a privileged path forward, insofar as today's postmodern materialists of the neo-Deleuzian variety tend to think of Jameson as someone dedicated to an old-fashioned—been there, done that—methodology: namely, dialectics. Well, like Foucault's nagging historical questions concerning power and exploitation (as he insists in his "Intellectuals and Power" dialogue with Deleuze, it took the entire nineteenth century for us to get a handle on what exploitation was, and surely it will have taken the twentieth and some chunk of the twenty-first before we have any workable sense of what "power" is), I wonder whether a certain *positive* Jamesonian itinerary surrounding the work of historicization or periodization remains unexplored or underexploited. We all know about dialectical method's attachment to the work of the negative; but surely any such work of negation must, in a dialectical system, be compensated for by an affirmation. What about this less-discussed "affirmative" Jameson? For a sense of that neglected Jameson, we need look no further than another '80s icon, his famous essay "Postmodernism; or, The Cultural Logic of Late Capitalism" (1984).

Holding at bay for a moment the many constative things we know or think we know about what the essay means or what it wants (a new totalization, a negation of consumer culture, a cognitive map, a return to this or that style of modernist subjectivity), I'd like to suggest that we concentrate instead on the essay's performative aspects—looking quite simply at how the essay does its work. For me, rereading Jameson's "Postmodernism" highlights a contradiction of the sort that we can only assume is intentional—antinomy being precisely the kind of shifting quicksand of an *Abgrund* on which dialectical thinkers influenced by Adorno often build their homes. In short, if Jameson is indeed a thinker of dialectical, progressive totalization (of the kind familiar from an old-fashioned reading of Hegel), then he certainly doesn't practice what he preaches. The style, range, and sheer volume of reference in the essay are anything but restricted or developmental in a recognizable sense—there's certainly no Hegelian movement from sense certainty, to unhappy consciousness, to the heights of knowledge, absolute or otherwise. Instead, from the opening paragraphs and their mishmashing of punk music and the minimalist song stylings of Philip Glass, through discussions of Nam June Paik, Andy Warhol, Heidegger and Derrida, E. L. Doctorow, Bob Perelman, the Bonaventure Hotel, Duane Hanson, Brian De Palma, and so on, we get less an analytical snapshot or critical dissection of postmodernism than a jump-cut-laden video starring it. We are presented, in other words, with many, many modes of postmodern cultural production but hardly any sense of postmodernism's sublated "meaning." And the hasty list of examples just provided doesn't even try to account for the heavy volume of seemingly passing reference so characteristic of Jameson's style on the whole: in the Austinean sense, he "uses" Doctorow or Warhol in "Postmodernism"; but he in addition "mentions" a truly dizzying array of postmodern cultural productions that would seem to have very little or nothing in common: Ishmael Reed, Godard, John Cage, *Reader's Digest*, Foucault, John Ashbery, Stanley Kubrick, Chinatown (both the Polanski movie and the San Francisco neighborhood referenced in Bob Perelman's poem "China"), Robert Wilson, David Bowie, the architecture firm Skidmore, Owings & Merrill, and William Gibson—as well as what must be the only extant reference to B-list movie actor William Hurt within the canon of poststructuralist theory.

On what's become the standard reading of this essay, the wide range of Jamesonian reference does indeed harbor a performative point, but it's largely a negative one: we, as readers, are meant to experience the dizzying array of centerless "intensity" produced by this laundry list of cultural productions; and as we try to deploy our outmoded categories to "read" or make sense of this puzzling, affectless flat surface, we're led inexorably to Jameson's conclusion: we need a new cognitive map. Without it, we're stuck with a meaningless and monotonous march of shiny, contextless consumer images. On this reading, the very intensity of the Jamesonian barrage—so much postmodern cultural production, so many examples— is meant not so much to highlight the positive (if sinister) force of postmodern cultural production, but instead to solicit our (modernist, all-too-modernist) inability to respond.

Fair enough, and—mea culpa—I've advanced just such a reading of Jameson elsewhere (1993, 144–52). But here I'd like to highlight the fact that there's another Jameson, one lurking beside (or maybe even in dialectical opposition to) the negative, stony, finger-wagging one we think we know. In classical dialectical fashion, Jameson insists that this negative inability can also provoke "a more positive conception of relationship":

This new mode of relationship through difference may sometimes be an achieved new and original way of thinking and perceiving; more often it takes the form of an impossible imperative to achieve that new mutation in what can perhaps no longer be called consciousness. I believe that the most striking emblem of this new mode of thinking relationships can be found in the work of Nam June Paik, whose stacked or scattered television screens, positioned at intervals within lush vegetation, or winking down at us from a ceiling of strange new video stars, recapitulate over and over again prearranged sequences or loops of images which return at dyssynchronous moments on the various screens. The older aesthetic is then practiced by the viewers, who, bewildered by this discontinuous variety, decided to concentrate on a single screen, as though the relatively worthless image sequence to be followed there had some organic value in its own right. The postmodernist viewer, however, is called upon to do the impossible, namely, to see all the screens at once, in their radical and random difference; such a viewer is asked to follow the evolutionary mutation of David Bowie in *The Man Who Fell to Earth* (who watches fifty-seven television screens simultaneously) and to rise somehow to a new level at which the vivid perception of radical difference is in and of itself a new mode of grasping what used to be called relationship. (1991, 31)

There's a lot going on here, in one of Jameson's most overt statements concerning "a more positive conception" of "what used to be called relationship" in and around postmodern cultural production. Most striking in this passage is Jameson's neo-Deleuzian (though he'd undoubtedly prefer the adjective "utopian") call for "a new mutation in what can perhaps no longer be called consciousness." Not a lot of nostalgia or mourning there.

Perhaps less obviously, this paragraph also constitutes the essay's most overt moment of reflexive self-thematization. We readers of Jameson are positioned as the hapless viewers of Paik's rapid-fire video installations: "bewildered by this discontinuous variety" of cultural stuff that Jameson so quickly offers us, we tend "to concentrate on a single screen"—this or that specific example—"as though the relatively worthless image sequence to be followed there had some organic value in its own right." However, this critical failure, far from being the negative and inevitable point of Jameson's essay, is overtly thematized as the trap to be avoided in reading it: "The postmodernist viewer, however, is called upon to do the impossible, namely, to see all the screens at once, in their radical and random difference; such a viewer [who is also Jameson's reader—*mon semblable, mon frère et soeur*] is asked to follow the evolutionary mutation of David Bowie in *The Man Who Fell to Earth* (who watches fifty-seven television screens simultaneously) and to rise somehow to a level at which the vivid perception of radical difference is in and of itself a new mode of grasping what used to be called relationship." Rather than primarily constituting a requiem for the non-schizo, somehow-still-centered mediating functions of modernist subjectivity, Jameson's essay is a call for revolution in this thing that can no longer be named by its quaint, old-fashioned handle: consciousness. On a performative reading—which will allow itself to speculate concerning constative effects only by first taking into account performative form—Jameson's work is far more schizo than it is centered, more "postmodern" than it is "modern." And this ambitious formal agenda should hardly surprise us, as Jameson is certainly a thinker who's had more than his share of things to say about the political and theoretical implications of "style."[2]

So, throughout this project I'll be taking up and intensifying both Jameson's call for a revolution in historical consciousness, and the immanent, experimental, well-nigh mishmashing style in which that call is announced. This book could be called "Jamesonian" not because it attempts to distill a method (dialectical or otherwise) from Jameson's texts and apply it to a horizon of new objects (the sort of thing Jameson himself would never do), but because *Post-Postmodernism* tries to follow along in the path that Jameson has set out for thinking about the present and its relations to the recent past. In short, I take Jameson's method to be immanent to his style of analysis, and it is precisely this style of analysis that I'm trying to inhabit, extend, and pay tribute to throughout *Post-Postmodernism*. As I noted at the outset, the project makes no claims to overcome Jameson's analyses or displace them. Rather, *Post-Postmodernism* follows his analyses precisely through intensifying them, and that movement of intensification and spread is what I try to stress by the infelicitous phrasing of post-postmodern (rather than that obsolescent valence of the dialectic where the "post-" might signal a simple historical overcoming). Postmodernism is not a thing of the past, any more than the 1980s are, precisely because it's hard to understand today as anything other than an intensified version of yesterday. But, of course, intensification is a movement that does alter things over time.

These Things Take Time

Jameson's "Periodizing the 60s" (1984) argues that the 1960s—or more precisely, the cultural, economic, and social upheavals that we commonly lump together and refer to as "the '60s"—actually began with the global decolonization movements of the mid-1950s and ended sometime in the early to mid-1970s. In other words, Jameson suggests that "the '60s" is not so much a calendar decade bounded by the years 1960 and 1970 as it is a period of transversally linked revolutionary historical developments that lasted nearly twenty years.

One might flesh out Jameson's claim by venturing that the '60s began politically sometime around the events of Dien Bien Phu in 1954, followed by the Algerian uprising starting on its heels, the Bandung conference in 1955, the strengthening of Indian independence in South Asia, and continuing struggles for decolonization in Africa in the '50s. Economically speaking, the postwar suburbanization of the US and Western Europe led to a sharp intensification of consumption-based capitalism in the "first world." Concomitantly, the "second world" of Soviet influence was solidified in the mid-'50s, with satellite nations becoming important players in the increasingly hot cold war. The rapidly decolonizing, nonaligned "third world" may have freed itself from direct political control by the former imperialist nations, but it quickly became sutured into a severe and controlling debtor relation with international capitalism: economics was already becoming the primary means of recolonizing the nonaligned nations, a movement that only intensified through the '60s and into the massive debt crises of the 1970s (with the increasing activism of the Bretton-Woods institutions, the World Bank, and the IMF). Culturally, the mid-'50s in the West saw a wide range of disparate global responses to the intensifying cold war: from the postcolonial theorizing of Fanon and C. L. R. James, to the increasing exhaustion of international modernism in the face of mutually assured destruction (one thinks of Beckett especially here, or at the other end of the spectrum the films of the French auteurs and the dreams of liberation and mobility connected to everything from abstract expressionist painting to beat literature). In any case, the revolutions we characterize as part and parcel of "the '60s" can be seen to have had their roots in the '50s, or at least it's a provocative and useful intervention to begin with that historicizing, periodizing premise.

On the other side of the '60s, the fall of Saigon in 1974 or the Watergate scandals of the early to mid-'70s are perhaps the most dramatic political markers of the end of the '60s, at least in the US. Economically, the most convenient break on the other side of the '60s is probably the Smithsonian Agreement (1971), which officially took the US dollar off the gold standard, allowing worldwide currency values to "float," their value determined by markets of supply and demand rather than by reference, however tenuous, to the "real" value of gold reserves in Fort Knox. Cultur-ally, the overdose deaths of '60s icons Jimi Hendrix, Jim Morrison, and Ja-nis Joplin—all in the early '70s—are often pointed out as definitive breaks with the joyful, experimental ethos of the culturally liberated 1960s.

Of course, what counts as a key cultural, political, and economic reference could be multiplied, refined, and argued exponentially—this is part of the gambit and provocation of Jameson's periodizing hypothesis. But here near the beginning of my analysis, I'd like to mine two relatively uncontroversial premises from Jameson's "Periodizing the 60s": first, cal-endar markers are not the be-all and end-all of grappling with historical periods; and, second, insofar as Jameson's "Periodizing the 60s" was pub-lished in 1984, it suggests that only from after the end of an epoch can one begin to size the era up historically or begin to "periodize" it (following, perhaps, Derrida's famous remarks on deconstruction and its relation to modernist philosophies of the subject: it is precisely from the boundary of a historical period, from inside its continuing end or closure, that one might hold out some retroactive or retrospective hope of naming what happened there).

In following up Jameson's periodizing thesis a few decades later, and focusing it narrowly on the United States, I am tempted to say that whenever "the '60s" finally ended in the US, the period that emerged in its wake was not so much "the '70s" as it was "the '80s": the conservative, "down with big government" period of backlash that fueled the Reagan revolution; and the intensification of that pro-business, market-take-all ethos in the 1990s. One might say that the '80s, that period of market-mad privatization, began in the mid- to late '70s, with the global reorganization of production. Fueled by the evisceration of unions and government regu-lation, the beginning of the leveraged buyout years in the US, and the un-precedented run-up of the equity markets, the Reagan '80s had quite a run through the Clinton go-go '90s. Indeed, if in the US "the '60s" functions politically as a kind of shorthand for resistance and revolution of all kinds, "the '80s" most immediately signifies the increasing power and ubiquity of markets and privatized corporatization in everyday life. And the '90s were clearly the years of full bloom for the conservative fiscal agenda hatched in the '80s. The market-tested Reagan truisms of the '80s were intensified to fever pitch throughout the 1990s (you remember: the government can't do anything right, we're not in the business of "nation building" abroad, Social Security should be wholly privatized, the wealthy getting wealthier is actually good for the rest of us, the Dow will run at 36,000).

And though it's a little hard to say exactly when the economic, political, and cultural regime we call "the '80s" began in earnest in the US (Reagan's election in 1980? the Iran hostage crisis of 1979? Talking Heads' first album in 1977?), one might say a bit more definitively when the '80s ended: if not with the bursting of the NASDAQ dot.com bubble in fall 2000, then certainly with the wave of corporate scandals (Enron, WorldCom, Arthur Andersen) that followed. And perhaps most definitively, the events of September 11, 2001 ended an era of antigovernment sentiment in the US. In the present social and political climate, where people in airports happily take their shoes off at the behest of government flunkies, it's hard to remember how omnipresent the tirades against big government were in the '80s and '90s. (Think about Waco, Randy Weaver, Tim McVeigh's Oklahoma City bombing. When merely to question United States hegemony is labeled "treason," in right-wing pundit Ann Coulter's catchy phrase, it's difficult to recall the hard-core intensity and ubiquity of antigovernment hatred during the '80s and '90s, especially among conservatives: so far, the Tea Party seems pretty tame by comparison.) In terms of foreign policy, the US government's forays into nation crushing/building in Afghanistan and Iraq seem possible only in a world that's very different from the isolationist corporatism that ruled the '80s and '90s (remember the conservative outrage against "nation building" in Somalia). Of course, there were a few cries of "socialism" during the US bailout discussions of 2008, but adding another several hundred billion dollars of taxpayers' money to the original package somehow silenced the critics of big government. The nation-state, which had looked like it was becoming an anachronism in the world of triumphant global corporatization, is back—and in a big way, though none of the things that progressives might like about the nation-state, such as widespread entitlement programs, seem to have much chance of returning with it.

On the affective level of everyday life in the US, it's pretty clear that whatever happened culturally and economically in the 1980s and '90s, we're living in a different period. We're still living that legacy, but many of the dominant economic, cultural, and political rules of the game have changed dramatically.

That being the case, I want to engage here in a kind of periodizing thought experiment, one that takes some of its inspiration from Jameson's "Periodizing the 60s." I want to suggest that, like Jameson's more global thesis about the '60s, the '80s in the US were a "period"—an era with a loose cultural, economic, and political affinity—that lasted roughly twenty years: from, say, Reagan's election in 1980 to the summer of 2000 or the fall of 2001. If that period is or feels like it is over today, we may be at a point where we can begin to describe and grapple with what happened there and to speculate concerning what's likely to come about in its wake: what has disappeared since the '80s, what has intensified, and what, if anything, has remained the same? In short, and in anticipation, I'll try to suggest throughout this book that over the past thirty years in the US, the major shift in economic and cultural terrain is within "capitalism" itself—which is no longer exactly the same thing it was in the 1980s. Less dramatically, one could say that the privatizing economic mandates of the '80s remained and intensified throughout the 1990s. And this perhaps is the most obvious way that the economic truisms of the '80s linger on today, even after the bubble burst. As Tom Frank writes, "The free-market faith is still with us. What's gone is the optimism" (2001, 3).

Still Ill

Jameson's "Periodizing the 60s" was published in 1984, the same year as his epoch-making "Postmodernism; or, The Cultural Logic of Late Capitalism"; and the two essays have much in common, each illuminating aspects of the other. One can, for example, more clearly understand Jameson's skepticism about the "cultural dominant" of '80s-style postmodernism by recalling one of the central themes of "Periodizing the 60s"—the 1980s is or was a period of cultural containment in the US, a dialectical inversion of the artistic, political, and economic energies unleashed in the '60s: artistically, the experimental avant-gardism of the '60s—pop art, performance art, Black Arts—is met in the '80s by the culture wars and the increasing corporatization of artistic production; politically, antiwar and civil rights movements of the '60s are countered by the "moral majority"

Reagan backlash of the '80s—the revenge of white suburbanites; economically, the global decolonizations of the '60s and the US's abandonment of the gold standard in the early '70s are met by the massive global debt crises and inflationary spirals of the 1980s (and the concomitant rise in power of finance institutions like the Federal Reserve, World Bank, and IMF). If, as Jameson writes, "the 60s were . . . an immense and inflationary issuing of superstructural credit; a universal abandonment of the universal gold standard; an extraordinary printing up of every more devalued signifiers" (1984, 208), then the bills unfortunately come due in the '80s: "The dreary realities of exploitation, extraction of surplus value, proletarianization and . . . class struggle, all slowly reassert themselves on a new and expanded world scale" (209). Needless to say, this description of the early to mid-'80s also has some considerable resonance with the present situation in the US, where we're reckoning with the staggering debts—human, environmental, and monetary—accrued by a go-it-alone style of global imperialism in Iraq and Afghanistan, America's longest war.

Reading Jameson's '60s essay next to his postmodernism essay also suggests that he harbors very little hope for nostalgia as a mode of critical engagement—that is, Jameson argues that the political and artistic strategies of resistance born in the 1960s aren't likely to be effective in the very different social and political climate of the 1980s. In diagnosing and contesting economic and social realities from the vantage point of 1984, Jameson notes that "the older methods [of the '60s] do not necessarily work" (1984, 208): "nostalgic commemoration of the glories of the '60s," he notes in the essay's opening line, is the first "error" to be avoided in any kind of historicist thinking about the present. Finally, "Periodizing the 60s" shows us that the historical transition from the '60s to the '80s is very poorly understood if we thematize that transition *solely* within the preferred terms of '60s-style narratives—as the unleashing of subversive social energy (the '60s) that's overcome by the repressive backlash of the '80s; '60s authenticity versus '80s co-optation; '60s resistance versus '80s normalization. In other words, the narratives by which we characterize that period called the '60s—narratives of unprecedented rebellion, resistance, and liberation—don't necessarily do much useful work in explaining or intervening within a very different historical situation. Taking a good deal of the wind out of the "wasn't that a time?" ethos, Jameson rather soberly suggests that the *economic* narratives of the '60s—rather than the artistic or political ones—may be most useful in thinking historically about the present. The social revolutions of the '60s, he writes, "may perhaps best be explained in terms of the superstructural movement and play enabled by the transition from one infrastructural or systematic stage of capitalism to another" (208). Leave it to Jameson to bring the wet blanket of economics to a '60s beach party.

Throughout this book, I want to follow Jameson insofar as he suggests we need to do a genealogy of the recent economic past, not so that we can nostalgically recall and celebrate the gains and losses, but finally so we don't delude ourselves into thinking that the oppositional strategies of the past can unproblematically and effectively be imported into the present. (I take this to be the force of the Jamesonian slogan "always historicize.") If Jameson's two 1984 essays suggest—however subtly—that many left-leaning academics in the mid-'80s were still stuck in an outmoded mindset of the 1960s, and that an economic analysis was the clearest way to show this, I want to fast-forward that hypothesis into our present. To put my concern baldly, it seems to me that much North American humanities "theory" of the present moment is essentially stuck in and around the "the '80s"; and perhaps the easiest and most effective way of breaking that spell is to try to think economically as well as culturally about the differences between the two periods.

If we consider only the most obvious example of such present-day theoretical anachronism, Jameson's "Postmodernism" essay itself remains the touchstone for cultural studies work on the present—it's a perennial syllabus favorite, and it continues to function as a term-setter for debates about economics and culture today. This, it seems to me, is quite odd (and quite un-Jamesonian). Remember that when Jameson's essay was published in 1984, the Berlin Wall was still firmly in place—the cold war was in fact heating up again, with Reagan's new morning in America still dawning; the Dow Jones was struggling to run at 1,200; Paul Volcker's inflation-worried Fed had US interest rates sky high; Japan, it seemed, was the economic power to be reckoned with and feared in the next century (recall that in the industrial Midwest of the mid-'80s, people would routinely vandalize Japanese cars and motorcycles—or, for that matter, just take a look at 1982's *Blade Runner* and its Japanized dystopian future); in

1984, Americans were just beginning to talk about AIDS; the first MAC computer—with 286 stunning k of RAM—debuted in North America in January 1984, introduced in a splashy, Orwellian Super Bowl commercial; the Internet—at least as we know it—was still the stuff of science fiction, as was the global ubiquity of cell phones and smartphones. Watching Michael Douglas talk on a billionaire's prize—a portable satellite phone the size of a shoebox—in *Wall Street*, who could have imagined that only two decades later, most middle school students would possess communication technology ten times smaller and a hundred times more powerful?

We live, in other words, in a very different world from the early to mid-'80s. Though we still live with the fallout of the '80s, it's clear that the economic component of our "cultural dominant" is no longer that particular brand of "postmodernism, or late capitalism." In fact, the neo-Marxist hope inscribed in the phrase "late capitalism" seems a kind of cruel joke in the world of globalization ("late for what?"). So among the tasks of periodizing the present, a collective molecular project that we might call *post-postmodernism*, is to construct a vocabulary to talk about the "new economies" (post-Fordism, globalization, the centrality of market economics, the new surveillance techniques of the war on terrorism, etc.) and their complex relations to cultural production in the present moment, where capitalism seems nowhere near the point of its exhaustion. Although the hopes contained in the phrase "the new economy" have all but dried up in recent years, the dreary realities of its market dictates remain very much with us—one hesitates to say permanently, but as far as the eye can see at the present moment. Also, I should note that I take mine to be a diagnostic project: any kind of tentative *pre*scription for treating current ills would have to follow from a thick *de*scription of the symptoms and their genealogical development over time. So it's to that descriptive or diagnostic project that I now turn.

Hand in Glove

How does or did this thing called economic "privatization" work? What exactly is the relationship of the '80s leveraged buyout craze, for example, and today's more seemingly sedate corporate orthodoxy? Not surprisingly, most economists—right and left—point to a fairly straight line of economic development from the '80s to today, from the death of the "old" economy to the triumph of the "new." As Michael Jensen, Harvard economist and leading theorist of the new market-take-all economy, writes in his 2000 *Theory of the Firm*, "LBO associations and venture capital funds provide a blueprint for managers and boards who wish to revamp their top-level control systems to make them more efficient" (56). Rather than an apology for the excesses of the '80s, Jensen's work constitutes a cheerleading tribute to "LBOs and their role in the restoration of competitiveness in the American corporation" (64). Indeed, if you want to ask why the Dow Jones Industrial Average shot up more than 12,000 points between 1985 and 2007, when it had managed only about 1,000 points of total growth in the half century between the 1929 crash and 1980, one need look no further than Jensen and his vision of "unlocking shareholder value."

Among all the other things that sprang onto the economic scene in the '80s, the most central throughout the 1990s was this Jensenite notion of shareholder value, which translated into an almost total corporate emphasis on maintaining a high stock price. For the better part of the twentieth century, American businesses didn't worry too much about their stock price, and the financial sector of the economy was certainly nowhere near the center. Production was king, with an economic and corporate structure dedicated to the Fordist courses of expansion, production, and liberal spending originally mapped by J. M. Keynes and tailored for the postwar mega-corporation by J. K. Galbraith. And Jensen is very much aware of the historical reasons for the triumph of production-based economics; the finance-based model lost considerable luster in the 1929 US stock market crash and subsequent worldwide Depression. Through the Depression and war years to the baby boom generation, the crash of 1929 resonated louder than bombs within the collective memory of American business. As a result, the financial sector of a midcentury corporation was hardly in any position to call the corporate shots.

Under a Keynesian or Galbraithian theory of the firm, shareholders and others in the "private" finance sector are a low priority—not exactly an afterthought, but certainly not the enterprise's primary reason for being. "Slow and steady growth" was the mantra of American business from the '50s through the '70s, and disgorging large amounts of "public" corporate cash to "private" stockholders is not a good way to manage such growth. Servicing the stockholder is, in fact, destabilizing for those who actually work at the firm—so-called stakeholders. Keeping the stock price and dividends high commits everyone at the firm to an uncertain, quarter-by-quarter, what-have-you-done-for-me-lately mind-set rather than a long-term pattern of steady growth.

Doug Henwood usefully sums up the orthodoxy of midcentury corporate America in *Wall Street*: "Galbraith dismissed profit maximization as the goal of a giant firm in favor of the growth in sales and prestige. To thrive, it needed not maximum profits, but 'a secure minimum of earnings' that would keep it from having to tap troublesome capital markets or cope with demanding outside stockholders. . . . The technostructure had little to gain from high profits, which would only be passed along to shareholders, and might even entail higher risk" (1998, 259). In such a Galbraithian scenario, it's more or less admitted that shareholder profits could always be greater; but the corporate management and workforce have little incentive to take the risks necessary to squeeze out every last little bit of profit—especially since such profit would, in the end, not help anyone *in* the corporation. Rather, such profits would be paid *out* to private individuals who don't work at the company but hold its stock. So goes the wisdom of corporate technocracy, the thinking attributed to "the man in the gray flannel suit": Why risk your job, your public reputation, and the jobs of your colleagues to secure higher profit for private shareholders, who have no stake in the everyday running of the corporation, no knowledge about the intricacies of the product line, no expertise in the industry? This corporate orthodoxy helps explain why, for example, the Dow Jones Industrial Average didn't break the 1,000 mark until 1972; and even then it didn't top 1,100 until more than a decade later, in 1983. During the period from 1990 to 2000, by contrast, rarely did three months go by without a hundred-point gain in the Dow. From 1995 to 1999, thousand-point yearly gains were the norm.

Indeed, the LBO era of the 1980s constituted nothing less than an assault on the Galbraithian corporation, the giant company and its truism that steady and predictable growth is good for all. For Jensen, this seemingly rosy picture of slow growth brings with it a horrible cost: inefficiency. Who's running these corporations, Jensen asks? The answer, in

Jensen's view, is middle managers—glorified production supervisors and halfwit business administration majors in cheap suits. And to whom are they loyal? The people who work for them and their immediate bosses; the private shareholder is nowhere to be seen in the equation. Jensen was outraged that businesses were not being run according to the interests of their ostensible owners, the shareholders. Jensen sums up the woeful rise of managerialism this way: "As financial institution monitors left the scene in the post-1940 period, managers commonly came to believe companies belonged to them and that stockholders were merely one of the many stakeholders the firm had to serve" (2000, 65–66).

The leveraged buyout movement of the '80s, fueled as it was by the mantra of "unlocking shareholder value," was nothing less than a civil war within American business, with shareholders (buoyed by the rise of the large institutional investor, the almighty mutual fund) demanding their piece of the corporate pie. And Jensen makes crystal clear the stakes of this internecine war: "The mergers, acquisitions, leveraged buyouts (LBOs), and other leveraged restructurings of the 1980s constituted an assault on entrenched authority that was long overdue" (9). True to his market orthodoxy, Jensen prefers to talk about the '80s LBO craze as a market itself, the "corporate control market" (3). And Jensen very much articulates the orthodox line in contemporary business—the history written by the winners—which understands the '80s as a kind of massive market correction: individual stockholders stepped in to discipline the lazy and unproductive practices of the old-line corporation. As Jensen smugly sums up, the '80s meant curtains for "those we used to call 'entrenched' management" (4). We all know the story, because we are still there: tens of thousands "lose their jobs as the inefficient and bloated corporate staffs are replaced by LBO partnership headquarters units" (78). Ahh, efficiency.

What was enshrined through the notion of "unlocking shareholder value" is a new-fashioned kind of class warfare, the revolt of the rich. Simply put, Jensen asserts that the people who put up the money should get the profits: "For control to rest in any other group would be equivalent to allowing the group to play poker with someone else's money and would create inefficiencies that lead to the possibility of failure" (2). Because rich people are so obviously and voraciously greedy, Jensen implies, they can be counted on to do anything necessary to maximize profits, which are hiding here behind the code word "efficiency." As Jensen baldly states, "In the private corporation, stockholders and bondholders, who bear the wealth effects of changes in firm value, have incentives to monitor managers to prevent them from making transfers of corporate assets to workers or permit workers from making such transfers" (194). This, the upward distribution of wealth to CEOs and shareholders while management and workers are ground under finance's heel, is the real agenda and effect of '80s-style corporate privatization.

With the high-profile crackdowns on corporate malfeasance in the US before and after the bubble burst, we might be tempted to say that the new barbarians finally got theirs. Note, however, that precious few Harvard MBAs or Wharton grads took the perp walk for the cameras in the first decade of the 2000s: the two CEOs actually led off in high-profile chains were Tyco's Dennis Kozlowski, an alum of Seton Hall, and the hapless John Rigas of Adelphia, a Rensselaer Polytechnic Institute graduate. Of the other infamous convicted CEOs and investment ne'er-do-wells, note that WorldCom's Bernie Ebbers was a working-class kid from Alberta, Canada, and unlikely alum of Mississippi Baptist College—which he attended on a basketball scholarship. Enron's Ken Lay was a graduate of the University of Missouri, and Bernie Madoff graduated from Hofstra College. The folks who took the heat were, in other words, aggressively *not* old-money Ivy Leaguers, and it's no coincidence that these upstarts are served up as scapegoats, while all the others repeat the line they learned from the Princeton frat-house scandals of their college days: it's just a few bad apples, not a systematic problem. Indeed, it's an instructive class lesson to recall that no one high up in the financial firms Lehman Brothers or Bear Stearns, lead perpetrators of Bursting Bubble 2.0 in 2008, has come anywhere near a federal courtroom.

Note also that the investigations that produced the corporate crackdowns of the early 2000s were instigated and fueled not by the outrage of unions, employees, the SEC, the Justice Department, or the general public, but by the shareholders of these corporations. While there's a nice populist feel to watching CEOs and CFOs being humiliated, their falls from grace owe virtually nothing to old-fashioned public outrage at the excesses of big business. They were taken down by the power and influence of Enron, Qwest, Adelphia, and WorldCom *stockholders*, which is to say that corporate scandals don't necessarily contradict the privatizing, shareholder-take-all logic of the '80s; they in fact confirm and intensify this logic. Since the '80s, CEOs have been paid lavish salaries to do what the shareholders hired them to do—drive the stock price sky high, by any means necessary. But when the proverbial shit hit the fan, the shareholders turned on their flunkies in a New York minute. So what you're seeing when you see a CEO in handcuffs is largely the continuation of an internecine war among the super-rich, and a concomitant extension and consolidation of the shareholders' power in corporate America. It most assuredly is *not* the result of a populist revolt against the fat cats.

What Difference Does It Make?

At some level, this is a familiar story: In the move from Fordism to post-Fordism and beyond, capital has become increasingly deterritorialized, floating flexibly free from production processes, and coming to rest more centrally in the orbit of symbolic exchange and information technologies. In addition, private notions of unleashed finance assert themselves over more public modalities of planned growth, in the corporation and in the public sphere at large. Lean and mean financial "efficiency" becomes the mantra; and in a nutshell, efficiency means privatization. That having been said, however, perhaps we need to follow those '80s masters of masochism, the Smiths, and ask, "What difference does it make?" Why rehearse this story, which tends only to make people on the left feel hopeless and resentful? Aside from bemoaning the state of advanced finance capital, what can we *do* with this genealogy of the recent past?

Regarding the present state of theory in the humanities and the possibilities for mobilizing response to the logic of privatization, this genealogy suggests it's no longer very productive to think in the terms of theoretical drama familiar from the 1980s—as Jameson notes, those terms themselves are already a hangover from the '60s. That is, it's becoming increasingly unhelpful to replay the drama that posits a repressive, normative "stasis or essentialism" that can be outflanked only by some form of more or less liberating, socially constructed "fluid openness." At this point, we'd have to admit that privatized finance capital has all but obliterated the usefulness of this distinction: to insist on the hybridity and fluidity of X or Y *is* the mantra of transnational capital—whose normative state is the constant reconstitution of "value"—so it can hardly function unproblematically as a bulwark against that logic. Think of the war on terrorism, for example. In order to be patriotic in this war, we in the US have not at all been asked to repress or downsize our desires: no collective, public efforts like wholesale rationing or conserving to enhance the war effort. Rather, in a 180-degree turnabout from the usual austere rhetoric of wartime, Uncle Sam now wants us to liberate our individual desires in the face of the axis of evil (defined primarily as anti-desire, anti-individual, fundamentalist repression): so we're asked to consume, travel, refinance our mortgage at lower rates, buy durable household goods. Follow our personal desires; that'll stick it to al-Qaeda.

Indeed, when Led Zeppelin plays over Cadillac commercials and a Rolling Stones tour can be brought to you quite literally by the housing bubble (the Stones' 2005 official tour sponsor was now-defunct Ameri-Quest Mortgage), you have to assume that the cultural rebellion narratives of the '60s, which often revolved around the liberation of an individual's or group's desire in the face of various social repressions, can now officially be pronounced dead. Under an economic logic that is in fact dedicated to the unleashing of multifarious individual desires and floating values (broadly speaking, a corporate-nation-state model), rather than desire's dampening or repressive territorialization on a gold standard of univocal value (broadly speaking, the traditional nation-state model), the role of social "normalization" (previously the purview of the state's Ideological Apparatuses) needs to be rethought from the ground up. Put simply, a repressive notion of "normalization" is not the primary danger lurking within contemporary capitalism. Though, of course, rigid normalization is still alive and well elsewhere in the political *socius*, as the xenophobic Arizona immigration laws of 2010 amply remind us; but we should also be reminded that *businesses* in Arizona and elsewhere are none too happy with these draconian laws. There are myriad social and political dangers latent in the neoliberal truisms of finance capital, but the rigid normalization of cultural options isn't paramount among them. (In only the most obvious example, it's not corporate capitalism that's at the forefront of discrimination against gays, lesbians, or immigrants—Disney offers same-sex partner benefits and produces large numbers of kids' TV shows in Spanish;

my blue-state university only recently started offering partner benefits, over the continuing objections of the state legislature; and don't hold your breath for lawmaker sessions conducted or broadcast in Spanish.)

So let me return to the methodological reconsideration of Jameson that I began earlier in this chapter and that I will likewise develop and perform throughout this book. On this kind of reading, what Jameson performs in the '60s essay and the "Postmodernism" essay—and, I'd argue, largely throughout his mature work—is nothing less than a rethinking of dialectical method, recasting it largely as an operation of what I would call "overcoding." What is overcoding? Recall that for Jameson the late capitalist social realm is inexorably "totalized" (Jameson's more provocative, Sartrean word for the mundane postmodern sense that there is no "outside": nature is gone forever, he writes, so culture is all there is). So, overcoding (or, to use Jameson's preferred word, "transcoding") is just one "dialectical" way of following out the logic, methodologically speaking:[3] if everything in our world exists on the same flat plane, then things that don't at first seem to have much in common quite literally have to be related in some way(s)—the cultural realm and the economic realm, avant-garde poetry and downtown skyscrapers, for example. Or, to put it somewhat more precisely, one should be able to take the claims and effects that surround the logic of X or Y cultural phenomenon (say, that contemporary literature is open ended, process oriented, not dedicated to the limitations of univocal meaning) and dialectically overcode or transcode these cultural effects in terms of economic ones (that, say, global capitalism is open ended, process oriented, not dedicated to the limitations of univocal meaning).

As Jameson puts it in *Valences of the Dialectic*, specifically in the context of trying to rethink base and superstructure as transcoding rather than subtending discourses: "The structure of production can, in other words, be translated or transcoded into the language of class struggle, and vice versa. To this proposition we can now add the imperative that the two codes must criticize each other, must systematically be translated back and forth into one another in a ceaseless alternation, which foregrounds what each code cannot say fully as much as what it can" (2009, 46–47). In other words, when one then dialectically "returns" from an economic coding of X postmodern phenomenon back to the cultural coding, one can no longer treat the cultural claims made for the thing in quite the same unproblematically liberating way. This is at least partially to say that, following out Jameson's overcoding logic, one can't make the kind of move that you still see rife within political theory: the ethos of liberation that surrounds cultural postmodernism (the transgressions of hybridity, the individual ethics of self-fashioning, Dionysiac celebrations of multiplicity, endlessly making it new) can't simply be walled off from the substantially more sinister work that these very same notions index within the economic realm—they're the watchwords of neoliberal capitalism as well. So when one dialectically overcodes the liberated cultural effects of postmodernism with the substantially more dire economic realities that rely on the same concepts, one can no longer assess the cultural effects in quite the same way. And vice versa—the inherently sinister claims of economic theory are cut down to size a bit when they're overcoded by less obviously grandiose or influential discourses like poststructuralist poetics.

Early on, in *Marxism and Form*, Jameson (1971) helpfully elaborates on the ways in which the "mishmashing" style of his work (taking on seemingly very disparate topics within the purview of a single analysis or essay) is intimately connected to these methodological aims. The style of his work, Jameson insists, is a direct overcoding of dominant political discourse: "The method of such thinking, in its various forms and guises, consists in separating reality into airtight compartments, carefully distinguishing the political from the economic, the legal from the political, the sociological from the historical, so that the full implications of any given problem can never come into view" (368). In short, Jameson's work, both the content and, just as important, the form, is targeted decisively against the theoretical and political imperatives of logical positivist empiricism—against separating out realms of social life into more easily policeable and controllable chunks, never confronting one social code with the values, language, and force of another.

In any case, I take the Jamesonian methodological starting point to be this: it's one logic, smeared across a bunch of discourses, and after the transcoding dialectical demonstration, you can't quite so easily or naively cherry-pick and affirm the stuff you like (say, the Yale School of literary criticism), while you simply denounce the stuff you don't like (say, the Chicago School of economics). Or, to put it more precisely, you can't unproblematically say that the logic of one of those things (American deconstruction, in this example) somehow inherently subverts or resists the logic of the other (neoliberal capitalism). I'd hasten to add that it's similarly unhelpful to assert, simply based on resemblance, that deconstruction causes global poverty: it's simply mendacious to suggest that Paul de Man is as responsible as Milton Friedman for the financial debacles of South America in the '70s and '80s. Indeed, as Jameson asserts in the context of a discussion of Marx's *Capital*, "The first casualty of this dialectic is of course any moralizing or ethical approach to the matter" (2009, 63). Rather than churn toward an inevitable moral conclusion (an outmoded understanding of dialectic), the transcoding or overcoding job becomes working out the connections, the sites of homology and difference, and the difference they make. If, as everyone seemingly agrees, there is no "outside"—if, as Jameson writes, "we are no longer in the position of evaluating whether a given thought system or aesthetic form is progressive or reactionary" (358)—then the question necessarily becomes, how are these various modes of production related; how do they configure a kind of odd, multiple totality? And what nodes of resistance and/or critique are locatable within such an altered diagnosis of the field itself?[4]

The real question this leaves us with is the question of today. Given the intensifications of privatized capitalism since the postmodern 1980s, what cultural, political, and economic routes of reconfiguration are opened up for us today? And what ones are gone forever? Will the financial crashes characteristic of the century's first decade really change the playing field of multinational capitalism, or will they simply rearrange the dominant players? Of course, it's a little too early to tell what will happen with the multiple cultural legacies of a shift in economic production, because such response is ongoing, multifarious, and largely experimental. That is, the work of critique, as Jameson reminds us, moves and gains foothold through an immanent and positive engagement with a present that is not a hole or a trap but is "rather to be imagined in terms of an explosion: a prodigious expansion of culture throughout the social realm, to the point at which everything in our social life—from economic value and state power to practices and to the very structure of the psyche itself—can be said to have become 'cultural' in some original and yet untheorized sense" (1991, 48). It is toward theorizing that "untheorized sense" of today as a kind of intense "cultural explosion" that the present book is dedicated.

CHAPTER 2

Intensity

EMPIRE OF THE INTENSITIES: A RANDOM WALK DOWN LAS VEGAS BOULEVARD

Capitalism no longer looks outside but rather inside its domain, and its expansion is thus intensive rather than extensive.
—MICHAEL HARDT AND ANTONIO NEGRI, *Empire*

Walking down the Las Vegas Strip at night, you can't help feeling that you're at the center of a brave new world of commerce. The Strip seems a perfect example of both the *product* and the *engine* of the American economy. Vegas, in other words, represents a kind of ground zero of the postindustrial American economy, with its just-in-time (which is to say, all-the-time) delivery of extremely high-concept sensory overload, staffed by wave after wave of service labor. As Marc Cooper writes, "If Lenin once summed up Communism as 'Soviet power plus electrification,' the highest formulation of the New American Economy might just be 'casinos plus part-time jobs'" (1997, 30). And every twenty-minute change of dealers and croupiers displays the flexible specialization integral to this post-Fordist economy.

However, one could argue that today's Las Vegas is an exemplary economic site in more ways than one: it obviously works according to the logic of the service economy, but it also figures the shift from such a post-Fordist world to the emergent and troubled new economy that one reads about every day in the *Wall Street Journal*. Those trying to name and diagnose this new economy often file it under the old rubric of neoliberal "finance capital," that regime in which speculative capital is wagered on a future of supposed or projected worth rather than invested in the production and mass marketing of new commodities or services. In other words, the future of capital seems to rest not so much on the innovation of products or manufacturing processes (a Fordist model) or in the colonization of new services or clients (the post-Fordist model), but in a futures market on capital itself, in a kind of gambling on the future worth of stocks and other speculation devices. As Fredric Jameson argues in "Culture and Finance Capital," the future of capitalism "resides no longer in the factories and the spaces of extraction and production but on the floor of the stock market, jostling for more intense profitability. But it won't be one industry competing with another branch, or even one *productive* technology against another more advanced one in the same line of manufacturing, but rather in the form of speculation itself" (1997a, 251.) The future of capitalism, in other words, rests not on the extraction of profit from commodities or services but on the production of money directly from money—making profit by wagering on an anticipated future outcome. And the future, it seems, is now.

This, I take it, is what Hardt and Negri point toward in the epigraph to this chapter: capitalism is no longer primarily "extensive" (seeking new markets, new raw materials, untapped resources), but rather has become "intensive." Capitalism today seeks primarily to saturate and deepen—intensify—its hold over existing markets, insofar as global capitalism of the twenty-first century has run out of new territories to conquer. And the intensities of finance (how do you squeeze more profits out of the stuff you already have?) become the linchpin practices of this risky new economy. Because it's a sector of the economy where capital is staked "intensively" (directly in order to generate more capital) rather than "extensively" (creating new tangible goods or services, which are then bought or sold to produce capital), the regime of finance capital has often been nicknamed "casino capitalism" (see Strange 1997). As Marx himself wrote, stock markets and futures markets work according to the logic of gambling—where no commodity is directly produced or consumed. According to Marx, it is precisely this gambling logic that gives bankers and other speculators "their nicely mixed character of swindler and prophet" (1997, 572–73).

In *Capital,* M-C-M' names the dialectical formula whereby accumulated wealth (M) is invested in the production of commodities, thereby becoming capital (C); the commodities produced by that investment capital are then sold to produce profit (M'). Thus begun, the dialectical adventure of money continues—with ever-more accumulation, ever-more investment in the production of commodities, and ever-more profits reaped by the capitalist: M-C-M'. Recalling this economic vocabulary of classical Marxism, one might say that finance capital skips a step, and its formula might be written as Marx writes the formula for all money lending and finance, M-M': "money creating more money," as Marx succinctly puts it in *Capital: Volume 3* (1894, pt. 5, sec. 24.2). In other words, an increase in finance capital requires no direct or overt mediation by a commodity or service: no commodity (C) mediates between investment (M) and profit (M'); no actual goods or services are required to represent or serve as a placeholder for the abstract value of invested money; and no labor power is required to account for the transformation or generation of surplus value as profit. One might say in a kind of shorthand that M-M' comprises the formula for all forms of gambling, where money is directly *intensified*—made greater or smaller—rather than transformed into a different state through the mediating work of investment, labor, commodity production, or exchange.[1]

Following this logic to its limits on the streets and gaming tables of Las Vegas, one might argue that contemporary Vegas doesn't primarily produce either goods or services; rather, it produces what Gilles Deleuze and Felix Guattari call actual and virtual "intensities"—the thrills of winning, the aches of losing, the awe of the spectacle, weddings and divorces.[2] Like the booming speculation markets in stocks, futures, and options that fueled its reinvention, Vegas's primary products are two: winners and losers. Twenty-four hours a day, seven days a week, capital of all kinds—phantasmatic, symbolic, monetary—is staked in the hope of producing *more.*

Insofar as Las Vegas specializes in the production of such intensities—direct, hypnotic states of excess, loss, and expenditure—it deserves some renewed attention as a privileged site in the emergence of the newest

American economy. If we spent the 1970s and '80s "learning from Las Vegas" the *cultural* lessons of a triumphant kitschy postmodernism (see Venturi 1977), I want to suggest that there are a number of emergent *economic* truths that we can learn from Las Vegas several decades later.

The most insistent thing we've already learned from Las Vegas is that so-called economic truths are inseparable from cultural or aesthetic ones. You don't have to spend much time in Vegas to witness the utter collapse of the base/superstructure model and obliteration of the classical Marxian idea that capital speculation is wholly parasitic and cultural, producing nothing of consequence for the real economic base.[3] From Bugsy Siegel's original gamble in the desert, through the Rat Pack years of livin' large, right up to the new Theme Park Las Vegas (rebuilt on junk bonds and culture industry profits), all of Las Vegas's economic power is built on a series of cultural speculations; and even today its economic power and well-being are based largely on its cultural identity as the home of excess: What happens in Vegas stays in Vegas. Vegas has plenty to teach us about the economic base of today, but we learn first and foremost from Las Vegas that this economic base is always already shot through with superstructural, cultural capital.[4]

Capital that's merely parasitic, that adds or produces nothing "real," can't build this kind of massive empire in the middle of the desert. Las Vegas is a kind of testimonial to contemporary modes of power and functions oddly like the symbols of bygone imperial dominance that Vegas so gleefully appropriates: the Egyptian Pyramids and the Sphinx (Luxor), the glory and decadence of Rome (Caesar's Palace), the Italian Renaissance (Venetian and Bellagio), the power of the Sultans (Aladdin), and even the utopian modernism of the City Center complex.

Ancient capitals of empire functioned as centers of both cultural and economic power, with the sheer spectacle of their symbolic excesses working to cement a pedagogical relation between the imperial force of empire and the symbolic spectacle of aesthetic expenditure. On a pilgrimage to ancient Rome from the provinces, one would be led to recognize very quickly (if somewhat unconsciously) that the awe-inspiring architectural spectacles of Rome were made possible by the very same forces of imperialism that rule your home village—just as the vacationing Iowa Knights of Columbus group learns, at some level, the truths of the new economy through Las Vegas's logics of intensity and speculation.

And there is still much learning going on in Las Vegas every day; it's a place of hard economic lessons, indexed by an old joke: "Vegas: I arrived in a $50,000 Mercedes; I left in a $500,000 bus." However, I want to shift ground somewhat and suggest that we don't so much learn from the spectacle of intensities that is Las Vegas ("learning" implies critical distance and rational judgment; it implies that we can decide to accept or reject the lessons played out there). Maybe these days we don't *learn from* Las Vegas as much as we are forced to *respond* to the emergent mode of power—the new global casino capitalism—that is Las Vegas. Or maybe, like an ancient Roman subject from the hinterlands, we are even compelled to *obey* Las Vegas.[5]

Hail Caesar!

Perhaps the best site to begin surveying this burgeoning empire of commerce and culture is Caesar's Palace Casino and Hotel, located at the center of the Las Vegas Strip, an appropriately labyrinthine imperial site. If Jameson had a hard time making his way around the Bonaventure Hotel in LA, one shudders to think of the disorientation he'd experience in the "Forum Shops at Caesar's": an unapologetic overlap of hotel, casino, restaurant, theme park, and shopping mall—all done up in some hyperpostmodern version of the ancient past. Around Caesar's shops are scattered mythological Greek figures like Poseidon, Homer, and the Trojan Horse—all emblems that, we may recall, were already ancient by the time of Plato, some four hundred years before the reign of Augustus Caesar. The statuary rubs elbows with a roaming live Cleopatra and her buff Roman Centurions, all of whom will gladly pose for pictures with Caesar's honored guests.

The Forum Shops are a hybrid of the contemporary suburban mall and the nineteenth-century flaneur's arcade (curiously decked out with ubiquitous Roman aqueducts—flows, everywhere flows). You're ferried into the Forum from the sweltering Strip along a series of covered moving sidewalks—a welcome fit for an emperor. When you want to leave, however, you have to trudge the five hundred yards back to Las Vegas Boulevard like a plebeian—through the Caesar's casino (if you can find the poorly marked exit) and out over the unforgivingly hot acres of blacktop set aside for horseless carriages. While you're there, the "experience" of the Forum Shops is rounded out by the usual American mall stores (Gap, Victoria's Secret, Abercrombie & Fitch) as well as unusual ones (Burberry, Versace, Cavalli); restaurants launched by ubiquitous uber-chefs Wolfgang Puck and Bobby Flay; and a huge aquarium, which both complements the statuary in "Poseidon's Fountain" (right next to the Cheesecake Factory in the Roman Great Hall) and serves as a backdrop for one of the rare free shows in Vegas, the "Fall of Atlantis."[6]

In Caesar's new empire, the myths of the absolute past and the promises of the deferred future are mishmashed together for easy, intensive, one-stop "experience" shopping. The heroes of Atlantis, Troy, Greece, and Rome did not die in vain; they perished to help create this new empire of "freedom"—which, as we all know, means subjective empowerment as consumer choice, the only water fit to satisfy our thirsts. But, one might ask the FAO Schwartz Trojan Horse (which curiously talks, making it an appropriately anachronistic mix of Mr. Ed and the Oracle of Delphi), What do you get for a crowd that has already experienced everything? The answer: more of the same.

Contemporary Las Vegas is not so much a figure for imperialist expansion or assimilation—the old-time "Fuck you, we're movin' in" Vegas of the Mob and the Teamsters—as it is an ongoing, live experiment conducted to see what happens when a certain imperial project has completed itself, when there are no more lands for Caesar to conquer: "the place where the wave finally broke and rolled back," as Hunter Thompson (1998, 68) put it. In other words, Las Vegas's current modes of power are no longer primarily deployed in the service of legitimating the enterprise or overcoming an enemy (the government, the middle-American prude, the other casinos); those battles have already been decided. Rather, emergent modes of both corporate and subjective power in Las Vegas are aimed at intensifying what you've already got: expanding market share and deepening the demographic base by deploying new forms of value-added entertainment "experiences."

In short, the economic force that's deployed in Las Vegas functions *not* by conquering or assimilating new territory but rather by intensifying new versions of familiar things: for example, Paris (with its own Eiffel Tower), the Venetian (with its replica frescoed ceilings and gondolas in the annexed shopping mall), and New York, New York (the building itself constructed as a faux version of Manhattan, complete with a Statue of Liberty). The wholly rebuilt Aladdin, a posh theme-park version of the eponymous Mob casino, was opened at the dawn of the new century— overtly completing the feedback loop of anachronism by taking the past of Las Vegas itself as the original historical script to be remixed and remastered. (That proved not "intense" enough a concept, so the Aladdin became the Planet Hollywood Hotel and Casino, with its Hollywood-film theme, including movie memorabilia in every guest room—the stars' throwaways serving as the altar relics of privatized capitalism.)

In such settings, you don't so much *consume goods* as you *have experiences* where your subjectivity can be intensified, bent, and retooled. In contemporary Las Vegas, you are offered opportunities for doing work on yourself (experiencing, seeing, feeling) rather than opportunities for confronting, overcoming, purchasing, or otherwise consuming some "other." As Michael Hardt and Antonio Negri write, "In the postmodernization of the global economy, the creation of wealth tends ever more toward . . . biopolitical production, the production of social life itself, in which the economic, the political, and the cultural increasingly overlap and invest one another" (2000, xiii). The force of the new globalized economic empire—the empire one spies from Caesar's Palace—doesn't primarily turn outward in an expansive, colonialist, or consumerist assimilation. Now it turns inward toward intensification of existing biopolitical resources. The final product, in the end, is you and me.

And gambling is the logical cornerstone of such an empire, insofar as *risk* is the perfect figure and vehicle for this new economy of intensities. In any endeavor, but especially economic ones, risk of various kinds is irreducible. You can't simply accept or deny risk wholesale; no actor has that kind of control over contingency. Any actor or collective can only *modulate* risk—speed it up or slow it down. Certainly, risk can be canalized—some outcomes made more likely, and some less likely; but risk per se cannot be subsumed or assimilated. Risk constitutes a flow that can't be overcome but one that can be affected only by being intensified—being made greater or smaller, faster or slower. This intensification, to take only the most obvious example, is what's on display when gamblers "chase" losses: increasing their bets, and their risk, in the hope of getting even.[7]

Such is the logic of intensity, then, on both the global and the subjective levels: in a world that contains no virgin territory—no new experiences, no new markets—any system that seeks to expand must by definition *intensify* its existing resources, modulate them in some way(s). This, in a nutshell, is the homology between the cultural logic of globalization and the economic logic of finance capital, neither of which is dedicated to discovering wholly new sources of human or economic capital: neither is set on cold war goals like seeking out raw materials or new territory to bring into the empire. Rather, the challenge for the globalized logic of finance capital is to find new mechanisms to work on money itself—new modes of risk intensification like derivatives, swaps, futures, currency trading, arbitrage.

On a subjective level of intensities, then, the paradigmatic Vegas casino experience is no longer modeled on the existentialism of Dostoyevsky's *Gambler*: a masculinized, heroic confrontation with a mysterious "other" (God, fate, chance, destiny, sex, money).[8] Here in Vegas, authenticity is no longer won extensively by challenging such an other but by a more direct, intensive retooling of the self. Even the strictly speaking corporate force in town is not aimed essentially at overcoming the competition. In contemporary biz-speak, the hostile corporate takeover or leveraged buyout (staple of the junk-bond era that provided the money to build the theme-park Vegas) is a distant memory—soooo '80s. "Mergers" and "synergy" are the new watchwords of empire.

Caesar, in other words, is not at war with the Flamingo or the Bellagio; they are all merely coexisting provinces within the same essentially peaceable kingdom. As a mundane example of this synergy, note that casino chips in Las Vegas are—unlike competing national currencies—essentially interchangeable: the other big casinos will treat Caesar's chips as the coin of their realm as well, which only makes sense, because you can't spend capital if you don't liquidate it—if you can't morph it into a form where it can immediately flow. Monetary chauvinism—like so many practices of the cold war nation-state—is just plain inefficient. At least since the fall of the Berlin Wall in 1989 and the millennial "defeat" of Soviet power worldwide, it seems that there is no "out there" for casino capitalism to vanquish, no dialectical other against which to define or test itself.[9] Such an empire can expand only by intensifying its victory, since there are no new lands to conquer.

Empire of the Intensities

Not coincidentally, such a very literal sense of empire's completion pervades another high-profile exercise in Romanesque anachronism at the dawn of the new millennium, Ridley Scott's Academy Award–winning film *Gladiator* (2000). In the opening scene, we're introduced to our protagonist, General Maximus (Russell Crowe, not channeling Charles Olson), who's about to lead his men into the final battle of the Roman Empire's last great campaign, circa AD 180. Maximus is the favorite general of the reigning emperor Marcus Aurelius (Richard Harris), the last Caesar of Rome's Golden Age. Victory against the "Germanians," we are told by the opening credits and by Caesar himself, will suture and complete the empire's imperialist expansion. After this battle, which the Romans are sure to win, the peaceable kingdom of Rome's Golden Age will have been wholly forged: there will be no more wars left to fight, no territory left to assimilate.

And seemingly no more movie, no more story to tell. Once this opening battle is over and the empire is secured, what's left to narrate? Audiences seem unlikely to respond favorably to a three-hour chronicle of an aged Caesar and his favorite general playing checkers and reminiscing over libations at the Old Soldiers' Club in Rome. As far as a promising Hollywood plot goes, the bureaucratic management of more-or-less peaceable kingdoms (whether Marcus's management of civil empire or Maximus's desired return to the domestic sphere of the family) hardly seems the stuff of spectacle-laden, epic cinema in the tradition of *Ben-Hur* or *Spartacus*. After seeing Maximus lead his men into the last battle for empire—a sweeping, gory, jump-cut-laden slaughter of the Germanians—do we then look forward to one hundred minutes of Maximus mowing the lawn and ordering the kids to clean up their rooms?

Luckily, Caesar's venal son Commodus (Joaquin Phoenix) steps in to save the plot. Seeing that Caesar distrusts him and favors Maximus— or, worse, that Caesar intends to turn power over to the Senate—Commodus murders his father and ascends immediately to the role of emperor. Aside from the simple motivating force of Commodus's lust for power, the audience can't help noting that Commodus also grasps a complex historical truth: after the defeat of the Germanians, the old emperor has outlived his usefulness. The skills of the father—assimilating and annexing land through warfare—are not the skills required for managing a vast transnational and multicultural empire. As Hardt and Negri write of a parallel in our globalized world, post–cold war politics becomes a matter of regulating "hybrid identities, flexible hierarchies, and plural exchanges through modulating networks of command" (2000, xii–xiii).

Paradoxically, *Gladiator*'s conquering Caesar has no place in the multicultural, global empire that he's brought about—where a kinder, gentler form of coercion, bloodshed, and violence will have to be invented and practiced.[10] Needless to say, neither does Maximus—commander of the tightly ordered and homogeneous world of the Roman legions—have any clue concerning the administration of such an unwieldy and complex new world order. But Commodus has some ideas. In fact, he's hip to the productive qualities of biopower and the coercions of the culture industry: keep the masses fat and happy by giving them entertainment, he surmises. Bring back the gladiators!

If we enter the world of *Gladiator* at the end of Roman imperialism proper—where the project for the foreseeable future becomes managing diversity rather than assimilating territory—what better tactic than bringing back the crowd-pleasing, heroically nostalgic intensities of gladiator battles? Scott's film—somewhat disingenuously, given its participation in this empire of nostalgia and representation—shows us that like our own colonial cold war, Roman imperialism was indeed brutal; but the film retroactively portrays those days of disciplinary imperialism as honorable, satisfying, and "real" in some way. We see this trace of authenticity repeated in Maximus's signature trope, deployed throughout the film: he picks up a handful of local soil before entering any battle, thereby cementing his existential bond with the earth and the land—with the forces of nature and the stability of the real.

Certainly *Gladiator* suggests that the imperialist world of the film's opening was a dangerous place—paradoxical, fraught with contradiction. Men had to act and fight for a nationalist abstraction, "Rome," without really understanding why. But the faux, staged gladiator fights of the post-imperialist empire (those that dominate the rest of the film) will never offer anything close to this kind of authentic subjective heroism. In the end, *Gladiator* shows us a world where the hard-fought battles of imperialism bring about the ancient analog to the slap-fights that festoon twenty-first-century reality TV programs. The eclipsing of Roman colonial expansion leads to an even more sinister kind of image-based totalitarianism: a spectacle economy staged for the amusement and, finally, *control* of the Roman masses—represented as decadent, fickle, Colosseum-bound couch potatoes. If Augustus ruled them with discipline, fear, and grudging respect, Commodus—a sort of Baudrillard in a toga—will amuse them to death.

I take this detour through *Gladiator* for a reason. First, the film quite overtly wants to function as a *Spartacus* (1960) for the new millennium; and like Stanley Kubrick's film, Scott's *Gladiator* offers—among other things—a historical allegory by which we might come to understand, and maybe even resist, the sinister powers of our own day. The most obvious target of Kubrick's film—and the blacklisted Dalton Trumbo's script—was the anticommunist hysteria of 1950s America. The (in)famous scene where dozens, then hundreds, of slaves stand up and pronounce "I am Spartacus!" functions as a kind of critical inversion and refusal of the US House of Representatives Un-American Activities Committee's practice throughout the 1950s—and, more broadly, the scene functions as a reaction to McCarthyist racial, ethnic, and political intolerance and hysteria in the US. Rather than offer up the names of others—"name names"—to absolve yourself of guilt, *Spartacus* models a mode of resistance to political blackmail: "I am Spartacus" could be roughly translated as, "If freedom of thought and action is the charge, then yes, we are all 'guilty,' and proud of it. We are all Spartacus—we are all communists, Jews, African Americans, poor people, homosexuals." In *Spartacus*, we see the slaves standing up to power through solidarity, and in the process the film provides a democratic model of collective action—a united subaltern strategy that promises to confront totalitarian threats of any stripe.[11]

Scott's *Gladiator* likewise uses the model of the ancient Roman Empire to comment on recent events. But, half a century later, Scott's presentation of global capitalism is inexorably different from Kubrick's cold war moment. Rome, for example, is depicted in *Gladiator* as a crowded, multicultural, and transnational city, much like contemporary global metropolises New York, Shanghai, or London. The gladiators, slaves with whom Maximus falls in after his family is slaughtered on the orders of

Commodus, uniformly hail from the distant, annexed Roman colonies: the Middle East, Africa, Spain, Germania. And among Scott's contemporary targets seems to be the exposure of a kind of postmodern plantation system, with all the shit jobs of our empire still performed by those from the so-called third world. More directly, however, *Gladiator* attempts to name and critique the globalized urban mass's obsession with media spectacle—the subtle voyeuristic coercions of "extreme" sports, political spin doctoring, trash talk shows, reality TV, celebrity gossip, millionaire quiz shows, and so on. Like the decadent Romans portrayed in the film, we post-postmodern capitalists are trained by our media masters to watch rather than act, consume rather than do.

Presumably, following the lead of *Spartacus*, *Gladiator* should try to produce a strategy for us, a model for resisting the commodified spectacle that the film so effectively demonstrates. There should be another way mapped—a response that might act as a vehicle for collective resistance, a road to some better place. But, alas, recall that the film is framed by the completion of empire, the literal absence of any such outside. In our world, as in the world of *Gladiator*, there's literally no place else to go: the dominant mode of power has succeeded in covering the known earth. And in the end, *Gladiator* responds to this situation fairly predictably—offering nothing but nostalgia for an older form of domination, longing for the good old days of discipline. Throughout, but especially in the end, the film rather shamelessly lauds the imperialist, masculine labor power of Maximus and Augustus ("good"!) and excoriates the feminized and incestuous practices of the image-monger Commodus (need I say, "bad"—even his name suggests heading for the toilet). Indeed, they don't get much more reprehensible than Commodus: incest and the hint of child molesting are bad enough, but this guy's even shown to be a *bad sport*, having fatally wounded a bound and helpless Maximus moments before their final battle in the Colosseum. So Maximus is forced to stumble through—and of course win—the battle while dying from this wound.

After the mutual death of Maximus and Commodus in the Colosseum, the Senate is poised to take power at the conclusion of the film, with Senator Gracchus (Derek Jacobi) as their leader. But this ending gesture toward "democracy" can't leave savvy, image-saturated movie audiences entirely happy. Senator Gracchus portrays himself as the ancient counterpart of a Kennedy liberal ("Not a man of the people," he reminds us, "but a man for the people"). However, Camelot hasn't fared so well in revisionary American history: Jack Kennedy was elected president largely because of his slick media savvy (or the 1960 Nixon's lack thereof), and he's remembered these days less for any populist credentials than for having brought about the Cuban Missile Crisis, Vietnam, and a level of White House philandering that would have made Bill Clinton blush. Besides, if audiences recall their high school textbook history, they know what's on the menu for Rome after the Golden Age of Marcus Aurelius: decline and fall. In the end, *Gladiator* suggests that only the reluctant but heroic leadership of someone like General Maximus—an Eisenhower for the ancient world—could have saved the empire: if we liked Ike, we'd have loved Max. But saddled as we are with our own venal, image-obsessed political and corporate emperors, we global capitalists in the United States should expect the same immanent moral and political decline as the Romans.

In *Gladiator*'s vision of the Roman epic film, a strategic mode of resistance to the violent othering of cold war imperialism ("I am Spartacus!") is replaced by a nostalgic mourning *for that very world of imperialism*: "I wish I could be like the conquering Maximus! But they don't make 'em like that anymore." *Spartacus*'s collective response is replaced by *Gladiator*'s atomized yearning for individual authenticity. And, needless to say, such a Golden Age of subjective authenticity is always already a thing of the past, an object of commodified nostalgia in late Augustan Rome as well as in contemporary Disneyfied Hollywood.

Taken as a contemporary political and historical allegory of cold war imperialism giving way to an even-more-dangerous, media-saturated globalized capitalism, *Gladiator* leaves us with very little strategic room to move, other than pining for the good old days of imperialism—when you knew who the good guys were, when you could be heroic and authentic, when the blood was real. Resistance to the global flow of fleeting images, the film suggests, can be found only in the intensive authenticity of your own private experience, turned up to Maximus: a quirky individuality that's available—maybe even on sale—at sublime locations like the Forum Shops at Caesar's, as well as mundane sites like your Netflix queue. And seemingly everywhere in between.

In any case, rest assured that it's coming soon—in fact, over and over again—to a theater near you, as virtually all Hollywood films contain a version of this message: resist the system by courting intense experiences, always modulating your own authentic, flexibly specialized subjectivity.

Post-Postmodern Empire

Of course, this new empire of postimperialist biopolitical production travels under a more recognizable pseudonym, one we read in the paper every day: globalization. In their mammoth book *Empire*, Michael Hardt and Antonio Negri point out that "Empire is materializing before our very eyes. Over the past several decades, as colonial regimes were overthrown and then precipitously after the Soviet barriers to the capitalist world market finally collapsed, we have witnessed an irresistible and irreversible globalization of economic and cultural exchanges" (2000, xi). It's all one world now, we're told over and over again, by people on the right and the left.

But how exactly is this new world of globalized, triumphant capital different from the old colonial hostilities of the cold war? Is this really a peaceable, postimperialist kingdom? The answer seems to be, yes and no. The new mode of empire's power—as *Gladiator* shows us—is different, but it's no less forceful. Hardt and Negri write, "Although the practice of Empire is continually bathed in blood, the concept of Empire is always dedicated to peace—a perpetual and universal peace outside of history" (xv).

As Foucault puts forth in his work on disciplinary regimes, iron-fisted mechanisms of regulation are both expensive and inefficient—a lesson that international business learned long before the cold war nation-state did. Foucault argues that the disciplinary apparatus was born gradually alongside imperialist expansion in the seventeenth through nineteenth centuries, and reached its height in the twentieth. As Hardt and Negri explain, "In a disciplinary society, the entire society, with all its productive and reproductive articulations, is subsumed under the command of capital and the state, and that the society tends . . . to be ruled by criteria of capitalist production. *A disciplinary society is thus a factory society*" (243). For Hardt and Negri, the American New Deal represents the apex of this disciplinary vision of society as a vast but centrally controlled and regulated factory.

By all accounts, however, this kind of Fordist New Deal welfare state has been systematically dismantled by worldwide conservative political hegemony and the rise of the new economy. In a world of cyber-work, e-commerce, wireless communication, distance education, virtual markets, home health care, and the perpetual retraining of flexibly specialized labor, the disciplinary world of partitioning and surveillance (the office, the school, the bank, the trading floor, the mall, the hospital, the factory) seems like it's undergone a wholesale transformation. As Deleuze argues, "We're definitely moving toward 'control' societies that are no longer exactly disciplinary. . . . We're moving toward control societies that no longer operate [primarily] by confining people but through continuous control and instant communication. . . . In a control-based system, nothing's left alone for long" (1995, 174–75). Deleuze further elaborates on the distinction between discipline and control: "In disciplinary societies, you were always starting all over again (as you went from school to barracks, from barracks to factory), while in control societies you never finish anything—business, training, and military service being coexisting metastable states of a single modulation, a sort of universal transmutation" of power (179). So, while societies of control certainly extend and intensify the tactics of discipline (by linking training and surveillance to ever more minute realms of everyday life), they also give birth to an entirely new form of power.

Discipline itself constitutes a form of power different from its predecessors—the sovereign power of the spectacle, the banishment of the leper, or the confinement of the plague victim (see Foucault 1979, 195–200). The panoptic power characteristic of modern discipline acts not directly on bodies but on the body's potential for actions: as Deleuze explains in *Foucault*, "Force is exercised on other forces" (1983, 35). In short, the Foucauldian power of surveillance doesn't directly mark bodies, as the sovereign power of the scaffold does; it is a (much more efficient and economical) regulatory mechanism—you don't know exactly when you're being watched, so you adapt your behavior at all times to the power of being seen. Such a form of power acts on your actions; its primary target is your "virtual" possibilities, which in turn more economically regulate your actions.

Surely, surveillance in the globalized world of control has been taken to a new, even more disembodied and therefore efficient state; your Web browser, your DNA, your credit or debit cards, your subway pass, cell-phone usage, or credit report all suggest that you are tracked in ways that make the warehousing of bodily traces (like photographs, surveillance tapes, fingerprints, or blood types) seem positively quaint by comparison. If you can't even escape your undergraduate alumni magazine, how can you hope to evade the grip of transnational corporations?

Discipline has been taken to the limit of what it can do; and in this intensive movement, discipline's limit has become a threshold, inexorably transforming this form of power into a different mode, a "lighter" and even more effective style of surveillance that can only accelerate the already lightning-fast spread of that monstrous form of power/knowledge known as globalization. And Hardt and Negri build their concept of post-postmodern empire precisely on this notion of the waning of disciplinary power and the waxing of the society of control: "The society of control might thus be characterized by an intensification and generalization of the normalizing apparatuses of disciplinarity that internally animate our common and daily practices, but in contrast to discipline, this control extends well outside the structured sites of social institutions through flexible and fluctuating networks" (2000, 23).

Hardt and Negri suggest that we are witnessing not so much the end of imperialist or disciplinary power, but its intensification and transmutation into another kind of power. At its completion, one might say that the disciplinary power of imperialism doesn't merely halt, but it's forced to work differently, to develop another modus operandi. As Hardt and Negri argue, the present-day empire of transnational capital comprises "something altogether different from 'imperialism.'" They explain:

Imperialism was really an extension of the sovereignty of the European nation-states beyond their own boundaries. Eventually, nearly all the world's territories would be parceled out and the entire world map could be coded in European colors: red for British territory, blue for French, green for Portuguese, and so forth. Wherever modern sovereignty took root, it constructed a Leviathan that overarched its social domain and imposed hierarchical territorial boundaries, both to police the purity of its own identity and to exclude all that was other. (xii)

As *Gladiator*'s Romans no longer fight the Germanians and Caesar's Palace is no longer out to slay the Venetian, so the logic of post-postmodern capitalism no longer works primarily according to the rigid disciplinary logics of exclusion, othering, and noncontamination. As GATT, NAFTA, the euro, and the WTO attest, the nation-state no longer functions primarily as a machine "to police the purity of its own identity and to exclude all that was other"; rather, the nation-state now seeks primarily to hold the door for transnational capital—though, of course, this task regularly requires crackdowns of a terrifyingly "old-fashioned" disciplinary nature.

Such brutal tactics are still in fact prominently on display wherever global elites—the leaders of the World Bank, IMF, WTO, G-20, major political conventions—meet, and where dozens of "potential" protestors and protest leaders are summarily arrested or banished to far-flung "free speech zones." And of course, the War on Terror has brought such first-world barbarity front and center—with "enhanced interrogation," arrest without warrant, and illegal rendition remaining approved US government tactics long after the George Bush administration has faded into unpleasant memory. And in times of economic downturn, you can still count on xenophobic political scapegoating of immigrants, or so we've seen globally in recent years: Turks in Germany, Muslims in Scandinavia, Mexicans in the American Southwest. In short, simply because the nation-state's primary reason for being has changed, we shouldn't therefore assume that it's been evacuated of its disciplinary power or its investments in confinement. This is especially obvious in the context of the US not only in terms of terrorism, but with its burgeoning prison-industrial complex: throughout the 1990s, the American prison industry boasted growth rates second to only one economic sector—that's right, gambling.[12]

So the emergent economy of globalized control doesn't simply supersede or wholly displace the society of the nation-state's discipline. However, in the world of post-postmodern capital, nationalism's political boosters dream not of purity or overcoming a threatening other but rather of the endless, smooth flow of capital and goods (though not so much people) across boundaries of all kinds. These days, everyone from politicians to CEOs to the Arby's fast-food chain joins in the global refrain "different is good": and, needless to say, one can't imagine any cold war leader worth his SALT talks saying such a thing. The world of imperialism is, by definition, a world where "different is bad"—otherness is an obstacle, there only to be excluded, demonized, or assimilated. But difference in the postmodern world isn't there to be overcome; it's there to be intensified.

The logic of *intensification* is the (non)site where the logic of the individual subject overlaps with the logic of globalization. As the subjective pole of existentialism—with its thematics of alienation, mutually assured destruction, binarized subject/object splits, its heroic confrontations with the other and with death—is inexorably tied to the era of *ex*tensive imperialism, so the subjective pole of contemporary experience *in*tensification is equally tied to the economic and political logic of globalization. The "flexible and fluctuating networks" of postmodern globalization function according to an intensification of Foucault's notion of productive power, which teaches us that power doesn't hold good unless the subject can take some pleasure or knowledge from its bargain with a dominant mode of power. There has to be something "in" it for the subject. This is the breakthrough modus operandi of empire, its direct linkage to subjective intensities, the complete "culturization" of political and economic life. As Hardt and Negri argue, "The society of control is able to adopt the biopolitical context as its *exclusive* terrain of reference" (2000, 24).

Unlike the discontinuous, desiring subject of Lacanian psychoanalysis (and the nation-state to which that subject was bound), the new globalized subject of empire requires no rigid boundaries to transgress, no central or Oedipal laws by which to orient itself. As Hardt and Negri continue, "In contrast to imperialism, Empire establishes no territorial center of power and does not rely on fixed boundaries or barriers. It is a *decentered* and *deterritorialized* apparatus of rule that progressively incorporates the entire global realm within its open, expanding borders" (xii–xiii). It is precisely its deterritorialized status—the biopolitical network of intensities—that inexorably links the individual subject to the logics of globalization and capital.

In the end, we may have to admit that *Gladiator*, at some level, has it right: the image-based intensities of the new culture industry *are* the ironic fruits of the West's economic "victory" in the cold war, the form of power that flourishes in our era of globalized finance capital. Rather than lament the victories of these intensive economies, we had best do some hard thinking about how these economies work, what they can and can't do, and how they might produce results otherwise. Because whether we like it or not, today it seems that Wall Street and Main Street are connected by the intensities we see played out along Las Vegas Boulevard.

CHAPTER 3

Commodity

THE SONG REMAINS THE SAME:
ON THE POST-POSTMODERN ECONOMICS
OF CLASSIC ROCK

The Rolling Stones lasting twenty, thirty years—what a stupid idea that would be. Nobody lasts that long. —LESTER BANGS, 1973

The Song Remains the Same

A decade into the new millennium, my American college-town life remains positively saturated with 1960s and '70s "classic rock." On the way to the gym the other day, I couldn't find anything but classic rock on the radio. Even our student radio station programs mostly classic rock throughout the day because, so they say, it's what people want to hear. So I got to listen to a nineteen-year-old kid intro Jimi Hendrix's "Purple Haze" as if it had never been played on the radio before. I arrive at the gym only to recall that even here classic rock plays all day, every day. Am I the only one who thinks that drug music is a little strange as a sound track for working out? (I heard the stoner anthem "White Rabbit" before I got my iPod up and running, a few seconds of "Comfortably Numb" on the way out the door.) This is all made even odder by the fact that the gym is owned and run by fundamentalist Christians. I get the impression that Jerry Falwell didn't work out much, but if he did, I'm reasonably sure it wasn't to the dulcimer tones of the Grateful Dead's "Truckin'." When I was a kid, serious Christians railed against the excess of rock music. No more, I guess. What a long, strange trip it's been.

Back in the car, inspired by the Dead, I decide to stop at the state-run liquor store. No respite there, though, as the state store also plays classic rock. As I search for bargains, I'm treated to a Doors two-fer: "Peace Frog" (you remember, "blood in the streets / It's up to my ankles") and "Five to One" ("trade in your hours / for a handful of dimes"). I wonder, should a state-run facility be playing music that, on the face of it at least, constitutes a sledgehammer critique of both the state and capitalism? But no one bats an eye. I'm back in the car just in time to hear Black Sabbath's "Sweet Leaf" playing under an ad for the local attorney who sponsors the classic rock show on the college radio station ("When that night of partying turns into a world of trouble, call us"). When I stop to fill up the gas tank, Kansas's "Dust in the Wind" pours out of the speakers at the self-service pump.

Watching a little TV after dinner bookends my day of classic rock. Surfing through the news stations, I find that nearly all US political candidates shake hands with supporters over the beats of classic rock, consistently dredging up the unpleasant reminder that Fleetwood Mac was the (white) house band of the Bill Clinton era. Meanwhile, Led Zeppelin, Blue Oyster Cult, and Aerosmith play over commercials for cars, while the Kinks, the Rolling Stones, and Bachman Turner Overdrive help to hawk office products, and Beatles songs play behind Blackberry and Target ads ("You say good buy / I say hello"). Oddly, though, it's not just the commercials that are saturated with classic rock. The Who has become the official theme-song provider for CBS's *CSI* franchise—"Who Are You?" functions as theme song for the original *CSI*; "Won't Get Fooled Again" introduces *CSI: Miami*, its first spin-off (clearly something's going on there, as the spin-off is a genre dedicated, one would think, to fooling you again). Finally, there's "Baba O'Reilly" for *CSI: NY*—"teenage wasteland" for the electronic wasteland? Turning to my Netflix queue for relief, I recently watched the futuristic drama *Children of Men*; but even circa 2027, the film suggests, we'll still be tapping a toe to Deep Purple, King Crimson, and the Stones.

Indeed, if you listen closely, as I have for the past few months, it seems that classic rock is everywhere—Santana in the doctor's office

waiting room, Janis Joplin at the hamburger joint, the Eagles in the gro-
cery store, Crosby, Stills and Nash in the dentist's chair (as if a root canal
weren't painful enough).

As an everyday occurrence more than forty years after classic rock's
summer-of-love heyday, all of this is quite puzzling. In a series of culture
markets dedicated slavishly to "the latest thing" (industries like advertising, music, and television), how can such decades-old popular songs
remain this ubiquitous? Much of my puzzlement around this question is
undoubtedly personal—I'd thought the reign of classic rock was over by
the time I graduated from high school more than thirty years ago. My
sophomore year of high school, 1979, seemed like the end of the line: it saw
the release of Aerosmith's pathetic *Night in the Ruts* (*Right in the Nuts*,
get it?) and Led Zeppelin's tepid last gasp *In through the Out Door*. Pink
Floyd's *The Wall* was also released that year, and while it was a gallant
attempt to restage the consumer-friendly alienation of 1973's *Dark Side of
the Moon* (fourteen-plus years on the Billboard album charts—talk about
legs!), it did seem pretty repetitive and formulaic, even to high school
ears. Bad Company's unintentionally hilarious 1979 single "Rock 'n' Roll
Fantasy" ("Here come the jesters / One, two, three") seemed pretty much
to nail the coffin shut. It must have seemed to anyone who was listening
that the Clash's *London Calling* (also released in 1979) was right: "phony
Beatlemania" had indeed "bitten the dust."

In fact, the category "classic rock" was invented by US radio stations in the fateful year 1979, precisely as a bulwark to protect this sag-
ging, increasingly anachronistic musical entity against the dominance of
disco, on the one hand, and against an emergent punk music, on the
other. At the dawn of the 1980s, it seemed that so-called classic rock was
a bloated, irrelevant self-parody. In fact, the very invention of a name and
retro radio format for it would seem enough to signal its loss of cultural
currency—"classic rock" being a thinly veiled updating of the familiar
"oldies" format, in somewhat punchier language (any variant of the word
"old" being poison throughout the contemporary culture industry). Just as
the popular music of the 1950s had faded into the background by the late
1960s, the classic rock of the '60s and early '70s was, it seemed, largely a
cultural throwback by the dawn of the 1980s. Classic rock seemed headed
the inevitable way of the Vegas Elvis, destined to be forgotten by all but

the most loyal fans by 1985—just as the music of Bill Haley or Chuck Berry had rendered the crooners of the 1940s anachronistic in their day. For better or worse, that's the inevitable consumer dialectic of popular music—almost by definition, nothing can last for long in the viciously trend-driven business of popular culture. Already by 1975, for example, underground rock critic par excellence Lester Bangs wrote of the superstars of the late '60s: "They're washed up, moribund, self-pitying, self-parodying has-beens" (2002, 39). Indeed, as early as the summer of 1973, when Mick Jagger had just celebrated his thirtieth birthday, Bangs suggested that the Rolling Stones were already finished. He called *Goat's Head Soup* "the epitaph of old men. . . . In other words, why don't you guys go fertilize a forest?" (143, 151).

However, classic rock did not go gentle into that good night of cultural oblivion. Quite the opposite. In fact, classic rock to this day remains a stubborn, really quite singular exception to this otherwise iron rule of culture-industry anachronism, the rule of the "new." Hence for me the impetus for this chapter—trying to understand the unprecedented success and longevity of this cultural product called classic rock. Besides asking questions concerning whether or not the staples of classic rock are any *good* or not on aesthetic terms, we're left to deal first and foremost with the raw cultural fact of their absolutely unprecedented longevity—the spectacular long-term success of "Ramblin' Man" or "Black Magic Woman" within a viciously short-term market for cultural commodities. What exactly do I mean by that unprecedented quality? Think about it this way: if you turned on the TV in 1965, you most certainly wouldn't see ads with songs from the '20s playing under them. College students in the 1970s didn't routinely listen to music from the '30s or '40s, and the TV shows of the '60s wouldn't think of using Rudi Vallee or Al Jolson tunes as theme songs. Will anyone in the near future be listening to '80s-era Mission of Burma on "all-punk radio"? One doubts it.

Or, as a more concrete example, think about this conundrum: the Rolling Stones' "Satisfaction," universally acclaimed as one of the finest works of classic rock, was released in 1965 and quickly climbed the pop charts in the US and Britain. It was a number-one hit in the US for four weeks in the summer of 1965, until it was knocked out of the box by "I'm Henry the VIII, I Am" by Herman's Hermits. In England, the single likewise went to number one, displacing Sonny and Cher, until it was in turn displaced by a Burt Bacharach song recorded by the now-forgotten Walker Brothers. The point, you ask? Well, how is it that, several decades hence, the pop sensibilities of Herman's Hermits or Sonny and Cher have gone the inevitable way of musical obscurity—becoming degraded and even laughable markers of cultural old-fashionedness—while tunes like "Satisfaction" continue not only to sell themselves ("Satisfaction," a song ostensibly about the alienation caused by rampant consumerism, is happily being consumed somewhere on classic rock radio right now), but to brand everything from beer to cars to TV shows? How can or does classic rock survive the seemingly iron laws to which other popular cultural phenomena are subject? I'd venture to say that few college students today think of Herman's Hermits as "cool" or would be willing to pay to download any of their songs. Not so the Rolling Stones. Leaving aside for the moment the puzzling question of why today's teenagers happily consume a "youth culture" that was originally produced over four decades ago, somehow or another the music of classic rock continues to thrive. It's speculating about the status of that "somehow or another" that will interest me here.

The Beat Goes On

In broad outline, the musical youth culture story of the past half century in America seems pretty clearly a story of innovation and obsolescence. The birth of mass-appeal popular music in the Al Jolson–Rudy Vallee era gave way to the swing of the late '30s and the crooners of the '40s, who in turn faded into the background in the rockin' '50s, paving the way for the folk and soul of the early '60s, which waned during the waxing of the second wave of rock in the late '60s and '70s. In its turn, that so-called classic rock seemingly should have made way for the disco of the late '70s, the punk of the '80s, the grunge and rap of the early '90s, the hip-hop and emo of the late '90s, and so on.[1] So my initial question here is simply this: Why has everything else on this list been subject to the popular dialectic of innovation and obsolescence, while classic rock has somehow remained not only immune to anachronism but actually continued to thrive far beyond its initial successes, with several new generations of mass consumers? Kate Smith, the Slits, Sam Cooke, the Weavers, MC Hammer, Frankie Valli, Fats Domino,

Michael Jackson, the Partridge Family, Minnie Ripperton, Jerry Vale, Conway Twitty, and the Gun Club: all of these artists, and hundreds more like them from widely varying traditions and decades of the twentieth century, enjoyed some measure of popularity in their day, followed by a slow slide into cultural obscurity. Not so classic rock: Aerosmith is more popular and culturally ubiquitous today than it was in the late 1970s; one certainly can't say the same for the disco and punk music of that same era.

In beginning to answer the question of classic rock's longevity, it's always tempting to fall back again on its internal aesthetics—maybe classic rock has lasted so long because the songs are in fact what the gray-haired, pony-tailed DJs on the radio say they are: just plain great, timeless classics. Classic rock songs survive for the same reason other cultural classics have survived—they stood the test of time. And "You Really Got Me" does have a great hook. But surely one would also have to agree that Chuck Berry's "No Particular Place to Go" or "Maybellene" are likewise great songs with memorable rhythms, but I haven't heard either of them on commercial radio lately, much less playing under TV ads for cars or makeup (for which they would seem particularly ripe pickings). However great the cornerstones of classic rock are, one would have to admit that intrinsically or aesthetically (as songs qua songs), they are at the end of the day no "better" than the best of Nat King Cole (listen again to "Straighten Up and Fly Right"), Buddy Holly, the Ramones, Grandmaster Flash, or Benny Goodman for that matter. But the great songs of the '40s, '50s, early '60s, and even the '80s and '90s, have gone the inevitable way of cultural anachronism, while the classic rock of the late '60s and early '70s has positively flourished. This cultural fact would seem to call for explanations that are not simply internal or aesthetic ones—explanations that attempt to grapple with the cultural uses and functions of classic rock rather than (or at least in addition to) its internal aesthetic makeup. That is, I'm interested here in thinking primarily about classic rock's unique long-lived status as a cultural commodity.

I should also make it clear that in treating classic rock as a commodity, I don't harbor any interest in denunciations concerning classic rock's having "sold out"—an odd claim on the face of it in our era of totalized commodification. Rock music may be all kinds of things in addition to being a commodity—it may be a way of life for people, a personal investment, a sound track for driving or partying, a nostalgia trip, or a new discovery. But in any case, such popular music most assuredly is a commodity. Indeed, what you might call the "way cool / sold out" dialectic of authenticity is, in my view, the least helpful—and, unfortunately, also the most ubiquitous—way to begin (and end) a discussion about popular music. "They were cool when I liked them back in the day; then they became popular and sold out." Of course, anyone who's ever been in a band, or thought seriously about cultural production of any kind, can see the dead-end quality of this thinking— where authenticity can only be purchased (and make no mistake, authenticity too is a commodity) at the price of utter obscurity.[2] It would seem odd indeed to make a record, produce a sculpture, or write a play hoping in your heart of hearts that no one will ever support it materially, so that you can save your prized authenticity. Ironically enough, it's precisely classic rock's stubborn attachment to a discourse of subjective authenticity—"I'm Not like Everybody Else," as the 1966 Kinks song insists—that helps it to survive and thrive in culture markets several decades removed from its native historical moment.

Of course, when one insists on treating classic rock first and foremost as a commodity, one has to be ready for an onslaught of objections. Initially those disagreements come from people who stubbornly refuse to think of rock music as a commodity at all (fans of varying intensities), but resistance to commodity-talk comes even more often from academic critics of rock music, who tend to object to that vocabulary as being tainted from before the fact by the specter of Adorno and Horkheimer's "culture industry" thesis. To treat rock as a commodity seems for many critics to have already (dis)missed much of what interests people about popular music—how various fans use and respond to the music. As Larry Grossberg sums it up, academic rock criticism has been premised on the "belief that music had the potential to serve as an organizing site if not force of resistance and alternative possibilities" (2002, 30). To talk about cultural products primarily as commodities inevitably conjures the specter of "vulgar Marxism," which treats the music as simply one product among others (Skittles, tires, classic rock) and thereby inevitably casts the rock consumer as a passive dupe of marketers and sinister business executives.

I think we've learned from a few decades of very good academic rock criticism—the work of Simon Frith, Grossberg, and Greil Marcus, among many others[3]—that consumers of cultural products like rock fans are anything but dupes for the Man, and there's very little understanding to be gained by treating them as such. This strikes me as absolutely true, and the starting point for any analysis of rock music's place in the present. Following along from those insights, however, I think a somewhat less-commented-upon parallel lesson should have been gleaned from this work: namely, that consumers of tires or Skittles are likewise not simply dupes, passive robots manipulated by Machiavellian businessmen at M&M Mars or Michelin. In short, I think we've learned from several decades of crucial work in cultural studies that the word "commodity" is no longer simply a fighting word, one that signals a top-down model of cultural force-feeding. Methodologically, thinking about contemporary culture is not confined to rooting out the inauthentic commodities (e.g., Boy Bands) and pitting them against the authentic flowerings of spontaneous creativity (e.g., DIY Punk). Certainly, the lightning-fast turnaround time between an innovative cultural phenomenon and its mass-market repackaging ("turning rebellion into money," as the Clash song puts it) is an interesting phenomenon to study. But the terrain of cultural studies, for rock music as much as for Skittles, is no longer well described by the old-fashioned lingo of inauthentic commodities versus authentic cultural expressions of uncommodified desire.

Classic rock is—like it or not—a commodity, and in that sense it is just like candy, tires, academic essays, and virtually everything else in our market-take-all world. If anyone still wants to fight this battle, I'd point out that in July 2008, *Condé Nast* estimated that the ultimate classic rock standard, "Stairway to Heaven," has by itself generated more than $562 million for Led Zeppelin (see Datskovsky 2008). Here it's probably worth noting that like the Rolling Stones' "Satisfaction," probably its only serious contender for most revered tune in the history of classic rock, the lyrics of "Stairway" quite overtly function as a critique of such rampant commodification: the song opens with "a lady who's sure all that glitters is gold"—she is so commodity obsessed that she envisions even the afterlife as a shopping mall. "Stairway" rejects this opening image of a life (and death) territorialized on "buying" in favor of the fuzzy, aneconomic affects of subjective authenticity, that "feeling you get when you look to the west." Luckily, "there's still time to change the road you're on," and the sonic progression of the song itself functions as a kind of allegory: from the grammar of the commodified pop tune (the opening section, recognizable and radio-friendly enough) to the unfettered jam-anthem that takes up roughly the second half of the song. In the end, the thing that "Stairway" wants to avoid at all costs is stagnation or commodification, "to be a rock and not to roll." As with its older sibling "Satisfaction," it's the song's commitment to personal authenticity as bulwark against stifling consumerism that, without the least hint of irony, helps make it one of rock's most enduring consumer products. To paraphrase Marx, if classic rock commodities could speak, they'd say "commodities suck"—which is partially what makes them such enduringly salable products.[4]

That classic rock is big business, however, doesn't mean that classic rock is inherently uninteresting, sold out, crappy, or anything else in particular—just to say that it swims in the same sea that most everything else does these days. The remarkable thing about classic rock, from this point of view, has been its ability to swim so far, wide, and long from its original historical moment—not only to buck the seemingly inexorable trends of cultural obsolescence, but to foil them outright. Indeed, one of the biggest differences between tires, candy, and popular music—considered strictly as commodities—is that successful brands of tires and candy can expect a certain market longevity, while successful rock bands almost by definition cannot. Lemonheads, the Ferrara Pan candy invented in 1962, still sells briskly today; while Lemonheads, the "alternative" rock band du jour of 1992, has not been so lucky.

I'm trying here neither to celebrate nor to denounce classic rock, but to try to understand classic rock's continuing and singular place in American cultural life—and to think about whether its unprecedented continuing popularity suggests any changes in what cultural studies theorists have to say about the fraught relations among American cultural production and economic production. To anticipate my conclusion in this chapter, I'll argue that classic rock's longevity can be read as a symptom of Fredric Jameson's famous understanding of postmodernism (in shorthand, the complete collapse of cultural production into the logic of economic production, and vice versa); but in addition, the continuing reign of classic rock as a cultural commodity shows us the emergent logic of something else: not necessarily something "new," but a different, more intense mode of production/consumption that I've been calling throughout, for lack of another word, post-postmodernism.

Iron Man: A Case Study; or, Now He Has His Revenge

Black Sabbath's "Iron Man" (from 1970's *Paranoid*) has always been a bit of a puzzler within the classic rock canon. In my day, nothing could get a group of stoner teenagers more worked up than a post-bong-hits discussion of the song: He's an *iron* man, but we learn that he was turned to *steel* in the great magnetic field (when he traveled time for the future of mankind). Just to add to the problem, he has boots of lead. Surely, Ozzy knows that iron, lead, and steel are not the same thing—what's he trying to tell us? And why has the iron-steel man decided, upon return from his time travels, to turn on "the people he once saved"? Because "nobody wants him"? Do men of iron really care that much if they're not loved by an adoring public? How do magnetic forces turn iron to steel, anyway? And steel is of course stronger than iron—it's iron with most of its impurities removed. Is it the impurities that made us love Iron Man, and now that he's Mr. Perfect Steel Man, people don't like him anymore? Was he somehow disabled by becoming stronger? Bogus, man.

Hermeneutic complexities notwithstanding, "Iron Man" has had quite a ride. Its guitar riff is one of the most recognizable in the classic rock canon, and the song is now a standard pop cultural reference, showing up everywhere from commercials for Nissan to Christmas song parodies ("I am Santa Claus")—and it's become a staple on band playlists at high school football games and served as a theme song for the Hollywood blockbusters of the same name. "Iron Man" is, then, an excellent case study in trying to come to grips with the life and afterlife of classic rock—primarily because, if you had told me thirty-five years ago that any song from Black Sabbath's drug-addled *Paranoid* album could be used to sell cars, or would soon become a favorite of high school administrators everywhere, I would have said you were high (and, it being the '70s, you very well might have been). In the American business world of the 1970s, it would simply have been *unthinkable* that the music of loud, heavy-metal druggies from England could help you move Japanese pickup trucks. And anyone who was in an American high school at any point in the '70s can, I think, attest to the fact that suggesting Black Sabbath songs be added to the school-band playlist would bring on a locker search rather than a nod of approval. So how does "Iron Man" go from being a confused underground stoner anthem about a mixed-media B-list superhero who goes on a killing rampage, to being a nifty way to sell products and/or boost school spirit?

Again, one could always attribute this (literally) commercial success to some version of "selling out"—Ozzy's quest for fame in the wake of his reality-TV stardom. As I have intimated earlier, however, in our thoroughly commodified world this kind of accusation doesn't make much sense: popular music is a commodity, so accusing it of being more or less of a commodity seems somewhat of an argumentative nonstarter. To vernacularize for a moment, one can certainly argue that X or Y song sucks, but it can't suck simply *because* it's a successful commodity—insofar as all recorded music is a commodity. Also, even if it's true that Sabbath (or any other classic rock band) desperately *desires* to be featured in endless commercials for all kinds of products, that could never explain why classic rock is *in fact* featured in endless commercials for all kinds of products. Regardless of whether or not you're willing to *sell* out, someone first has to offer to *buy* you out—ad agencies, TV producers, the folks who put together sheet music for high school bands.

To suggest that Black Sabbath has sold out because they allowed "Iron Man" to be featured in a 2006 Nissan commercial doesn't explain how or why anyone would connect a 1970 Black Sabbath song with selling pickup trucks in the first place. Indeed, authenticity-talk aside for the moment, the real oddity here is not that rockers approaching retirement age will accept big dollars for the thirty-second use of a song they recorded decades ago; the truly puzzling thing is that ad agencies are willing to pay huge coin for the thirty-second rental of a forty-year-old product. (I'm sure that Fats Domino, his life left in ruins by Hurricane Katrina, would happily have "sold out" his songbook to advertisers; problem is, no one was that interested in buying—while the remaining members of the Doors routinely continue to turn down million-dollar offers to use snippets of "Light My Fire" or "Break on Through" in advertising campaigns.)[5]

In short, it would seem that what's changed in the last several decades is neither the imperatives of dominant discourses like advertising (sell stuff!), nor high school administration (keep order!), nor even really the imperatives of classic rock (which still promises to "come into your town, and help you party down!"), but the relation among these imperatives: what's different, it seems, is the larger cultural and economic sea in which these discourses, once so very divergent or even antithetical, now somehow swim synchronously.

The Sun Is the Same, in a Relative Way, but You're Older

The easy answer to this conundrum can be summed up in two words: "baby boomers." The prime demographic target for crime dramas, classic rock radio, or luxury car commercials (forty- to sixty-year-olds with disposable income) has become one with the demographic of people running the advertising agencies, and they're both sets of folks who grew up with "classic rock"; so an advertiser can easily and economically index all that "youth" supposedly stands for with one easy riff or song lyric: lust for life, just push play, start me up, been a long time since I rock 'n' rolled. On the easy explanation, in other words, classic rock is all over the place because baby boomers are all over the place, on both the production and consumption side of much of our dominant culture. Sure, my crew-cut-wearing high school principal wouldn't go for Black Sabbath, but he was born in the 1920s and came of age during World War II, well before the first wave of rock 'n' roll in the mid-1950s. "Cool" was not his métier. However, today's suburban high school principals, who one presumes follow CEOs and politicians in asking students to call them by their first names, would have grown up on rock 'n' roll, and many of them were in fact weaned on the classic rock of the 1970s.

So, if you want to know why Cadillac plays classic rock under its ads, just think about Cadillac's target market and who's producing the ads: aging white baby boomers trying to recapture some of their rockin' youth. Cadillac needs to rebrand itself, from your Uncle Bernie's car to yours. What better way to rebrand a stodgy car line for baby boomers than to play Aerosmith or Led Zeppelin under your ads? In short, one answer to the question "how does 'Iron Man' end up as a truck commercial?" is quite easy: the riff from the song recalls for middle-aged, white, exurban consumers some sense of carefree nostalgia, being yourself, taking risks, having fun, rockin' out. You're cool, a little bit subversive, and so is the car, so throw away your inhibitions, like you would back in the day, and spend some dough! Classic rock, then, has migrated from its roots as site-specific music of the '60s and '70s and been reinvented as a kind of contentless cultural style: the mandarin commitment to an always "rebellious" subjectivity, identifiable by platitudes that are at this point as easily applicable to right-wing blather of Rush Limbaugh as they are to the music of Canadian power trio Rush. "Do your own thing" has become the Hegelian law of the whole.

This "authenticity nostalgia" explanation also holds for the unusual popularity of classic rock radio (oldies for people who hope they die before they get old) and helps explain why I had to suffer through the entirety of "Rikki Don't Lose That Number" while looking for some hardware at Lowe's the other day. Classic rock's ubiquity is a sign of white suburban baby boomers stubbornly hanging on to the authenticity of their youth, in a series of spaces—the home-repair store, the orthodontist's office, Cleveland's classic rock station—that could hardly get any less authentic.

On this line of reasoning, the prescription for classic rock's cultural longevity is then relatively easy to reconstruct: drain the leftist political stances and the druggy danger out of rock music, and conveniently forget or downplay rock's roots in African American culture, and there you have it—not exactly the "durable Republican majority" that Karl Rove had openly dreamed about, but something parallel. Let's call it a durable cultural style of subjective empowerment, perhaps—one that Robert Christgau (1991) lays out (with maximum prolixity) in his discussion of "how politically retrograde the classic-rock mindset is": "Not for nothing did classic rock crown the Doors' mystagogic middlebrow escapism and Led Zep's chest-thumping megalomaniac grandeur. Rhetorical self-aggrandizement that made no demands on everyday life was exactly what the times called for." In other words, classic rock at this juncture functions in popular culture as little more than an endless incitement to become who you want to be, being your own person, not following everyone else, and all the other stuff that cultural subversives like Miss America contestants and former sports stars talk about in their Sunday prayer breakfast speeches.

What's changed most radically in culture at large is the very status of authenticity itself—or, more precisely, the relation between consumption and authenticity. In the not-so-recent past (even in the classic rock past, if songs like "Satisfaction" and "Stairway to Heaven" are to be believed), there was an outright antagonistic relation between commodity consumption and personal authenticity: the more you consume, the more you're like everyone else, the less authentic you are, mostly because you're simultaneously buying stifling social norms when you buy products (as "Satisfaction" ironically puts it, "he can't be a man because he doesn't smoke / the same cigarettes as me"). In the past twenty or thirty years, however, the work of commodity consumption has been rebranded as part and parcel of the work of individuation and subversion, and thereby a certain style of consumption has become a royal road to authenticity (rather than an assured off-ramp).

In the process, the concept of authenticity in and around rock music has become completely portable and completely personal—it's not so much located anymore in the music or even the ostensible "scene" surrounding the music; nor is authenticity to be found in keeping up with the Joneses, or in the collective consciousness of the age, but in *you*, whoever you may be. The commodities you collect around you are authentic signs of the real you, not evidence—as the Buzzcocks would have it—that you're "hollow inside." Classic rock has become, for better or worse, the sound track of choice for becoming who you already are, and as such it mirrors and extends the baby boomers' slide from the "We" generation of the '60s to the "Me" generation of the '70s, a generational ethos proving to have legs far beyond the usual ten years allotted. And wild, wild horses couldn't drag your authenticity—or your classic rock—away.

Following along after Jameson's mammoth analyses of postmodernism as a phase where the innovation-driven logic of cultural production ("make it new!") becomes central to the logic of economic production as well (consumer capitalism that has consistently to churn out new objects for consumption), one might venture something like the following thesis about the longevity of classic rock as a cultural commodity: *It's the workings of capitalism itself that have changed most radically over the past forty years.* The rock 'n' roll style of rebellious, existential individuality, largely unassimilable under the mass-production dictates of midcentury Fordism, has become the engine of post-Fordist, niche-market consumption capital-ism. Authenticity is these days wholly territorialized on choice, rebellion, being yourself, freedom, fun; and these, what one might call the "values" of classic rock, today hold for your choices in music as for your choices in cars (Saab: Choose your own road), computers (Microsoft: Where would you like to go today?), and virtually every other commodity you can think of. Even hyperconservative, fundamentalist Christian political candidates these days run as "mavericks."

In short, capitalism today promises the same subjective authenticity as the once-outlaw commodity called classic rock. So it's not at all that classic rock has "sold out" to capitalism, but that capitalism has morphed into the kind of thing that, at its center rather than at its margins, now has a use for classic rock. Fly high, free bird.

Young Americans

This explanation makes some sense of classic rock's long-lasting run in what seems to be a short-term market for cultural commodities, but it does leave at least one bustle in the hedgerow completely unexplained. I certainly see why people like me (b. 1963) might remain invested in clas-sic rock—nostalgia for authenticity, the days of carefree teenage discovery, sex and drugs and rock 'n' roll, and so on. The more puzzling question is why anyone born in the meantime would gravitate toward classic rock. Why or how, one wonders, do today's teenagers and young adults happily consume a "youth culture" that was originally produced by people who are now old enough to be their grandparents? (Alas, both Mick Jagger and Keith Richards became eligible for full Social Security benefits when they turned sixty-six back in 2009.)

In other words, this analysis helps explain why someone like me might listen to classic rock radio or be interested in buying a truck because Sabbath plays under its commercials, but it doesn't necessarily shed any light on the enthusiasm that younger folks feel for classic rock. If indeed the classic rock canon was pretty much set when the moniker was in-vented in 1979 (with many of its cornerstones more than a decade old even at that point), it's hard to imagine how today's freshman class of college students would have much investment in this music. How can today's teenagers and young adults receive another generation's music as relevant any more than the crooning of Perry Como struck young people as timely in the late '60s?

Surely, the pull of a nostalgia-based "authenticity" has something to it for younger folks as well, but for people who are today in middle age, that "authenticity" at least has a tenuous referent, even if it's only the vague memory of bell bottoms, bongs, or disco demolition night at the local ballpark. In other words, if you're over forty-five, you may have a classic rock past to romanticize—not so much if you're presently in high school. So, about the only thing that's left for young folks, on this "classic rock's longevity = baby boomer nostalgia" reading, is that they function as the Adorno and Horkheimer–style cultural dupes who have been patiently waiting in the wings of this story.

While I suppose that this a tempting conclusion (people who grew up during the last decade or two in the US have no "authentic" or common cultural identity to speak of, other than as a consumer), at another level, this also strikes me as ridiculous, yet another manifestation of baby boomer exceptionalism. Commercial radio or arena rock reunions are probably not the right place to go looking for "what's happening" in popular music today. Surely, young people listen to classic rock. But that's not all they listen to, by a long shot.

Ironically, it's precisely this new eclecticism of musical tastes that presents a problem to the founding assumptions of rock criticism, which holds as an article of faith that subjects' investments in the music are supposed to be deeply felt and strongly held markers of cultural identity: you can't wear your "Disco Sucks" T-shirt on Thursday and head for a disco on Friday. But it's just such an "anything goes" aesthetic that seems on the ascendancy today—download them all, and let the iPod shuffle sort them out. According to Larry Grossberg's "Reflections of a Disappointed Popular Music Scholar," this emergent youthful eclecticism of musical taste (what he sees as the new "dominant apparatus" for consuming music) is less a progressive evolution of musical listening habits than it is a retrograde reversion to a '50s-style "Top-40" model of corporate force-feeding:

The apparatus that is becoming dominant is a new mainstream that actually looks a lot like and is committed to much of the logic of the Top 40. . . . Top 40 has always been hybrid, bringing together in a statistical sample the disparate tastes of various taste cultures. The result is a collection of music the totality of which no one actually liked, but that, given the alternatives, many people listened to. Yet I believe today the dominant apparatus embraces a similar kind of eclecticism. Rather than claiming some sort of rock purism, it celebrates rock hybridity at its most extreme and celebrates as well its own eclecticism. . . . In fact, this apparatus—and the individuals within it—embrace an extraordinarily wide and (at least to my musical sensibilities) jarring range of music. The fans within this formation may like some classic rock, some country, some punk, some disco, some rap, and so on. And because these fans happily switch among these genres from song to song, spending an evening with them can be a strange experience for someone who still lives within the becoming-residual formation. (2002, 47)

For Grossberg, what's primarily lost in the withering of the "residual" formation of rock culture is a hard mediating logic of subjective authenticity. In the dominant "rock" cultural formation of an earlier era, investments in the music were inseparable from investments in identity: anyone who insulted your music's authenticity also implicitly questioned your personal authenticity. However, for Grossberg, this is increasingly not the case. Within the new cultural dominant, he argues that younger music fans'

tastes are not taken as the grounds for other larger and more significant types of judgments of other people or groups. They have largely given up the differentiating function of rock even as they attempt to hold onto its "territorializing function" in relation to a politics of fun and everyday life. They are tolerant beyond anything that the once dominant, now residual, paradigm could understand. Taste is increasingly lived as if it were merely a site of individuality and shared entertainment, nothing more and nothing less. . . . People dislike what they dislike (or what particular individuals in the group dislike) but they do so largely without the mediations of a logic of authenticity. (48)

In short, young people still happily consume classic rock, but it's precisely the content-free *consumption* of music that's the problem for Grossberg. No one's willing anymore to get into screaming matches about the relative merits of *Wish You Were Here* because people's investments in Pink Floyd are now unmoored from larger claims to (their own or their group's) subjective authenticity. Grossberg's claim (or maybe his "disappointment") is that classic rock is now just another product—"shared entertainment, nothing more and nothing less." In the rock era, by contrast, it used to be a cornerstone of authentic identity formation and a potential site of oppositional cultural resistance.

The question of classic rock's present-day "authenticity" has taken another somewhat bizarre turn in a recent flap among rock critics concerning the "whiteness" of contemporary "indie" music. In a 2007 essay called "Paler Shade of White," *New Yorker* rock critic Sasha Frere-Jones wonders "why rock and roll, the most miscegenated popular music ever to have existed underwent a racial re-sorting in the 1990s. Why did so many white rock bands retreat from the ecstatic singing and intense, voicelike guitar tones of the blues, the heavy African downbeat, and the elaborate showmanship that characterized black music of the mid-twentieth century?" Such "miscegenation" is yet another way to make a retroactive claim for the authenticity of classic rock—and quite a bizarre one at that: the claim seems to be that Led Zeppelin, with its full-blown appropriation of African American blues forms, was somehow racially more progressive than bands like the Decemberists or Arcade Fire, whose sound doesn't rely heavily on such forms.

In responding to Frere-Jones, *Slate* critic Carl Wilson (2007) takes the opportunity to pile on, arguing that not only is contemporary indie music too "white," but it also lacks classic rock's broad class appeal (cue Springsteen, and obligatory shots of football stadiums full of white kids raising a fist to blues licks served up by Grand Funk Railroad). Wilson calls contemporary indie music "bookish and nerdy," "blatantly upper-middle class and liberal-arts-college-based": in short, "class, as much as race, is the elephant in the room." Even though classic rock's most successful practitioners are aging white multimillionaires whose primary talents consisted of repackaging black music for white audiences, classic rock nevertheless somehow continues to function in contemporary music debates as a kind of unquestioned, authentic gold standard for racial openness and the classless society.[6]

Regardless of how (in)accurate such estimations of contemporary indie music may be, what interests me here is the notion that both Frere-Jones and Wilson share with the substantially more sophisticated analysis of Grossberg: the contemporary sense that the classic rock era was an unparalleled harbinger of cultural authenticity. This stance is summed up by no less an authority than *New York Times* editorialist David Brooks (2007) in his two cents on the issue: "Musical culture," he writes, "has lost touch with its common roots," which Brooks helpfully limns out for us: "Muddy Waters, the Mississippi Sheiks, Bob Dylan and the Allman Brothers." For Brooks, the memory of those "throngs who sat around listening to Led Zeppelin" function in the new millennium not as a pathetic portrait of aimless, white suburban stoners, but as the last vestige of a common culture that could "span social, class, and ethnic lines."[7] One could, of course, say much about the willful cultural amnesia of all this—more aging white male, baby boomer exceptionalism—but I'm particularly interested in noting here the myriad high-culture places where classic rock continues to function as a marker for authenticity of all kinds, ideological fantasies of both the left and right: classic rock functions as a common cultural heritage, a version of the classless society, a place of racial understanding and admixture, and a site of oppositional identity formation. It's also worth noting that this authenticity is, on all these accounts, completely lost on the younger generation, even if they profess to "like" classic rock among a series of other musical genres.

Oddly, though, even if one accepts this kind of tsk-tsking reading of the new generation, the young music fans of today are both dupes and not dupes enough—insofar as they have been tricked into falling for a once-vibrant, but now flatulent and reified product (a Top-40 version of classic rock); but interestingly enough they haven't fallen for the economic engine of these larger consumerist processes, the endless dialectic of commodity obsolescence. On the rock-critic reading, young people today are not supposed to like this product (yesterday's classic rock); they're supposed to like that one (today's hip-hop or emo)—and all the while they're supposed to be vaguely worried about the commodity status of music itself. But a product's a product, and it's getting increasingly hard to believe the baby boomer line that classic rock was ever anything but one—the fable that it actually had a great deal of political content that could somehow be siphoned off from its commodity status (for further skeptical ammunition, see here prepackaged protest songs like the Monkees' "Pleasant Valley Sunday," or Sonny and Cher's "The Beat Goes On," which poignantly reminds us that "the rock band's a business man today").[8] Ironically, it's those of us cultural-critic types (those who still stubbornly believe in the ultimate trumping value of the "new") who may be the real cultural dupes waiting patiently at the end of this story, as we are perhaps the last generation still holding out for the high modernist connection between stylistic/ formal innovation and cultural value, where the culturally new functions as the vanguard moment of the dialectic, that emergence that has yet to be completely assimilated.

One might define authenticity, on this line of reasoning, as a certain kind of refashioned modernist "make it new," that which remained most stubbornly left over from modernism in the work of postmodernism.[9] For his part, Jameson succinctly defines the postmodern condition like this: "What has happened is that aesthetic production today has become integrated into commodity production generally: the frantic economic urgency of producing fresh waves of ever more novel-seeming goods (from clothing to airplanes), at ever greater rates of turnover, now assigns an increasingly essential structural function and position to aesthetic innovation and experimentation" (1991, 4–5). In terms of Jameson's work on the concept, any number of critics have pointed out that his postmodernism remains driven by a kind of hypermodernism of avant-garde innovation—and this seems true enough. But, stepping from the diagnostic to the critical for a moment, I think we'd also have to locate the properly critical power of postmodern critique precisely in that same "make it new" modernism; that is, the critical moment in most economic or cultural analyses of the postmodern depends on the continuing sense of shock, indignation, or dislocation at the fact that cultural production does indeed share the same logic as high-end economic production; the impulse to point this homology out then functions as a kind of "aha" moment of critical revelation.[10]

So, you're postmodern in this Jamesonian sense if this collapse of economic production into cultural production (and vice versa) still strikes you as something that endlessly needs pointing out. For example, Grossberg sums up his analysis of the musically eclectic, post-rock present, as follows: "If those within this [dominant] apparatus embrace commodification without illusions, it is because they cannot imagine an outside to or a way out of commodification" (2002, 49). I think it's fair to say that you take up a "postmodern" position if such rampant commodification remains, strictly speaking, a "problem" for your analysis (in other words, if commodification functions as a conclusion or end point of your analysis, as it does for Grossberg). Conversely, if rampant commodification functions as a more or less neutral beginning premise for your analysis of popular culture, your position is "post-postmodern": if the tongue-in-groove meshing of artistic and economic production is all you've ever known, the very thing we learned from folks like Jameson in the early '80s, why should it shock or discombobulate you three decades later? In other words, insofar as today's youth (and this is really a global story—there's even a thriving heavy metal scene in Iran[11]) still has a great investment in classic rock, cultural critics should be able to find something to laud (maybe even something ironically "new") here. In embracing and recycling the rock music of the past, the current generation is simultaneously refusing the larger engine of the culture industries, the constantly updated tyranny of the culture industry's obsolescence machine. If nothing else, it shows young people staring down the reality of their times, marked by "commodification without illusions."

Ironically, though, in refusing the absolute tyranny of "authenticity" or "innovation" in their musical consumption patterns, today's classic rock youth are not so much throwback figures in this story (Adorno and Horkheimer's "victims" of the culture industry) or even ironic postmodern consumers who consume the faux authenticity of the old with a certain new cynical or knowing edge; rather, today's classic rock fans seem to function as what we might call quintessential post-postmoderns—those for whom the entire economic and cultural logic that holds "newness = value" seems a suspicious holdover of something else, or at least something that doesn't really name their experiences of consumption or life. And as we look back, it's a little hard to explain how the 1960s story of discovering a commodity like rock radio that then inexorably changes one's suburban white life— an experience enshrined in countless personal testimonies and in classic rock staples like the Velvet Underground's "Rock and Roll" or Queen's "Radio Gaga"—is qualitatively different from a subsequent generation's discovery of iTunes or the shopping mall: they both allow a certain sense of atomized belonging mixed with the potential for constant updates of your self-branding through commodity consumption. One undoubtedly seems "cooler" than the other (I'll leave it to the reader to decide which vhich), but in the twenty-first century, it's very hard indeed to suggest that knowing a lot about the Beatles is different in kind (or somehow more "authentic") than knowing a lot about the various styles at Abercrombie & Fitch. In contemporary parlance, they both allow you to be a quintessential "prosumer," that consumer who produces him- or herself through consumption.[12]

In strictly theoretical terms, the upshot of this would seem to be that Jameson's postmodernism hasn't at all failed or been overcome, but rather triumphed in a way similar to other classics of the late twentieth-century theory canon. Think of Roland Barthes's "Death of the Author" or Judith Butler's gender performativity: these are no longer concepts that you have to laboriously sell to freshmen. They already know this stuff; in fact, they live it. Postmodernism, performativity, and the death of the author are no longer "emergent" phenomena, but they've become "dominant" ones. For example, if you grew up with chat rooms and Facebook, the performative truisms that people have multiple identities and that identity is not "original" (it has to be cited and repeated from a social stock of available avatars) can hardly come as a shock. Concerning the death of the author, not even the most sincere freshman these days needs to be told that Emily Dickinson is not the ultimate arbiter of her poems' meanings—quite the opposite (if anything, students today are a little too confident in their own ability to produce meaning). In terms of postmodernism today, the links that Jameson highlights between cultural and economic production/ innovation have hardly disappeared in the new millennium; rather, they've been smeared across a broad range of other commodities. The connoisseur's care and attention that used to be reserved for wonking your favorite bands has made its way all the way up to the board room—where innovation and rebellion are touted as necessary to any healthy business model—and all the way down to the ever-changing minutiae of cell-phone applications and ring tones.

So, in the end, it may be that classic rock's unprecedented longevity is not an exception to the iron rule of planned obsolescence, but oddly, in classic rock's very obsolescent popularity, its long strange trip shows the cultural logic of authenticity and obsolescence itself becoming increasingly obsolete. Consumption in the present cultural market for music has largely become unmoored from newness as the ultimate test of authenticity and value; and in the offing this cultural shift gives us an inkling of the passing of the high postmodern phase of US cultural production into something not exactly new, hardly "better" or "worse," but something that's certainly different: cultural and economic post-postmodernism.

CHAPTER 4

University

THE ASSOCIATE VICE PROVOST IN THE GRAY FLANNEL SUIT: ADMINISTRATIVE LABOR AND THE CORPORATE UNIVERSITY

Family, school, army, and factory are no longer so many analogous-but-different sites converging in an owner, whether state or some private power, but transmutable or transformable coded configurations of a single business where the only people left are administrators.

—GILLES DELEUZE, "POSTSCRIPT ON THE SOCIETIES OF CONTROL"

The end of the cold war in the late 1980s could have brought with it a massive peace dividend in the US, a national welfare state of unprecedented expanse and largesse: a shiny new government-funded public sphere, fat with butter and short on guns. Couple the end of the cold war with the triumph of the "new" or "information" economy, where continuous training increasingly seems a must, and the last two decades might have been characterized by a huge boom in particular for government funding of higher education. Instead, the dreary reality is that the end of the cold war brought the triumph of '80s-style corporate neoliberalism, the economic name for privatization on a national, and increasingly global, scale. The leveraged buyout years in the US were fueled by now-familiar Reaganite slogans (Down with big government! No new taxes! Privatize for efficiency!), and those refrains intensified in the 1990s, wreaking particular havoc on government funding for education. And the economic downturns of the 2000s have intensified this crisis of funding, with new and unprecedented cuts in state appropriations for education. According to a 2011 report by the Center on Budget and Policy Priorities, "An Update on State Budget Cuts," at least thirty-four states have made deep cuts in K–12 education funding in the wake of the economic meltdown, and forty-three states have cut back assistance to public colleges and universities. In higher education, this conservative economic agenda (downsizing state spending) further opens the door for the triumph of the "corporate university," a set of practices and management styles that remains bitterly disputed around countless academic watercoolers nationwide, at both public and private schools, at large universities as well as small colleges.

While there's quite a bit of progressive or leftist discourse around the topic of corporatization and the university, very little of it actually takes up corporatization itself as a topic, explaining or considering how this larger economic process called "corporatization" works, where it came from, and how its stated ends might be refashioned in more progressive directions. Rather, the dominant mode seems to be worry over an immanent academic "crisis" and "corruption" caused by corporatization's creep into the ivory tower. One needs only to survey book and essay titles to get a flavor of the discourse surrounding this topic: *The Last Professors: The Corporate University and the Fate of the Humanities* (Donoghue 2007); *University Inc.: The Corporate Corruption of American Higher Education* (Washburn 2005); *Higher Education under Fire: Politics, Economics and the Crisis of the Humanities* (Bérubé and Nelson 1995); *Higher Education in Crisis: The Corporate Eclipse of the University* (Natale et al. 2001); *Will Teach for Food: Academic Labor in Crisis* (Nelson 1997); "Ivory Tower in Escrow" (Miyoshi 2000a). Masao Miyoshi gives us a concise, if polemical, version of the prevailing wisdom: "The corporatization of the university is destructive anywhere" (2000b, 692). He continues in an even more dire tone by arguing that, in the absence of some kind of intervention, it's bound to get worse, much worse. According to Miyoshi, we're in an "interim period," but there's a complete corporate readjustment of the American university on the way in a generation or so: the evisceration of tenure; even larger armies of poorly paid, part-time instructors; closing down or savage cutting of humanities programs; and the continuing upward redistribution of wealth and power to the top administrative ranks (presidents, deans, provosts, directors of development), while people doing the teaching and research labor get increasingly squeezed out of any say in the future directions of higher education.

Indeed, when former Treasury secretary Lawrence Summers succeeded a humanist as president at Harvard (2001–6), you had to suspect that the firewall between higher education and corporations had been breached, if not eradicated altogether. Stanley Aronowitz gives a concise picture of the present in *The Knowledge Factory*:

Since the 1980s, the academic system of American society has undergone another process of profound transformation. . . . Having adopted the framework and ideology of large corporations, universities and colleges—private as well as public—are "downsizing" in the name of rising costs and declining or stagnating revenues. . . . Presidents and chancellors resemble CEOs rather than academic leaders. For the most part, their grasp of the mission of the university has been articulated in terms of (a) the job market and (b) the stock market. The intellectual mission of the academic system now exists as ornament, that is, as a legitimating mechanism for a host of more prosaic functions. (2001, 62)

While some of the hard sciences got the gold mine as a consequence of university corporatization since the '80s, most of the humanities got the shaft, especially following the near depression of 2008: downsized departmental staff and faculty, furloughs and pay cuts for tenure-line faculty, not to mention less influence concerning university policy, higher teaching loads, intensified tenure requirements, and ruthless exploitation of part-time instructors. And those are the lucky programs. Liberal arts mainstays like classics departments are quickly becoming a thing of the past; any course of study that finds itself unable or unwilling to speak to the dictates of the contemporary "market" will be downsized out of existence in the new corporate university. Training students for new-economy jobs, applying for grants, and raising funds from donors on the side: these "prosaic functions" are "job 1."

In any case, Aronowitz here makes a point that virtually everyone agrees upon: since the 1980s, the university—along with the *socius* at large—has become increasingly like a corporation. Now, what's to be *done* about that corporatization, or how one *responds* to it—these are matters about which there's substantially less agreement. The debates surrounding the corporate university are well known, high profile, and too complex for me to summarize quickly here.[1] Suffice it to say, what I want to add to this discourse is neither an affirmation nor a condemnation of the corporate university; rather, I'd like to follow out the analysis I've begun of corporatization itself, to see if the internecine war for the soul of *corporate* America might offer any strategies or points of intervention for the *academic* struggle over the corporatization of the university. I want to see if the similarities and differences between university corporatization and corporatization at large can offer us different angles of intervention within this ongoing debate.

What I'm doing in this chapter is a continuation of the Jamesonian imperatives that I laid out in Chapter 1 (and tried to perform in both the Las Vegas and the classic rock chapters). Just to take a reflexive moment to recall the methodological gambit: take one set of cultural claims (about the '60s, gambling in Vegas, rock music's commodity status, or the state of education in the corporate university) and overcode those cultural claims with another set of economic imperatives or explanations. When one then returns to the cultural claims, this intensifies and modifies the claims, and one can no longer dialectically return to the initial, seemingly commonsense claims and see them in quite the same way. As Jameson writes in his provocative essay on Walmart as a kind of model for utopia, no one suggests that Walmart's sheer size is a "problem," but people suggest this about socialist government all the time. So he thematizes his engagement with Walmart "as an opportunity to exercise the Utopian imagination more fully, rather than an occasion for moralizing judgments or regressive nostalgia" (2009, 423). Just as Jameson suggests there may be some interesting things to be learned from juxtaposing the practices of Walmart with the possibilities of socialism (around the question of scale), here I'm trying to do something similar with neoliberal corporatization and higher education (around the question of downsizing or cutting). If socialism has to be big to be successful, as Jameson suggests, maybe it can learn something from the world's largest corporation. And if higher education has to cut somehow to stay alive in the near term, maybe it has something to learn from the people who brought you downsizing, '80s-style corporate practitioners.

The University in the Eyes of Its Accountants

The first and most obvious difference between universities and large corporations is that the vast majority of universities are ostensibly non-profit organizations—they issue no stock and have no shareholders.[2] With some trepidation, I'd argue that this is both a good and bad thing—good insofar as it keeps the university from engaging in the most savage kind of economic behavior that's become standard operating practice for most corporations; but it also creates a kind of difficulty, because, as one commentator puts it, "Universities are not accountable to anyone but the trustees, and can't be influenced in the way regular corporations can be pressured by shareholders" (White and Hauck 2000, 122).

In the war for the soul of American business, flexible specialization and shareholder influence won, while the univocal behemoth of slow, managed growth lost: recall Harvard economist Michael Jensen's glee as the "inefficient," "bloated" management of the old corporate world ("the man in the gray flannel suit") was sent packing, with the looming possibility of further savage cuts continuing, in Jensen's model, to "encourage managers to act in shareholders' interests" (2000, 244). Economically speaking, this has meant massive downsizing layoffs in the name of profit-mongering "efficiency." Blue-collar workers, and even more directly white-collar middle managers, were the targets of these cuts, while wealthy shareholders and CEOs were the beneficiaries. As the American Management Association wrote in its report on downsizing, "There is a consensus that middle managers . . . are among the hardest hit in this leaner, meaner business climate."[3] In the wake of the savage realignment of the 1980s and '90s, the *last* thing you want to be in today's economy is a middle manager, hopelessly "entrenched" among other levels of stagnated, slow administration. A sitting duck for downsizing.

Unless, that is, you work in *university* administration. Studies show that between 1975 and 1993 (roughly, the leveraged buyout years), student population increased in American higher education by 28%, "while non-teaching administration increased in personnel by 83 percent" (White and Hauck 2000, 163–64). The NEA offers slightly different numbers for its study of the period 1976–95, but it offers a similar conclusion. Over that twenty-year period, the NEA reckons that numbers of students and faculty rose at about the same rate, up 25% and 27%, respectively (though *full-time* faculty hiring in fact *dropped* 17% during this period, as mandates to downsize expensive tenure-track lines brought large numbers of part-timers into the teaching workforce). However, full-time executive and administrative staff grew at almost double the rate of new students, 45%, while the ranks of "other professional staff" rose a whopping 150% between 1976 and 1995.[4] A separate NEA study of the years 1993–2001 shows a further intensification of the administrative hiring boom that began in the '80s: administrative hiring for the 1990s was up an astonishing 48%; and while the hiring of "other professional staff" cooled somewhat, it was still up 36% in the period 1993–2001 (NEA *Update* 9.2). In comparison, the number of full-time faculty at American colleges and universities rose only 4% during that period (*Update* 7.4).[5]

There has been, in other words, a kind of puzzling anomaly or unevenness between academic corporatization and the economy at large during the leveraged buyout years: corporatization at large has shrunk the middle-management ranks and made business command structures more flexible, while the "corporate" academy has positively bloated itself on rigid layers of paper-shuffling administration. Shelia Slaughter and Gary Rhodes put it very concisely in *Academic Capitalism and the New Economy*: "In contrast to the pattern in industry, where the numbers of middle managers have declined, colleges and universities have greatly expanded middle management" (2004, 332).

As Richard Brown and Remi Clignet point out, academic institutions have lagged embarrassingly far behind business by remaining resolutely "inflexible and hierarchical in their management practices. Thus, colleges and universities remain dwarfs in relation to the giant major corporations, and there is a growing asymmetry between economic and educational institutions in their relative tactical agility, financial resources, and political powers" (2000, 22). In short, whether it's a good thing or not, '80s-style corporatization has made American business more flexible by cutting out large layers of management. By contrast, such an "entrenched" management in American academics has flourished. Corporatization in the economy at large has spelled certain doom for large, slow bureaucracies, in the public as well as the private sector. But corporatization in the university has seen exactly the opposite movement. Aronowitz highlights the all-too-familiar scenario: "At many public universities in the past two decades, faculty hiring has been virtually frozen while administrative hiring has experienced a veritable boom" (2001, 66–67).

In fact, in retrospect it seems clear that the building of a permanent managerial academic class has been among the most important cogs in the wheel of university corporatization. Aronowitz savvily points out the problem:

The formation of a permanent administrative bureaucracy in education was the crucial internal precondition for the gulf that now separates faculty and students from educational leaders, leading to the development of the corporate university. . . . The learning enterprise has become subject to the growing power of administration, which more and more responds not to faculty and students, except at the margins, but to political and corporate forces that claim sovereignty over higher education. (164)

In a kind of inversion of economic developments since the '80s, the university has resolutely refused to disgorge or deterritorialize its cash flows, paying them out neither to students (through reduced fees or tuition) nor to faculty (by hiring more tenure-line professors). The university has, rather, sunk its resources resolutely into building a labyrinthine administrative bureaucracy, and one that's become a permanent career track: largely gone are the days when a provost or dean rotates back into the faculty when his or her term is finished. Like a Roach Motel, you can "check in" to administration, but increasingly you can't "check out."

And this is where another seeming homology between academic and economic corporatization breaks down: from a leftist perspective, the "entrenched bureaucracy" of the midcentury corporation begins to look positively progressive when compared to its downsized, lean-and-mean heir. But in academics, it's precisely the bloating of entrenched administration that has furthered the negative effects of corporatization. In other words, managerialism was the clear *target* of '80s-style corporate warfare; but such managerialism has paradoxically been both the *vehicle* and continuing *effect* of academic corporatization. As Brown and Clignet argue, those in university administration have seen

an alliance between the faculty and the students as a threat to their own positions and the funding base of their institutions. Educational administrators no longer acted as leaders of a community of scholars and learners, nor as national spokespersons for enlightened values, nor even as intermediaries between the ivory tower and the fields of government and business. Instead, they became specialized bureaucrats engaged in tasks more narrowly defined. . . . Their primary functions became those of quelling internal dissent and securing external funds. (2000, 30)[6]

And Aronowitz clearly concurs, citing the evisceration of "faculty sovereignty" as having been the hidden agenda driving university corporatization all along: "It should be evident to all but the most myopic observer that the worst abuses of the collegium have been in the abrogation of faculty sovereignty by the corporate university" (2001, 66).

Of course, faculty themselves bear no small responsibility for the abrogation of their sovereignty and the rise in power of corporate administrators. In my experience, most tenure-track faculty members want absolutely nothing to do with the administrative functions of the university, and many restrict their involvement with those functions to complaining bitterly about work they've left others to perform: "Why are my classes so overfull? Who admitted these unprepared students? Where's my new computer, my raise, or my travel funding?" It may simply be that, as Thomas Tighe puts it, "there is a sense in which faculty can be said to be too involved in the world of theory and thought to be violated by the world of practical affairs" (2003, 58), and hence the faculty has simply ceded those practical functions to the administration.

There's another line of reasoning, however, that paints tenure-track faculty not merely as the passive dupes of an administrative takeover, but as the primary culprits in the triumph of the new lean-and-mean corporate university. And oddly enough, this discourse often comes from the left side of the political spectrum. The argument goes something like this: At some point not that long ago, teaching loads and administrative responsibilities were relatively consistent across a wide range of institutions—most tenure-track faculty taught three or four courses per semester, in addition to rotating in and out of administrative duties. At some point, though, a rising class of full-time administrators offered a Faustian pact to tenure-track faculty at research institutions: "We'll make you a star, kid—we'll reduce your teaching load, give you more research time, enhance your travel budget, take away any administrative responsibilities. All you have to do is tacitly agree to sit by silently while we hire an army of exploitable part-time workers to take up the teaching slack." Desperate for recognition and perks, lacking in vision but fully "equipped with efficient mechanisms for deluding themselves" (Nelson and Watt 2004, 30), the faculty fell for this deal hook, line, and sinker.[7]

On this line of reasoning, the publish-or-perish rise of research-driven "theory" (and the subsequent death of an agreed-upon teaching mission or "core curriculum" for many disciplines) is largely responsible for an academic world where there are fewer seats on a more comfortable tenure-line boat,[8] a situation that Cary Nelson and Stephen Watt very pointedly cash out in their critique of tenured faculty at research institutions: "For every person earning $50,000 to $100,000 or more for teaching a course there are hundreds more earning about $1000 or $2000. . . . With every budget cut the exploited group typically suffers more while the protected class remains protected. Can we continue to pretend that one group is not living off the exploitation of the other? Is not the indifference of the lucky, the wealthy, the comfortable, the empowered, fast becoming an intolerable scandal, at least for an industry that seeks to be admired and supported for commitments of a higher order?" (2004, 32). While it's hard for any leftist not simply to say "right on, man" in the face of this kind of critique (and then to ask back channel how one can apply for the $100k-per-course job), there remain some problems with this explanation for the rise of contingent teaching labor in the university.

Nelson and Watt here round up the usual suspects within most popular discussions of the university's decline: people with tenure at research universities, pampered folks who make good coin and spend a lot of time writing books on arcane topics (which is another way to say, not enough time teaching). In short, people like Nelson and Watt (and, I guess, me—as I am also a professor in a Big 10 English department). While blaming research-obsessed faculty for the problems of academe is a proven argumentative winner (right-wing pundits in particular love it), I wonder what real power it possesses in the context of the academic labor crisis, either as an explanatory mechanism or as a blueprint for effective future action. Indeed, Nelson and Watt's zero-sum reasoning—person X has a crappy job *because* person Y has a good one—doesn't necessarily do much work in thinking about distributions of wealth and goods, in the university or elsewhere. Despite what your dean tells you at every faculty meeting, there is no inherent scarcity of resources in the corporate university: if there were, where did they find the money to build a highly paid army of college administrators, or the dough to give a fat raise to that colleague who got an external job offer? And who's paying to put up these new buildings and dorms? Not to mention the CEO-style salaries for the president and his circle, and the seven-figure football coach? There is no shortage of resources coursing through the corporate university—the question is how they're allocated and how they might be reallocated more equitably. And turning part-timers against the faculty in this struggle over academic labor is bound to lead to the same problem that one sees whenever one population is turned against another in the fight for supposedly scarce resources: an unproductive war among those who should be allied against a common enemy.

The relationship between tenure-line positions and the exploitation of contingent labor, in other words, was not *created* by the well-paid tenured professor with the arcane research agenda and the light teaching load; rather, this labor system was created and is maintained by university administration. And the scandal is not that someone or another has a good tenure-line job, but that there aren't a whole lot more of them. The problem, in short, is the administration's maintenance of a scarcity discourse around tenure-track lines—a containment strategy made easier to maintain by liberal doses of faculty guilt. And, even if one agrees with Nelson and Watt that the faculty are often silent partners in the contingent labor crisis (which strikes me as true enough), the present academic labor situation could hardly have been *avoided* if the Faustian research bargain had somehow been refused by tenure-track faculty—if there were no "stars," less of a research focus, and everyone taught more classes for less money throughout the humanities and social sciences.[9]

My point here is simply this (and here Cary Nelson and I are clearly back on the same page):[10] any fix for these problems of part-time labor will have to involve the intensification of faculty sovereignty—more jobs and more control over administrative functions—rather than personal scapegoating or self-loathing, and any future activism worth the name will have to strive to make all teaching jobs (inside *and* outside the university) into something like "good" tenure-line faculty jobs. Yes, too few of the privileged are presently spending their institutional capital agitating (or even thinking seriously) about this issue of labor and distribution of resources. But in the end, I think it's hugely disempowering to propagate the party line that is heard over and over concerning tenure-line faculty: one person's tenure-track success adds up to the wholesale exploitation of others. This zero-sum line of reasoning only drives tenure-track faculty further underground, rather than mobilizes them around this crucial workplace issue.

"You're fired." —Donald Trump

So what do we do? Put bluntly, it seems that the corporate university is in need of an '80s-style leveraged buyout by its shareholders—those who, as Jensen reminds us, "guarantee the contracts of all constituents" (2000, 2). In the case of the university, it seems that such a stockholder position is occupied precisely by those who have been ousted by academic corporatization: faculty and students, the people who put up the intellectual capital that runs the entire operation, and those who bear the real brunt of the university's gains and losses. From a business perspective, it's hard not to conclude that the administration is the cash-wasting "entrenched bureaucracy" that needs to be savagely downsized in the corporate university, or at least this is what we might learn from doing a genealogy of '80s-style corporatization.

If the corporate university is here to stay, it pays for those within the structure to strategize and think through strategic problems on corporatization's own terms. And while I'm sure that this seems perverse to many, '80s-style economic theory offers some provocative tools and arguments to folks who would want to strengthen the position of those ousted by corporate managerialism in the university. Recall, as Doug Henwood points out in his indispensable book *Wall Street*, that the "argument is, in a phrase, that stockholders can't trust the managers they've hired to run their corporations, and a radical realignment is in order" (1998, 265). This, it seems to me, very concisely names the present state of the corporate university.

But, aside from a provocative analogy, what exactly does this brief history and transcoding operation offer us? First, I think it makes us wary of the way the academic corporatization debate has been diagnosed or framed. Too often, the enemies in the corporate university game are diagnosed as outsiders—stingy grandstanding politicians or control-mad donors. While donor influence and shrinking state funding are real problems, I think we learn from this genealogy that the more pressing problem is right in front of us—no farther away than the administration building. In fact, the rise in importance of academic "development"—outside fundraising—is routinely lamented by my friends and colleagues and is one of the first lightning rods for resentment among progressive critics of university corporatization. But let's remember that virtually every "important" left-leaning critic or theorist in America sits in a donor-funded chair. And let's also recall that donors, savvy businesspeople that they ostensibly are, don't like to think about their monies going to feed a bloated bureaucracy. Donors overwhelmingly want to fund the intellectual work of the university—students and curricula, not assistant vice provosts for academic excellence. Development contributions are treated by donors as charity, and no one will continue to give to a nonprofit that soaks up huge amounts of donor contributions in administrative costs. In the end, nobody ever attended a university or donated money to it primarily because he or she was smitten by the administration.

If, in the final analysis, academics is beholden to corporate forces, it may pay for us to look at the genealogy of corporate "downsizing" and make our case directly to donors and other funders: faculty and students are not the "fat" in higher education. Indeed, as corporations demonstrated in the '80s, the army of highly paid but largely unproductive middle administrators is the expendable sector in any command structure.

Though we should recall that future possibilities for faculty leverage looked very bleak only a few years ago, when it seemed that distance education and for-profit online universities, with their fast-food version of knowledge production and consumption, would all but obliterate faculty and student input in higher education. However, the distance ed craze has cooled considerably, and the for-profit university world has been rocked by scandal. In fact, it seems clear that a combination of faculty refusal to cooperate, copyright problems concerning uploaded materials, and the continuing cultural capital of an old-fashioned, face-to-face university education have severely damaged the distance ed dream. Faculty are refusing to have their expertise instrumentalized by distance ed, and students (as well their potential employers) aren't buying this myopic vision of "university education." Indeed, this rollback of distance ed is, it seems to me, something that promises faculty even more leverage in the future: in short, the major funding streams—the students and the donors—continue coming to the university largely because of its symbolic capital, that is, *faculty* and what they have to offer. As David Noble points out in his authoritative work on the subject, distance ed was fueled by the university administration's dream of finally wiping out faculty sovereignty. But if the administration lost that battle—if as Noble writes, "the bloom is off the rose" (1998) of distance ed—then the battle itself surely confirms the centrality of faculty-student interaction in higher education. Likewise, the bursting of the distance ed bubble evidences yet another expensive blunder of the corporate university's administration. And, if the *Wall Street Journal* is to be believed, corporations don't look kindly upon those responsible for such expensive mistakes.

To put it somewhat perversely, I'm suggesting that in many ways *the corporate university isn't corporate enough*, or that it isn't corporate in the right way, insofar as the present configuration of the corporate university isn't really dedicated to the dictates of the so-called new economy: excellence of the product, and the maintenance and well-being of the people who invest the (cultural and monetary) capital that sustains the operation. Indeed, the most pressing "problem" in the corporate university has been building an entrenched management structure that seems to believe the university exists for its administrators.

Of course, there are several caveats immediately attached to such a perverse call: first, clearly not *all* administrators constitute the problem. For several recent years, I served as a half-time administrator myself; and, as they say, some of my best friends work in administration. I hasten to add that positively heroic work goes on in these ranks every day. It's easy to complain from the academic sidelines or the classroom lectern; but it's much harder actually to get involved in the day-to-day economic battles of administration. So this is not simply to slag administration wholesale. However, as those who serve in the administrative trenches recognize, much of the heroic work therein has to be directed *against* a creeping "administration-think": the increasing sense that education—the work of students and faculty—is no longer the raison d'être (the "core business," if you will) of the university.[11] At its worst, such administration-think is guilty not merely of displacing the educational and research mission from the center of the operation, but of actually framing the higher education debate in such a way that faculty and students constitute the principal "problem" to be "managed" in higher education. As far as administration-think is concerned, eviscerating faculty tenure and upping student test scores are the core "educational" issues in the university. The line of thinking seems to go something like this: in responding to the challenges of the twenty-first century, universities finally require more management—part-time instructors ruthlessly overseen, post-tenure review for full-time faculty, and more intensive testing for students. Intensified administration seems to be the prescription for the future health of higher education.

Economically speaking, such cries for increasing the scope and power of management in higher education are truly astonishing. Bar none, every other business sector in the current economic climate is struggling to find more ways of tapping the potential of its creative wing—the peer-to-peer synergy of symbolic analysts and other "idea" people—by cutting out entrenched layers of 1950s-style, top-down management and intrusive centralized regulation. Not so in the university, however. And this constitutes the real perversity of the current economic discourse surrounding the university: the sense that, unlike any other "cutting-edge" business in America, higher education somehow needs *more* management, rather than *less*, for it to thrive in today's flexibly specialized world.

Second caveat: I'm certainly not suggesting that the university adopt wholesale the downsizing fever of corporate America. Such a fever has to be treated aggressively wherever it appears. However, insofar as such a virus has clearly spread to academia, and calls for further cuts are inevitable, we should at least be clear concerning the potential targets and desired outcomes of such university "rightsizing." And the choice for the future of academics is increasingly stark: Is the "rightsized" future one that looks to increase the intensity and scope of the educational mission? Or does the future health of higher education call for increasing layers of top-down management? Put in this way, the future choice should be clear—even to the most ruthless MBA accountant.

Mea culpa: This diagnosis and prescription exist in some tension with calls for faculty unionization. While I can see and support the reasons behind such calls, and I think it makes all the sense in the world for graduate students and part-timers to unionize, it remains an open question whether unionization is the best path for revitalizing tenure-track faculty sovereignty. My university, for example, insists that tenure-track faculty are "management," and as such we're not able legally to organize as labor. Rather than continuing to insist that we're "labor" to the administration's "management," I'm suggesting here that we shift tactics somewhat—that we accept and amplify the role that the administration has given to faculty. Instead of fighting the label of "management," we might in fact embrace it, and in turn ask the administration: "OK, we're management. But if we're managing the place, what the hell are you doing here?"[12]

Final caveat: At the risk of engaging in outright blasphemy against a book that is almost universally adored, I have to confess that I've long been baffled by the reception surrounding Bill Readings's analysis of the corporate U, *The University in Ruins* (1996). Readings recalls, in broad strokes, the early theorizations of the modern university carried out by Von Humboldt and Kant, and shows (quite deftly) that the modern university was conceived as a vehicle for the transmission of national culture, a sense of shared *Bildung* for a nation. For a host of historical reasons, not the least of which is the weakening of the nation-state under a regime of global corporate capitalism, that "cultural" reason for the university's being has eroded, leaving something of a void in the discourses that would justify the work that university professors do. Enter "the university of excellence." Readings's primary thesis (that corporatization was brought to the forefront in the university through a focus on contentless "excellence") strikes me as largely correct, if a tad confused about how excellence is somehow the ruination of the university, and even more confused about whether that ruination was visited upon the university from without.

Some version of excellence has never been far from the gold standard in academics; however difficult excellence may have proven to define, it's clearly been at work in academics long before business self-help guru Tom Peters made it into an official guiding principle of globalized corporatization in his 1988 book, *In Search of Excellence: Lessons from America's Best-Run Companies*. Long before the categorical imperative to "be excellent to each other" was driven home to us in the 1989 film *Bill & Ted's Excellent Adventure*, academics were in the business of accessing whether or not students' or colleagues' work meets a standard of excellence: what else is the work of grading, student admissions, faculty hiring, reviewing dossiers to determine raises or promotions and awards, organizing conference panels, or the blind reviewing of manuscripts for publication? Of course, to denounce a "contentless" notion of excellence doesn't necessarily commit you to a flat-footed notion of "content," policing acceptable topics for scholarship. But Readings's beef, embarrassingly old-fashioned it seems to me, boils down to this: an emphasis on excellence suggests that university training doesn't "mean anything," one hastens to add "anymore." Indeed, for Readings the crisis of the contemporary university is first and foremost a crisis of *meaning*, of referentiality. "To understand the corporate university," Readings insists, "we must ask what excellence means (and does not mean)" (1996, 12). And in the end, excellence doesn't mean a damn thing—it has no referent—and this is precisely why it's taken off as a buzzword in academic administration. While this seems true enough as an observation, it seems to me that the primary task before us is to examine what excellence *does* in the corporate university (around questions of academic labor, acquisition and distribution of funding, etc.), rather than quibble endlessly about what it *means* (the favored bait-and-switch tactic of social conservatives: trade a properly economic question for a question about "values").

So, what does excellence do, in terms of progressive or left-leaning scholarship and teaching in the academy? Oddly enough, the university of excellence (where "meaning" or "content" doesn't drive the discourse) is the place where leftist academic scholarship, whether it likes it or not, is most clearly on the same page as university corporatization. Donors, for example, are not squeamish about funding chairs for Marxists, postcolonial critics, feminists, cultural studies types, or queer theorists—as long as they're *excellent* Marxists, postcolonial critics, feminists, cultural studies types, or queer theorists. Conservative deans and provosts will fall all over themselves to hire lefties of all stripes, as long as they have an impressive publication record. Just in my own backyard, for example, staunch Republican ex-coach Joe Paterno donated the money for a chair that's occupied by Michael Bérubé. My former colleague Henry Giroux, a savage critic of corporate media, has taken a chair at McMaster, funded by the Canadian equivalent of Rupert Murdoch. My point here is most certainly not that these folks are "sellouts," but that the university of excellence has been very, very good to theory, feminism, gender studies, cultural studies, poststructuralism, postcolonialism, African American studies, visual culture, and the like, precisely because work in these areas dominates the "excellent" university presses. (Got a formalist reading of Shakespeare that focuses on the universal theme of heroism? Good luck getting it accepted for a Modern Language Association panel or published by an "excellent" journal. Got a manuscript that focuses on sodomy and economics in *Hamlet*? Your chances just got a whole lot better. Is this a loss of "content" or "meaning"? If so, good riddance.)

Indeed, it's not clear to me why we're to lament the loss of the university of content or meaning, *Bildung* on the German model. I point this out not so much to pose a question to Readings's book, as he harbors little nostalgia for it himself, but to stress the near ubiquity of a stance or set of stances that puts leftist critics of the corporate university inevitably in league with social conservatives, as if there were no other possible critical alliances to be built or critical concepts to use as tools in restructuring the outcomes of the corporate university. My alternate genealogy of corporatization suggests that a contentless emphasis on excellence (as a synecdoche for conservative economic policies) isn't the primary problem with the corporate university: the problem isn't, in other words, that the university has caved in on its moral obligations and become just like every other business in the contemporary global economic field. In fact, the problem with the corporate university is almost exactly the opposite: we have adopted a model of management-driven corporatization that is completely anachronistic. The hierarchical managerial structure of the corporate U looks a lot more like the IBM of the 1950s (or at times, like the medieval Catholic Church) than it looks like the horizontal, streamlined, high-tech Silicon Valley firms of the 1990s. Returning to my own backyard for just a moment, this pervasive hierarchical structure of university administration (protect the other administrators at all costs) was on tragic display in the Jerry Sandusky child molestation scandal that rocked Penn State in 2011.

Historically or economically speaking, the emphasis on excellence is as much an academization of the corporate world as it is the opposite. In production-based modes of corporate assessment, symbolic analysts have relatively little to say; but finance capital's measures, like the academy's, are largely if not wholly symbolic—not just *how many* widgets you produce and sell, how many books you publish, or degrees you grant, but the *excellence* of those widgets, publications, degree candidates—hence, the cash value of cultural theorists, who are flexibly specialized symbolic analysts par excellence. University degrees have long derived their value from brand-name recognition, or what Pierre Bourdieu more portentously calls "symbolic capital" (1987). Decades before ad agencies and corporate governance gurus became obsessed by building and maintaining brand loyalty through excellence, colleges and universities understood and maintained themselves largely as brands. For example, while the content of higher education is more or less similar across a wide range of institutions, everyone knows that an Ivy League degree is worth more than one from a state university, which in turn is worth more than one from a community college. A Harvard degree is excellent just like a Prada bag is: the inherent excellence of the raw materials isn't what makes either one valuable (all history degrees, like all leather bags, are made of pretty much the same stuff). So it's the brand (which is partially to say, the initial cost paid) that guarantees the continuing value of either commodity, on both economic and social registers. And this hyperattention to brand names was standard procedure in the higher education business long before anyone dreamed of paying $2,500 for a shoulder bag.

To sum up, my critique of Readings's book is a simple historical one: corporatization has not been visited upon us from the outside, imposed by a creeping business-think that makes academic work look and feel increasingly like corporate work. Indeed, the work of corporations over the past twenty years has come to look increasingly like the traditional work of academics (symbolic analysis, virtual labor, information production and evaluation, brand management), rather than vice versa. This is an important difference in diagnosis of the problem, because when we start looking to treat the ill effects of corporatization, this genealogy offers us different tools for intervention and different (more easily locatable) targets. In the university, we have met the "corporate" enemies, and they are our managers, not some faceless, distant businesspeople. And as shrinking public funding increases the moves toward corporate privatization for the big public universities, this analysis suggests we need faculty sovereignty again to be front and center on the agenda, as we talk to donors and corporate interests about what's both unique and valuable about the American university model (more about this in the Coda). Bloated management is not what's made the American research university the undisputed global leader in higher education.

In the end, regarding progressives fighting corporatization in the academy, I'm arguing that an alliance with the enemy may still be in order, but that the provisional ally is not the *cultural* conservative (who also wants to take the university back, by rebuilding the national canon, refocusing education away from trendy PC theories and back onto the "great" texts, etc.). For example, the most controversial aspect of Aronowitz's *Knowledge Factory* (subtitle: *Dismantling the Corporate University and Creating True Higher Learning*) concerns his proposing a kind of alliance with cultural conservatives to fight corporatization. At the end of his book Aronowitz offers, as a practical example of the education that will bring back "true higher learning," a core curriculum that would make E. D. Hirsch very happy indeed. While I agree with Aronowitz in many ways—more Spinoza more often!—such a strategic alliance is limited in my view, and not because it's an alliance with a conservative canon, but rather because it continues trying to fight corporatization on the grounds that the university is somehow tainted by being or becoming a business. Insofar as the university is *already* a business, the question is not how to keep it from becoming one, but rather, How is it going to be run in the future? For what reasons? For the substantial benefit of what populations inside and outside the university community? And according to what labor protocols?

So if we want to take the university back, perhaps we should take our inspiration not from *cultural* conservatives but from *economic* ones, who'd teach us to "unlock shareholder value" in higher education by severely trimming and streamlining the administrative ranks of middle management and disgorging that excess cash back into the "core business" of teaching and research, thereby turning the university back to the people who bear the real brunt of its success or failure: the faculty and the students.

SECTION 2

THEORY GOING FORWARD

Rereading

ON THE "HERMENEUTICS OF SITUATION" IN
NIETZSCHE AND ADORNO

In "Reading on the Left," Christopher Nealon (alas, no relation) lays out a concise version of the Jamesonian drama I've been trying to stage here in *Post-Postmodernism*. Jameson is of course well known as a symptomatic reader, insofar as he is often reading for allegory, for a political unconscious or an inferred stance toward capitalism in texts that would seem otherwise to have very little to say about economics. As he infamously writes, "Every position on postmodernism in culture—whether apologia or stigmatization—is also at one and the same time, and necessarily, an implicitly or explicitly political stance on the nature of multinational capitalism today" (1991, 3). Given this stance, one could take Jameson's project (as many people do) to be uncovering or exposing these buried, "symptomatic" economic imperatives secreted away within cultural artifacts. This, as I suggest at the outset, might be thematized as the "negative" pole of Jamesonian dialectical analysis—undermining and uncovering.

However, in addition to these symptomatic "depth" readings, Nealon highlights a second kind of "historical" reading practice in Jameson, one that's especially evident in Jameson's representation of "untimely" thinkers like Adorno and Sartre. (Recall that Adorno's stock was not particularly high when Jameson published his Adorno book in 1990, at the fall of the Berlin Wall; and Sartre couldn't have been less fashionable when

Jameson was touting him in the high poststructuralist era). In short, precisely at the historical moment when "those thinkers seem discredited or superseded" (2009, 25), they become most useful again. At these historical junctures, Nealon argues, a Jamesonian "'symptomatic reading' involves figuring out how history and the text have come around to meet each other once again, how what once seemed like weakness in an argument, or in a mode of presentation, can come to find new force, or even truth, in a later period. . . . In these moments, Jameson's symptomatic style of reading emerges not as a hermeneutics of suspicion but as a hermeneutics of situation—a kind of reading that proposes texts for our attention because they seem useful for historicizing the present" (25).

It is in this spirit of rereading thinkers (and the recent history of theory itself) not for any supposed truth-content or meaning, but for some useful tools in thinking differently, that I want to perform this interruptive excursus right in the middle of this book, and then go on to take up the question of theory qua theory in the present and the future. It should be obvious by now that the overcoding practice that I've borrowed from Jameson is precisely such a "hermeneutics of situation"—aimed at offering tools for thinking differently about the present, rather than primarily either exposing or undermining the supposed "truth" of this or that cultural position. Here in this excursus, I'll be working with two figures (Nietzsche and Adorno) who are on the surface blisteringly hostile to the very idea of any kind of positive "situational" relations among thinking and capitalism. The overcoding experiment is to see if they may offer us some very valuable tools for rethinking those questions, specifically in and through consideration and deployment of the unique *styles* of Nietzsche's or Adorno's thought. In other words, following along from my opening gambit with Jameson, here I'm interested in leaning less on *what* Nietzsche and Adorno have to say about culture and economics (their negative, undermining exposure of its lies), than in *how* they say it—maybe in the service of wondering whether, as Deleuze asks, a person has to be sad to be militant? I begin with a brief untimely excursus on Nietzsche, and move on to discuss Adorno—two cranky "hermeneutics of suspicion" thinkers to be sure (especially when they turn to questions of culture and economics). But it's precisely that kind of offhand, even gruff crankiness that I think offers us some stylistic tools in the present, and why I want to steal *mon frère* Nealon's phrase "hermeneutics of situation" to think about ways to redeploy their thinking in the present. So what follows are two short experiments in theory that are played out stylistically in a slightly different way than the rest of this book, but that I think nonetheless sum up the ethos of the entire project and the practice of overcoding reading that it's trying to develop through intensification. The corrosive, undermining "hermeneutics of suspicion" style of negative analysis practiced by both Nietzsche and Adorno has been well documented;[1] but, as I'm doing with Jameson throughout this text, I want to suggest that perhaps Nietzsche and Adorno's less-discussed modes of affirmation or positivity—literally, the way they do their work, how it works rather than what it means—may be more useful to us in responding to our situation in the present.

Excursus 1: Nietzsche's *Money!*

Confronted with the ways in which our societies become progressively decodified and unregulated, in which our codes break down at every point, Nietzsche is the only thinker who makes no attempt at recodification. He says: the process still has not gone far enough.   —GILLES DELEUZE, "NOMAD THOUGHT"

It's somewhat odd that Nietzsche's corpus is looked upon as the cross-disciplinary progenitor of our contemporary "post-" world. For all its slippery descriptions and heterogeneous definitions, there is perhaps nothing more universally recognized as "postmodern" or "posthuman" than the triumph of consumption capitalism—the obliteration of humanist use-value and the concomitant domination of mechanistic exchange in this, the age of money as the ultimate general equivalent. Though there's still a lot of disagreement on the microlevel—for example, over what constitutes posthumanist visual art, or what might be the distinctions between postmodern and post-postmodern literature—everyone seems to agree on the macrolevel that a certain style of consumption-based capital both puts the "posts-" in post-postmodernism and runs the "human" out of posthumanism.

One can, for example, see this consumption anxiety as the central conundrum of recent cultural studies in North America, which seems hopelessly stuck squabbling over what one might call (after Elvis Costello) the "I used to be disgusted, now I try to be amused" quandary: Are everyday consumer practices of "post-" society to be condemned as the inauthentic canalizing of desire by capitalist masters? Or are such practices to be celebrated as forms of subversive agency performed by savvy consumers? Following the Frankfurt School, are we to be "disgusted" by contemporary consumerism? Or, picking up on Michel de Certeau's analysis of everyday subversion, are we to be "amused" by the multifaceted, posthumanist subjectivities that are born in and around contemporary economic practices?

So my starting point in reconsidering Nietzsche's relevance for the "post-" world is here—or, rather, *beyond* this debate. The ubiquity of third- (or fourth-)wave capital is, for better or worse, what Gilles Deleuze and Felix Guattari call the "body without organs" of our era of globalization, its most wide-ranging plane of consistency, the field within which the posthuman desiring machines of capital nomadically roam. As Deleuze and Guattari write about our globalized world, "The universal comes at the end—the body without organs and desiring production—under the conditions determined by an apparently victorious capitalism" (1983, 139). A capitalism that, they remind us, is "the only social machine that is constructed on the basis of decoded flows" (139). Capital, in other words, is simultaneously the "problem" we must learn to respond to, and the field of forces wherein that discontinuous response will be worked out or worked over: "Capital," Deleuze and Guattari argue, "is indeed the body without organs of the capitalist" (10); and insofar as we are consuming producers, whether we like it or not, we are all de facto capitalists here at the beginning of what promises to be a very disputatious millennium.

Certainly, one way to revisit Nietzsche's relevance at the contemporary post-post-moment would be to examine what his corpus has to say about these debates over economics and contemporary culture. But this introduces a bucket of problems right away: even his staunchest admirers might have to admit that Nietzsche has very little trenchant to say about consumerism and bourgeois culture—other than that he hates them both. In regard to a mandarin condemnation of popular culture, Nietzsche can often make Adorno look like Joe Sixpack. In fact, the bourgeois type is the most obvious figure in Nietzsche for the "base" individual, who looks only to accumulate wealth, work long hours, and please the herd at work. What he calls this "common type" lives quite happily "in the midst of an age of 'work,' that is to say, of hurry, of indecent and perspiring haste" (1982, 5). Such a base bourgeois type, it seems, cannot understand Nietzsche's corpus at all, "cannot comprehend how anyone could risk his health and honor for the sake of a passion for knowledge" (1974, 78).

Indeed, insofar as the claim to Nietzsche as the grandfather of the post-isms makes any sense at all, he seems best understood as the grandfather of a certain strain of "aesthetic" post-ism, obsessed with questions of self-overcoming, performative subjectivity, living with multiplicity and flow. He is *not*, as far as I can tell, seen as the grandfather of much productive work on "economic" post-ism. One doesn't often see Nietzsche cited in discussions of post-Fordism or post-Keynesianism, for example.

This short excursus is a modest attempt to change that. It seems to me that Nietzsche has much constructive to offer, even in his ambivalence, for a hermeneutics of situation designed to size up and respond to contemporary capitalism. Territorialized as it is on global flows of money, flexibly specialized labor markets, symbolic economies, transvaluation, and the dice throw that is the stock and futures markets, Nietzsche's work should have much to tell us about the situation of transnational capitalism—the speeds and slownesses inscribed on the body without organs that is our world of global capital. More specifically, I'll try to suggest that Nietzsche has much to teach us about capital's most slippery symbolic materiality: money. Following Nietzsche in *The Gay Science*, perhaps today we should ask ourselves, "Do you understand this new law of ebb and flood" (1974, 76)?

To add an additional hurdle, I'd like to structure this excursus as that most contemporary of consumerist textual forms, the business "self-help" manual, much like bestsellers *The Seven Habits of Highly Effective People* or *Leadership Secrets of Attila the Hun*. So the subtitle of this experiment is "The Five Most Will-to-Powerful Laws of Nietzschean Personal and Financial Growth." All of which we'll get to in a minute.

But first, another obstacle: Nietzsche's critiques and comments concerning economics are not only mandarin, but they also seem hopelessly romantic and negative—a kind of neo-Wordsworthian pining for a life not territorialized on "getting and spending." As Nietzsche writes, "The most industrious of all ages—ours—does not know how to make anything of all its industriousness and money, except always still more money and still more industriousness" (1974, 94). Or, as he writes about "the American lust for gold": "The breathless haste with which they work—the distinctive vice of the new world—is already beginning to infect old Europe with its ferocity and is spreading a lack of spirituality like a blanket. Even now one is ashamed of resting, and prolonged reflection almost gives people a bad conscience. One thinks with a watch in one's hand" (258–59). This particular critique—a kind of slacker's critique of the "Man"—may seem oddly resentful, especially coming from our greatest proponent of *amor fati* and diagnostician of resentment. Some of Nietzsche's sentiments, in fact, seem ready for easy translation to the jauntily resentful workplace antics of the comic strip *Dilbert*—a character whom nobody ever mistook for the *Ubermensch*: "Oddly," Nietzsche writes, "submission to powerful, frightening, even terrible persons, like tyrants and generals, is not experienced as nearly so painful as is this submission to unknown and uninteresting persons, which is what all the luminaries of industry are" (107). Post-postmodern translation: Work sucks—and Nietzsche certainly knew a thing or two about remaining on disability for long periods of time.[2]

But, as true as it is, "work sucks" is *not* the First Law of Nietzschean Personal and Financial Growth, and I would hesitate quite a bit before suggesting that Nietzsche's only practical advice for hacking the situation of contemporary capitalism is to complain about your boss's incompetence or to Xerox your ass on the company copier. His critiques of modernity and its discontents—the triumph of clock time, the banalization of work, the leveling of all culture by the general equivalence of money—certainly suggest a refusal of work, but I think his intervention goes further than that: if we learn first and foremost from Nietzsche that one must diagnose a sick system if one is to "treat" it in any effective way, performing such a genealogy of capital will more fruitfully lead us to discovering lines of flight from that system, the Laws of Nietzschean Personal and Financial Growth.

For Nietzsche, money's leveling effect on modern life is an extension of the triumph of general equivalence that he traces in the *Genealogy* and elsewhere: the capitalist, in other words, is the new ascetic priest. Capital continues and completes that special kind of violence that characterizes the triumph of the weak. As he writes in *Daybreak*,

For if one man employs false weights, another burns down his house after he has insured it for a large sum, a third counterfeits coins; if three-quarters of the upper classes indulge in permitted fraud and have the stock exchange and speculations on their conscience: what drives them? Not actual need, for they are not so badly off, perhaps they even eat and drink without a care—but they are afflicted day and night by a fearful impatience at the slow way in which their money is accumulating and by an equally fearful pleasure in and love of accumulated money. In this impatience and this love, however, there turns up again that fanaticism of the *lust for power* which was in former times inflamed by the belief one was in possession of the truth and which bore such beautiful names that one could thenceforth venture to be inhuman *with a good conscience* (to burn Jews, heretics and good books and exterminate higher cultures such as those of Peru and Mexico). . . . What one formerly did "for the sake of God" one now does for the sake of money, that is to say, for the sake of that which *now* gives the highest feeling of power and good conscience. (1982, 123)

Post-postmodern translation: God is soooooo money! And, as Nietzsche makes clear, this is the case not because God and money both *represent* something similar—far from it. What they represent or what lies behind them is wholly beside the genealogical point, because God and money are not metaphors or signifiers at all; rather, they're modes of power. In fact, they are networks of interrelated practices that enact or attract the lowest forms of reactive force (swindling, counterfeiting, insider trading), fueling that "lust for power" that makes a mockery of the "will to power."

It's not surprising, perhaps, that this genealogy leads us to discover the First Law of Nietzschean Personal and Financial Growth: God is dead, but the NASDAQ remains volatile. Both God and money, in other words, have a common face or enact a common truism: it's all about the practices of *force* and *power*, not about the states of *truth* or *representation*. Like God, an Internet or tech start-up NASDAQ stock doesn't really represent anything at all—there's nothing tangible or authentic "behind" it; but both certainly do comprise and enable certain kinds of *command*.

In short, as Deleuze and Guattari (those relentlessly post-post heirs to Nietzsche) insist, language is not primarily meant for interpretation, but obedience and resistance: "Writing has nothing to do with signifying. It has to do with surveying, mapping, even realms that are yet to come" (1987, 4–5). One might say that the performative in Deleuze or Nietzsche doesn't succeed negatively by showing the inevitable failure of the supposed constative; rather, it succeeds the old-fashioned way—as a positive deployment of force, as a provocation. For this reason, Nietzschean or Deleuzian *amor fati* is about transformation of the present, not about fatalistic acceptance of an inevitable future or pining for a golden past. The cash value of truth or representation is beholden to a deployment of force, rather than vice versa.

This leads us to consider Nietzsche's most famous commentary on the interrelations between money and truth:

What is truth? A mobile army of metaphors, metonyms, anthropomorphisms, in short, a sum of human relations which were poetically and rhetorically heightened, transferred, and adorned, and after long use seem solid, canonical, and binding to a nation. Truths are illusions about which it has been forgotten that they *are* illusions, worn-out metaphors without sensory impact, coins which have lost their image and now can be used only as metal, and no longer as coins. (1989, 250)

In recent commentary, this passage from "Truth and Lying in an Extra-Moral Sense" is often folded interpretatively back upon the essay's larger point about conceptualization and the forgetting of an originary experience: the concept is base coin, the faded representation of a representation, the residue of a metaphor that is itself guilty of forgetting the originary experience. Because truth and money are twice removed from the unthematizable experience of singularity, the history of money thereby becomes a figure for the history of truth, as both dress up a historical regression—increasing abstraction and conventionalization—as "progress." In *Symbolic Economies*, Jean-Joseph Goux argues along these lines that "the substitution of the concept for the image means a loss. . . . For Nietzsche, the imprinted head, the visible trace, is at the root of the concept; but from image to concept, what disappears, by attrition, is the vivacity of the impression. . . . For Nietzsche, the concept is a paltry reality in comparison with the image: it is an eroded, diminished, faded image—a cliché" (1990, 104, 105, 106).[3]

As compellingly "right" as Goux's interpretation is as an example of the undermining hermeneutics of suspicion (the supposed truth is actually a lie), I would argue that the stake or upshot of Nietzsche's intervention on coins and truth is not finally metaphors or images or falsifying significations at all. Rather, perhaps the stake of this passage (read for a hermeneutics of situation rather than suspicion) concerns the "binding" (*verbindlich*) function that confers an obligatory or compulsory signification upon this chaotic "mobile army" of discontinuous relations. Near the origin or far away from it—either way, it's all about *force*. "Truth and Lying in an Extra-Moral Sense" is not merely a lament for lost original experience; rather, Nietzsche's challenge is to affirm the fact that truth and lying are not treated in any serious way if they are treated moralistically or judgmentally—as if truth or lying referred to any preexisting moral standard. Money is akin to truth, then, not because both fail to represent some *Ursprung* of preexisting value and thereby figure the loss of some kind of originary "vivacity." Rather, both the worn coin and the clichéd truth show you the wisdom of the Second Most Will-to-Powerful Law of Personal and Financial Growth: What does not kill my portfolio only makes it stronger.

In other words, Nietzsche would always show us that markets (of money, of truth) are sites of struggle and risk: the coin, like the concept, (already) has a face—the Janus face of power, which is manifest in social *exchange*: measuring, calculating, valuing. Nietzsche's intervention concerning truth and/as a coin teaches us that the value of truth or money is the product of a *dynamic action*, not the mere referencing of a *static state*. When one determines value, it finally doesn't make any difference what's printed on the coin or what one calls the truth—a thing's value is enforced not by the thing itself, but from elsewhere, from a relation of social force and strife. As Antonio Negri holds in *Marx beyond Marx*, "Money has the advantage of presenting me immediately the lurid face of the social relation of value; it shows me value right away as exchange, commanded and organized. . . . Money has only one face, that of the boss" (1996, 23). Like the general equivalent that is the truth, Negri insists on the Nietzschean point that "money is a *tautology for power*. A power that extends everywhere" (35).

Recall, in this vein, Nietzsche from the *Genealogy*:

The feeling of guilt, of personal obligation, had its origin, as we saw, in the oldest and most primitive personal relationship, that between buyer and seller, creditor and debtor: it was here that one person first encountered another person, that one person first *measured himself* against another. No grade of civilization, however low, has yet been discovered in which something of this relationship has not been noticeable. Setting prices, determining values, contriving equivalences, exchanging—these preoccupied the earliest thinking of man to so great an extent that in a certain sense they constitute thinking *as such*: here it was that the oldest kind of astuteness developed; here, likewise, we may suppose, did human pride, the feeling of superiority in relation to other animals, have its first beginnings. . . . Man designated himself as the creature that measures values, evaluates and measures, as the "valuing animal as such." (1967, 70)

This quotation leads us straightaway to the Third Nietzschean Law of Personal and Financial Growth: All good things are bathed in blood at their origin (including your TIAA-CREF Social Choice Account).

Nietzsche's genealogical insistence on "thinking" as a kind of exploitation, a price-setting mechanism, shows us why the rampant consumerism of the postmodern is never about "choice"—or why more consumption oftentimes adds up to fewer choices: the ubiquity of consumption is a problem, everyone agrees, but one can't simply accept or reject consumerism. As Deleuze and Guattari write, "Capitalism . . . proceeds by means of an axiomatic and not by means of a code" (1983, 251). So-called third-wave capital, for example, works according to the axiom "consume!," and you really can't choose to ignore or refuse that axiomatic pronouncement—it's not up to "you," whoever you might be. As Fredric Jameson explains, capital's "axioms . . . are operational: they do not offer anything for commentary or exegesis, but are rather merely a set of rules to be put into effect" (1997a, 398). One doesn't get to *decide* to denounce capitalism or appreciate it—or even really to comment on it or understand it. But you do have to *respond* to it, insofar as capitalism is all about axiomatic deployments of force—from its significations right through its border patrols. Contemporary capitalism, one might say in a slightly different idiom, is not the sort of thing that hides—it's everywhere, all the time—so a depth-oriented hermeneutics of suspicion may not offer the most effective tools to diagnose it. If the truth's not hiding, maybe it doesn't need to be uncovered. Likewise, we all probably already recognize the hermeneutics of suspicion truism that driving a Prius or eating local foods is not actually to resist capitalism in any meaningful way (insofar as it's just more consumption capitalism, all the way down); but it's not clear that such a guilty realization or truth is worth much as a response to the totalizing situation of globalized consumption capital.

As *amor fati* teaches us, judgment and condemnation are weak tools indeed: condemning capitalism, like condemning thinking, will get you nowhere, and only catch you up in a kind of Habermasian "performative contradiction." From where "outside" can you judge capitalism wholesale? Simply condemning something is the weakest, most resentful form of power's deployment—the reactive puffing up of "human pride" and self-righteous "good feeling." On a Nietzschean reading, exchange and valuation are clearly deterritorializing, "affirmative" values: the problem with modern or postmodern consumerism is that this notion of exchange or valuation gets territorialized on the human subject and the concomitant "feeling of superiority" that comes with possession and ownership. As Deleuze and Guattari write, "Capitalism is inseparable from the movement of deterritorialization, but this movement is exorcised through factitious and artificial reterritorializations" (1983, 303)—private property, subjectivity, the desire for control. Such reterritorializations configure the *socius* as a negative body without organs—closed, privatized, suffocating. And it is this junky body that haunts the air-conditioned totalitarianism of late, later, or just-in-time capitalism.

So, for Nietzsche, Deleuze, and Guattari, it seems one can broach the question of value only by attempting to leave behind the organic, the authentic, and finally the privilege of human consciousness itself, because the kind of subject we are is the most reactive pustule of resentment. As Nietzsche points out, "Our pleasure in ourselves tries to maintain itself by again and again changing something new *into ourselves*: that is what possession means" (1974, 88). Such a "ridiculous overestimation and misunderstanding of consciousness" (85) being the case, "how," Nietzsche asks, "should explanations be at all possible when we first turn everything into an *image*, our image" (172)? Humans are reactive pockets of consumerist interiority, and that's also why we have to *become something else* if we are to be capable of transvaluing values. The problem, in other words, is not capitalism but the style of subjectivity that capitalism has produced, selected for, and rewarded—appropriation, judgment, denunciation: these are the residues of humanism that must be overcome if bourgeois subjectivity is to be transvalued.

But in the service of this project (on the other side of the coin, as it were), we should keep in mind the fact that capitalism is a great deterritorialization machine. Response to its axioms is the social manifestation of force, flight, and reconfiguration. The electronic flows of multinational capital are perhaps our version of Nietzsche's faceless coin, traded at a dizzying pace across national, monetary, and linguistic boundaries. It is this movement of capital, this flow, that forces us to confront a different kind of power, and thereby to search for something other than the weak weapons of humanism—the resentful judgments and condemnations of moralism. Recall Deleuze: "Judgment prevents the emergence of any new mode of existence. . . . It is not a question of judging other existing beings, but of sensing . . . whether they bring forces to us, or whether they return us to the miseries of war, to the poverty of the dream, to the rigors of organization" (1997, 135). Following in the footsteps of Nietzsche's analysis of reactive force turning on itself in the will-to-nothingness (and thereby opening the possibility of an exfoliation of ascetic priesthood into overcoming-man), both Nietzsche and Deleuze urge us to find ways to surf capital out of capital, through the deployment of the Fourth Law of

Personal and Financial Growth: Don't moralistically denounce or judge capital, but rather experiment with its speeds and slownesses—see what (else) it can do!

"Which," Deleuze and Guattari ask in *Anti-Oedipus*, "is the revolutionary path? Is there one? To withdraw from the world market . . . in a curious revival of the fascist 'economic solution'? Or might it be able to go in the opposite direction? To go still further, that is, in the movement of the market, of decoding and deterritorialization? For perhaps the flows are not yet deterritorialized enough. . . . Not to withdraw from the process, but to go further, to 'accelerate the process,' as Nietzsche put it" (1983, 239). As Nietzsche writes in his own ethical idiom, "I do not want to accuse; I do not even want to accuse those who accuse. Looking elsewhere [*Wegsehen*] shall be my only negation. And all in all and on the whole: some day I wish to be only a Yes-sayer" (1974, 223, translation slightly modified).[4] Little is clear on this itinerary, but it is clear that the only way *out* is *through*. A difficult navigation, but Nietzsche has some helpful advice: "I favor any *skepsis* to which I may reply: 'Let us try it.' But I no longer wish to hear anything of all those things and questions that do not permit any experiment" (115). "We have to improvise—all the world improvises its day. Let us proceed today as all the world does!" (95).

In the service of this project, perhaps we need to consider the prescription written out by Deleuze and Guattari in *A Thousand Plateaus*, where they outline "How to Make Yourself a Body without Organs" (BwO):

This is how it should be done: Lodge yourself on a stratum, experiment with the opportunities it offers, find an advantageous place on it, find potential movements of deterritorialization, possible lines of flight, experience them, produce flow conjunctions here and there, try out continuums of intensities segment by segment, have a small plot of new land at all times. It is through a meticulous relation with the strata that one succeeds in freeing lines of flight, causing conjugated flows to pass and escape and bringing forth continuous intensities for a BwO. Connect, conjugate, continue: a whole "diagram," as opposed to still signifying and subjective programs. (1987, 161)

This, the way through that is the only possible pathway out, is what *amor fati* teaches us as a concrete strategy for constructing a positive body without organs—as a map or a pack made up of lines of becomings, "populated by multiplicities" (30). Like any plane of consistency, the body without organs that is capital "is neither totalizing nor structuring, it is deterritorializing" (144), made up of lines of flight.

This leads us finally to the end of this first excursus/experiment, and the revelation of the Fifth and final Law of Nietzschean Personal and Financial Growth: You are a mutual fund, not a subject. So forget about enjoying your symptom; try diversifying your portfolio. And who is the one who can offer a toolbox for such becomings? Nietzsche—that dude is *money*!

Excursus 2: Speed and Slowness in Adorno's
Minima Moralia

Prelude

If the Frankfurt School seems "dated" to many contemporary theorists, it may have something to do with the *style* of Frankfurt School
analyses—often caricatured as heavy, labored, highly abstract, and hu-
morless. The Frankfurt School seems slow, lumbering, a bit clumsy even.
Adorno's monograph on the "irrationality" of the *LA Times* astrology col-
umn is perhaps paradigmatic here: bringing a sophisticated and ultrase-
rious brand of ideology critique to bear on astrology is a little like using
a bazooka on an anthill. Really, shouldn't there be more levity in such
an analysis? And does Adorno seriously think he's discovered something
here? Isn't virtually any reader of astrology columns stricken by the suspicion that "the stars seem to be in complete agreement with the estab-
lished ways of life and with the habits and institutions circumscribed by
our age" (1994, 59)? Can an exposé on the sinister ideology of the fortune
cookie be far behind? Adorno's unmasking hermeneutics of suspicion is,
as I suggested previously about Nietzsche, probably not the most productive version of his work for responding to the present moment of ubiquitous, post-postmodern capitalism, whose unofficial theme song might just
be Leonard Cohen's "Everybody Knows" ("Everybody knows the fight
was fixed / The poor stay poor, the rich get rich / That's how it goes / Everybody knows").

Difficult contemporary questions are raised by Adorno's seemingly
high-handed style of suspicious hermeneutics: Does treating cultural texts
so laboriously—so slowly and didactically—offer any relevant tools to intervene in the fast world of late, later, or just-in-time capitalism? How, if at
all, can the seeming slownesses of Adorno's work be adapted to confront
the speeds of contemporary culture? In taking up these questions here,
I want to suggest that there's another Adorno lurking beside his finger-
wagging, stony persona. I argue that it's precisely in close attention to and
(re)deployment of Adorno's *style* that one might find a more affirmative—
dare I say speedy—Adorno at work: the style of Adorno's hermeneutics of

suspicion may offer more and better tools for what we've been calling the hermeneutics of situation, diagnosing and responding to the present.

My Dogma Ran Over My Karma

The fact that inversion or chiasmus is the dominant trope of Adorno's thinking is so obvious that it scarcely seems worth mentioning—especially in *Minima Moralia*, where it's prominently on display from the very beginning. The title itself is an inversion of Aristotle's *Magna Moralia* or "Great Ethics"—though we should note a meta-inversion here at the very beginning, insofar as Aristotle's ethics (based as it is on everyday exchanges like friendship, household matters, urbanity, and commerce) is itself already an inversion of an even "greater" (that is, more metaphysical) Platonic ethics. As we open *Minima Moralia*, the inversions continue in the text's first sentence, where Adorno famously characterizes his work as a "melancholy science," in chiasmic contradistinction to Nietzsche's "joyful science" (again, itself already an inversion of idealist metaphysics). From the book's epigraph (Kürnberger's "Life does not live") to its most famous sentence, "The whole is false" (1974, 50) (an inversion of Hegel's dialectical dictum that only the whole is true), chiasmic reversal is all over *Minima Moralia*.[5]

It's hard *not* to recognize this, I suppose. But the more thorny question is, what's the *upshot* of Adorno's chiasmic hermeneutics of suspicion? Clearly, Adorno's is a highly performative discourse—the "form" of his thought can hardly be separated from its "content"—and it seems obvious that the interruptive and open-ended quality of chiasmus lends itself very well to a thinking dedicated to demonstrating that the whole is false: the chiasmus frustrates any kind of gathering into a unity—even the impossible unity that Hegel posits.[6] In *Minima Moralia*, it seems that the reader is meant to confront contradiction qua contradiction—on the sentence level as well as the social level.

Indeed, if the bumper sticker or the advertising slogan is ideology writ small—the keenest expression of what Adorno calls "organized tautology" (66)—then the work of ideology critique would almost have to include a kind of negative or critical moment—a chiasmic *slowness* that interrupts the smooth movement of tautological self-reassurance. If, as Adorno writes, the culture industry "expels from movements all hesitation" (19), then chiasmus is clearly one way of reintroducing (at the level of form *and* content) an ethical hesitation into the otherwise too-swift movement to a conclusion. If "the splinter in your eye is the best magnifying glass" (50), then the chiasmic fragments of *Minima Moralia* would seem to be best understood as little splintering machines, magnifying contradictions by slowing thought down and deforming closure. And through his interruptive inversions, it seems that Adorno hopes actually to enact (rather than merely describe) his "minor ethics"; through a slowing down and breaking of ideological tautology, *Minima Moralia* hopes to "to teach the norm to fear its own perversity" (97).

Confronting the chiasmic slowdowns of Adorno's thought, one might be forced to realize, "*Damn*! My karma *is* my dogma." Or, as Adorno puts it, "Relativists are the real . . . absolutists" (128).

Slower Traffic Keep Right

OK, this makes a certain sense of Adorno's odd "method" in *Minima Moralia* and makes him more recognizable within a series of postmodern family resemblances: this method of chiasmic interruption was, for example, the coin of the realm for American deconstruction;[7] and certainly any Lacanian would recognize these kinds of chiasmic moves, where the rock of the real is finally shown to be contradiction itself.[8] Or one might see Adorno's method as a kind of ideology critique writ small—an open-ended "minor" critique of cultural ideologies, in contradistinction to the "major" determinist critiques of the economic base.[9]

But Adorno, like a chiasmic inversion of your drunk uncle Ted at a holiday dinner, will quickly make you reconsider those postmodern family resemblances. For example, on the deconstructive move of returning rights to the nonprivileged term within an opposition, Adorno's discourse retorts: "In the end, glorification of splendid underdogs is nothing other than glorification of the splendid system that makes them so" (28). About psychoanalysis, Adorno likewise has very little kind to say: it's the complete suturing of the social to bourgeois subjective ideology—it's the karma that slows down to give your dogma a ride—and "he who calls it by name will be told gloatingly by psycho-analysis that it is just his Oedipus complex" (63). In fact, even the general project of slowing thought down to reveal its ideological contradictions seems to come under Adornian fire: "Serenity is becoming," he writes, "the same lie that purposive haste already is" (99). Indeed, Adorno will go as far as to say that irony and ideology critique are literally impossible, insofar as both presuppose some chimeric notion of the real and some fiction of aesthetic or political distance: "The difference between ideology and reality has disappeared" (211).

So if the chiasmic reversals of the melancholy science aren't attempts to highlight exclusion (not about the "underdog"); and if they're not attempts to return a slowness or deliberation to thinking; and if they're not exactly ideology critique either, then exactly what are they? What kind of hermeneutics of suspicion is this, if it doesn't hold out the promise of a truth (possibly a negative one, the impossibility of truth) at another level? If, as Adorno writes, his aphorisms are meant to be *active*—if they "are all intended to mark out points of attack or to furnish models for a future exertion of thought" (18)—why would he want to depend so heavily on the slowness of a "melancholy" science? One usually doesn't think of an ass-kicking melancholia: the Irish wake, at least as I've experienced it, hardly seems "to furnish models for a future exertion of thought," and "Danny Boy" is hardly the kind of rousing protest song that might offer "points of attack." So what exactly is the point or use-value of this melancholic slowing down?[10]

Speedball

Of course, *Minima Moralia* is not all slowness, chiasm, and slogan. Although not many people write about this, one of the things that always strikes me about Adorno is the *ranting* quality of his prose—the way it moves from the slowness of the chiasmic slogan to the speed of the seemingly uncontrolled rant. Consider, for example, part 1, no. 38 of *Minima Moralia*, "Invitation to the dance." The section is named after Carl Maria von Weber's piece, often touted as the first modern dance music. For Adorno, we can only assume that this section is *not* going to be sweetness and light, named as it is after a music that serves as precursor to the commodified dance music that he rails against elsewhere.

Not oddly, then, this section takes up what Adorno calls "the capacity for pleasure" and its supposed cultural liberation by psychoanalysis. The screed against the commodification of pleasure is recognizably Adornian (it is in fact the sort of thing that cultural studies scholars complain about all the time in Adorno), but as you read it, note (at least initially) how it's very much *not* a melancholy lament that works by aphoristic "slowness." Though it does begin with a slogan:

Prescribed happiness looks exactly what it is; to have a part in it, the neurotic thus made happy must forfeit the last vestige of reason left to him by repression and regression; and to oblige the analyst, [he must] display indiscriminate enthusiasm for the trashy film, the expensive but bad meal in the French restaurant, the serious drink and the love-making taken like medicine as "sex." Schiller's dictum that "Life's good, in spite of all," *papier-mâché* from the start, has become idiocy now that it is blown into the same trumpet as omnipresent advertising, with psychoanalysis, despite its better possibilities, adding its fuel to the flames. As people have altogether too few inhibitions and not too many, without being a whit the healthier for it, a cathartic method with a standard other than successful adaptation and economic success would have to aim at bringing people to a consciousness of unhappiness both general and—inseparable from it—personal, and at depriving them of the illusory gratifications by which the abominable order keeps a second hold on life inside them, as if it did not already have them firmly enough in its power from outside. . . . The admonitions to be happy, voiced in concert by the scientifically epicurean sanatorium-director and the highly-strung propaganda chiefs of the entertainment industry, have about them the fury of the father berating his children for not rushing joyously downstairs when he comes home irritable from the office. It is part of the mechanism of domination to forbid recognition of the suffering it produces, and there is a straight line between the gospel of happiness and the construction of extermination camps so far off in Poland that each of our countrymen can convince himself that he cannot hear the screams of pain. (62–63)

This is vintage Adorno, but not a vintage that gets the same critical attention as the chiasmic, "slow" Adorno. There is, of course, a kind of chiasm at work here: the discourse of commodified happiness *is* the discourse of the Holocaust. But if this particular "fast" or ranting Adorno gets any critical attention at all, it is generally the stuff that gets him painted as a snob or a prude: critics of Adorno often say something like "I take the point about the Holocaust—I'm down with that; but, hey, let's not be so hasty in dismissing French restaurants and sex."

Supposedly, Adorno doesn't understand pleasure—this is, after all, the guy who said that "fun is a medicinal bath" (Adorno and Horkheimer 1993, 140). In order to argue this position against Adorno, however, one has to ignore the immense pleasure evident on the surface of this screed. It's like a Lenny Bruce routine: it's cranky and obsessive enough to be hilarious, even while it's deadly serious. It in fact screams to be read as a kind of superego gone berserk—but that's the inversion, no? The superego isn't supposed to be berserk. If this passage is at some level an ode to the joys of "repression and regression" in the face of "fun," flashy cultural surface effects, it certainly doesn't practice what it preaches.

We could go on picking away at Adorno's supposed high-culture biases, but I'm less concerned here with the content of this passage than with the form—though I hope finally to show how the two are inseparable. First, note that the way this passage is set up and the *speed* at which it makes links. It simply won't allow you to slow down, isolate, and affirm some form of "entertainment" (whether it be film, drinks, or witty banter) without being chiasmically entangled and forced to respond to the passage's other pole of engagement, the horror of the Holocaust. This passage seems to follow the Adornian "maxim that only exaggeration per se today can be the medium of truth" (1998, 99). In fact, this kind of ranting discursive "speed" and the outrageous linkages of this passage constitute a seemingly unruly—but actually quite deliberate—inversion of Adorno's chiasmic "slowness," and as such it seems yet another crucial role for the legacy of *music* in Adorno's work. Certainly Schönberg interrupts the reassuring flow of the popular song by slowing it down; but he also interrupts the popular song by speeding it up—intensifying music to the point of provocation, in addition to undermining it to the point of stasis.

Speed and slowness are crucial composition techniques in music, and one of the primary ways in which music "means" something. In other words, in art—and recall Adorno, "Perhaps the strict and pure concept of art is applicable only to music" (1974, 223)—*what* something means is always inseparable from *how* it works, and this is in fact why immanent analysis is so important to Adorno's aesthetics and his politics. Music never allows a simple answer to the question, "What does this mean?"

I want to suggest that Adorno's "minor ethics" is a kind of "musical ethics" of speed and slowness—an ethics that *does something*, produces effects, over against the transcendental ethics of resentment, judgment, and condemnation. What Adorno insists about the dialectic and about aesthetics seems equally true for the discourse of ethics: you don't *use* it;

you *become* it. As Adorno suggests in his work on Beethoven, we don't play music—rather, it plays us.[11] This, it seems to me, is finally what *Minima Moralia* is all about: not applying metaphysical ethical standards in a uniform way, but giving oneself over to the complexity of the situation, *responding* rather than handing down predetermined judgments. A symphony is no more contained in its notes than an ethics is contained in its rules.

Pot Calling the Kettle White: A Meta-interruptive Meta-excursus on Adorno and Jazz

We all know the song, so just let me hum a few bars for you: Adorno has a tin ear for jazz, which he reads as a wholly commodified form; his Eurocentric high-culture biases—and, by extension, his latent antiblack racism—make him unable to hear jazz's obvious abilities to be precisely the sort of challenging music that Adorno champions in his essays on atonal composition. If he weren't such a snob or closet racist, he'd be giving it up for Monk or Bud Powell in the same breath in which he's praising Schönberg.

Problem with this song: it seems to ignore that Adorno's argument is pretty much the same as, for example, Amiri Baraka's critique of jazz's commodification in *Blues People* (1963)—where, in the famous chapter "Swing: From Verb to Noun," Baraka shows how swing has been hermetically sealed and packaged for white listening audiences. Admittedly, Adorno doesn't go out of his way to find out much about atonal jazz—he knows what he hears on the radio (Benny Goodman, the king of swing) and knows that it's flatulent and reified. And, of course, one assumes you wouldn't get very far with him arguing the merits of Cecil Taylor's piano style over Glenn Gould's—not so much because he'd disagree (though he probably would), but because he likely knew as much about Cecil Taylor as Charlie Parker knew about Gregorian chants. In any case, it's important to remember that the jazz that Adorno critiques is *not* the atonal, "free" jazz that critics like Baraka tout—Charlie Parker, John Coltrane, Ornette Coleman.

In fact the swing that Baraka rails against *is* the jazz that Adorno hates—and they both say pretty much the same thing about it: swing is commodified slop; it's music as noun, to be consumed, not as verb, to be responded to. Adorno calls it part of the "blind conformity of . . . radio-listeners" (1974, 36); Baraka sees it as a pillar of the "vapidity of mainline American culture" (1963, 182). Of course, nobody calls Baraka a racist—or at least no one calls him an *antiblack* racist—because of this critique, and he's seldom accused of being too high culture for his own good.

So a word for the future of Adorno jazz critique: if you disagree with Adorno, be prepared to tell the world what's so interesting or crucial about the swinging grooves of Fred Waring and the Pennsylvanians—or, more important yet, have something affirmative to say about the current "swing revival" and its attendant accessorizing lifestyle products. In terms of commodified whiteness, the success of the Brian Setzer Orchestra or Big Bad Voodoo Daddy seems quite a large (if noxious) confirming flower on the kudzu vine of Adorno's fifty-year-old analyses. Listening to the swing sounds of the Cherry Poppin' Daddies on so-called alternative radio, one might even yearn for Tommy Dorsey: as Adorno notes, "Even the out-dated, inconsistent, self-doubting ideas of the older generation are more open to dialogue than the slick stupidity of Junior" (1974, 22). Close excursus within excursus. We now return to our regularly scheduled program.

Speed Kills

Speed and slowness, then, work together to diagnose or name a situation. For example, if you want to know what an aphorism "means," Adorno urges you to read it according to "its tempo, compactness, density, yet also by its tentativeness" (1974, 100). As in music, one extreme (slowness) doesn't mean anything except in relation to the other (speed); and that relation must always be worked out immanently, in terms of a specific piece or situation and its social contexts. If slowness is primarily interruption of tempo or rhythm, then speed is primarily linkage to other cadences. And one might say that for Adorno there's no shortage of haste in contemporary culture, but there's certainly not enough speed. The slogan, for example, is always "false," until it's introduced into a larger field of multiple social and theoretical linkages. Or as Adorno writes, "The statement that things are always the same is false in its immediateness, and true only when introduced into the dynamics of totality" (235)—again, plenty of haste or "immediateness," but not enough speed or cultural "dynamics." Speed and slowness are dialectical elements of composition, but as extremes they allow no simple (or even complex) sublation. They enact the "dynamics of totality."

Speed and slowness are, at some level, another set of names for Adornian mediation, but as musical terms they importantly have no essential or immediate link with the individual (karma) or the whole (dogma), and as such they comprise the watchwords for an ethics that doesn't dictate, but rather works through and modulates extremes in a dialectical way. As Adorno writes in *Three Studies,*

> For Hegel, mediation is never a middle element between extremes, as since Kierkegaard, a deadly misunderstanding has depicted it as being; *instead, mediation takes place in and through extremes, in the extremes themselves.* This is the radical aspect of Hegel, which is incompatible with any advocacy of moderation. (1993, 9, my emphasis)

Given this sense of dialectic, Adorno's can never be an ethics that advocates any kind of moderation or the giving of cracker-barrel advice; his is not a dialectical or chiasmic slowing down for the sake of edification.[12] As he recalls about the leisure industry, the imperative to slow down is "a formula borrowed from the language of the nursing home, not of exuberance" (1974, 217). Oddly enough, then, "exuberance" seems to be a key animating principle of the melancholy science.

So the project of an Adornian minor ethics is not solely to limit, slow down, or truncate a too-hasty move to totalization. Certainly, such a slowing down is one effect of *Minima Moralia*, but the text itself demonstrates that there is no privileged or final way to produce "ethical" effects: slowing thought down would always have to be dialectically combined with speeding it up in other registers in order to establish the fluid dynamics of a complex, concrete singularity.

In and of itself, however, the dialectic is not a privileged mode of inquiry—just as chiasmus or inversion is not a trope that necessarily guarantees anything in the realm of ethics. As I suggested previously, the Adornian dialectic is a performative, rather than a constative, discourse. In other words, the dialectic "is" something only insofar as it produces effects; learning from the music that is a kind of template for the dialectic, the philosophical question "What does it mean?" will always be subordinated to the ethical question "What does it do?" Think here of Adorno's interest in the slogan: Is the slogan a rightist or a leftist tool? For Adorno, this is the wrong question. Better, one might ask, What slogan? Uttered where and by whom? What effects does it produce? The slogan itself does not contain meaning or truth; however, they're not simply false either—or they are true and false within a dynamic hermeneutics of situation, rather than within a supposedly timeless mode of hermeneutic suspicion. "Slogans . . . are the index of their own untruth" (1998, 41) precisely insofar as they attempt to downplay and simplify their own dynamic cultural interactions and linkages. Nike's catchphrase "Just do it!," for example, seems to index its own untruth pretty quickly: "Don't do it without the proper accessories!"

Dialectic for Adorno is finally not an ontological or epistemological discourse. As he argues, "Just as the dialectic does not favor individual definitions, so there is no definition that fits it" (1993, 9). The dialectic is too "fast" to be defined; in fact, it is nothing other than a complex modality of *speed*, linkage, response. As Adorno sums up the work of dialectic in *Minima Moralia*, he insists that

limitation and reservation are no way to represent the dialectic. Rather, the dialectic advances by way of *extremes*, driving thoughts with the utmost consequentiality to the point where they turn back on themselves, instead of qualifying them. The prudence that restrains us from venturing too far ahead in a sentence, is usually only an agent of social control, and so of stupefaction. (1974, 86)

It is this insistence on the "driving" *extremes* of thought—the *speed* of linkage—that propels both the sentence and the dialectic forward, that projects thought and forces it to move both forward and back upon itself. Speed, rather than slowness, finally seems to be the immeasurable measure of dialectical ethics in Adorno.[13] Indeed, if we follow this dialectical path, it seems best to describe his thought as both a *Minima Moralia* (a "minor" ethics of melancholia or originary loss), as well as a kind of "maxima immoralia": an anti-ethics that proceeds by "venturing too far ahead" of transcendental and ideological certainties—an ethics of speed, affirmation, and futurity.

Speed as Hope

Inevitably, the question posed to the "slow" or "chiasmic" Adorno is the question of hope: sure, you can slow down ideological closure, frustrate totalization, keep open questions, relentlessly reveal the contradictions of capital; but how is that any kind of effective intervention? How does that interruption offer any hope to *change* things? In an already hopelessly contradictory society, to insist on contradiction and chiasmic impasse seems kind of like pissing in your wishing well.

In trying to answer such questions, Adorno will often write in a Benjaminian vein: "No other hope is left to the past than that, exposed defenselessly to disaster, it shall emerge from it as something different. But he who dies in despair has lived his whole life in vain" (1974, 167). Certainly, one could argue, Adorno's insistence on slowness, contradiction, and chiasmus has an upshot in a kind of paradoxical Benjaminian "hope," something like the "messianism without messianism" that dominates Derrida's late thought (see, e.g., Derrida 1994). And, of course, such interruption is key to any post-Holocaust thinking, which must honor the dead precisely by standing in the way of any kind of "final solution." This hesitation itself is a kind of hope.

But I'd like to suggest another kind of intense, post-postmodern hope in Adorno—not the hope of slowness as interruption, but the hope engendered by speed as linkage. Adorno insists throughout his minor ethics that the ethicist is inexorably caught up in the situation that she's diagnosing; as he insists, "The detached observer is as much entangled as the active participant. . . . This is why the very movement of withdrawal bears features of what it negates. It is forced to develop a coldness indistinguishable from that of the bourgeois" (27). I'd argue that what Adorno here calls "coldness" is akin to what I'm calling "speed," the necessity of linkage. If one always learns from Adorno that "there is no way out of entanglement" (28), then there are only situations, and tools for transforming them. Entanglement inexorably calls for critical response. Active, engaged praxis within existing conditions is the first and last principle of Adornian ethics.

Gillian Rose concludes her book on Adorno by arguing that "his 'morality' is a praxis of thought, not a recipe for social or political action" (1978, 148); and while I take her point (Adorno's ethics doesn't offer dogmatic courses of action), I think that the provocative quality—the *speed*—of his minor ethics is precisely a kind of recipe, or, as I suggested earlier, even a musical score: a set of organized potentials that must be performed, responded to, acted out. The recipe or musical score presents a set of provocations that must be modified—sped up or slowed down—in the process of "enacting" them at a specific time or place: even if you follow the recipe, the cake is never the same twice, just as the *Goldberg Variations* are different in each performance. And, importantly, such a notion of difference can't merely be explained away by the individual idiosyncrasy of the cook or the performer; difference is always wrapped up and manifest in the complexities of social and contextual response. You don't get to write the recipe or the musical score, but nevertheless it doesn't simply control you. You have to respond to it, work with and around it, resist it at some points.

Certainly, the chiasmic Adorno shows us how negation or withdrawal is a response; but in the end Adorno also shows us that such withdrawal or slowness isn't effective until it is dialectically coupled with an "extreme" movement of speed or affirmation. Critique is effective and ethical only insofar as it's "forced to develop a coldness indistinguishable from that of the bourgeois": cultural criticism is called not only to interrupt or critique, but literally to forge multiple linkages. As Adorno argues concerning cultural critique, "Repudiation of the present cultural morass presupposes sufficient involvement in it to feel it itching in one's own finger-tips, so to speak, but at the same time the strength, drawn from this involvement, to dismiss it. This strength is by no means of a merely individual nature" (1974, 29).

In the end, or from the beginning, this necessity of involvement or response—this ethical "strength" of continued engagement, this coldness of future linkages—is what one might call the legacy of hope as speed in Adorno. While the slowness of chiasmic reversal ruins thinking as totalization and thereby offers its own kind of future hope, the movements of speed as linkage offer another kind of open-ended ethical "hope" in his texts: the tools for reinscribing culture elsewhere. As Adorno writes in one of his last essays, "Thought is happiness, even where it defines unhappiness" (1998, 293). And we learn from Adorno that it's never too late for such a speedy critical intervention, no matter how dire the hermeneutics of situation may seem. "Hurry up, please. It's time."[14]

CHAPTER 5

Deconstruction

POSTDECONSTRUCTIVE? NEGRI, DERRIDA,

AND THE PRESENT STATE OF THEORY

Nobody needs French theory. —JEAN BAUDRILLARD, 2005

It seems that we live in discouragingly posttheoretical, or even an-
titheoretical, academic times. Venerable interdisciplinary journal *Critical
Inquiry*, whose advertising materials used to hail it as "Theory-Driven,"
held a kind of high-profile wake for theory after 9/11, with many of theory's luminaries (now somewhat flickering, as they approach retirement
age) pronouncing the entire operation dead in the water. Even Terry Eagleton (who, to hear the *New York Times* tell it, in fact *invented* theory
sometime in the late 1970s) pronounced the enterprise over and done with
in his 2004 book, *After Theory*. The *Times* story on Eagleton's book ran
under the headline "Cultural Theorists, Start Your Epitaphs." Indeed, an
epicedial discourse surrounds theory in the North American press: from
Christopher Hitchens in the *New York Times Book Review*, to articles in
Slate, Salon.com, and the *Chronicle of Higher Education*.[1] Even the *Christian Science Monitor* ran a feature-story obit for theory. And, according
to its Web site, "Christian Science . . . speaks to the dumb the words of
Truth, and they answer with rejoicing"; so when Christian Scientists speak
these words of Truth, you might begin to think there's something to them.

However, having already lived through several deaths of theory, I'll have to say that I'm not very impressed with the pitch and tonality of this latest rendition of "Danny Boy," though I think it is undeniably true that a certain kind of theory (let's call it English department or comp lit theory circa 1980-something) is in fact over and done with, and effectively has been for at least a decade. From the vantage point of the present, it's very hard to understand why, if I recall the statistic correctly, a late-'80s MLA survey found that more than 10% of English professors surveyed thought their primary job was to show students how binary oppositions in a text cancel themselves out. If that version of "theory" is over, good riddance, one might say.

You'd never know theory was dead, though, if you ran a citation index on the big names associated with it. In 2010, the Arts and Humanities Citation index turns up 1,498 hits for Michel Foucault, 1,310 for Jacques Derrida, 699 for Gilles Deleuze, and 455 for Jacques Lacan. And these citation numbers have in fact grown steadily in recent years, up more than 60% across the board since 2003. And, contra the "theory is over" hypothesis, these numbers are substantially higher than those from the supposed heydays of theory: Foucault, always leader of the citation pack, scores only 699 hits for 1986, and 700 for 1993.

Of course, Derrida's death in 2004, still so personally difficult for the many people whose lives he touched, has only intensified this anxiety in the theory world, broadly conceived. As the *New York Times* put it shortly after Derrida's passing: "With the death . . . of the French philosopher Jacques Derrida, the era of big theory came quietly to a close" (Eakin 2004). Derrida's death also painfully reminds us that all the "master thinkers" are gone, with the most-cited theorist (Foucault) having been dead for more than a quarter century, which inevitably brings up these kinds of hand-wringing marketing questions: Who's next on the throne? Rancière? Agamben? Badiou? Can Zizek continue to write several books a year? Or is the age of big theory and big theorists indeed over?

Negri and Derrida

The last "big thing" on the North American theory horizon, arguably, has been the work of Antonio Negri. Among all the provocations contained in Negri's recent work (with and without Michael Hardt), perhaps none is more memorable than a series of polemical provocations concerning postmodern thought in general, and the legacy of deconstruction in particular. Recall Hardt and Negri's assessment of the contemporary, post-postmodern state of "theory" in *Empire*:

When we begin to consider the ideologies of corporate capitalism and the world market, it certainly appears that the postmodern and postcolonialist theorists who advocate a politics of difference, fluidity, and hybridity in order to challenge the binaries and essentialism of modern sovereignty have been outflanked by the strategies of power. Power has evacuated the bastion they are attacking and has circled around to their rear to join them in the assault in the name of difference. These theorists thus find themselves pushing against an open door. (2000, 138)

While they rail wholesale "against all [philosophical] moralisms or positions of resentment or nostalgia" (218), and have biting things to say about a number of theorists (Homi Bhabha's postcolonial "hybridity" and Foucault's supposedly totalizing conceptions of "power" come under heavy fire), there's a particularly severe dismissal saved for Derrida and deconstruction. In short, they proclaim that today "the deconstructive phase of critical thought, which from Heidegger and Adorno to Derrida provided a powerful exit from modernity, has lost its effectiveness" (217).

These polemical statements by Negri and Hardt are generally read as a kind of theoretical ground clearing: if *Empire* is to be, as the *New York Times* hailed it, the "next big idea" (Eakin 2001) in North American avant-gardist theory, it has to proclaim the old king (deconstruction) dead. In other words, Negri and Hardt's comments concerning deconstruction are easily dismissed as rhetorical flourish, a kind of theoretical one-upmanship that functions largely as an ad campaign for the arrival of a new market maker at the theory store: there's a new meta-theory in town, ready to dominate the theoretical marketplace as deconstruction has, on and off, for the last quarter century.

While this kind of theory MC-boasting happens all the time in academic circles, and the theory industry's star system is an interesting site of reflection in its own right, my question or line of inquiry here will be somewhat different. I'd like to take Negri and Hardt's statements about deconstruction on the face of them, rather than primarily as triangulated symptoms of some marketing war or attempted cornering of the futures market on conceptual paradigms in the humanities. Taken quite literally, what might this provocation mean: "the deconstructive phase of critical thinking . . . has lost its effectiveness"? Is there a way of understanding this intervention outside the "theory marketplace" explanation, which would suggest that deconstruction has had its run, saturated the market, but it's now passé and needs to step aside for a new trend to take over? Though such a "market" explanation is true enough (for this and, let's face it, virtually any other phenomenon today), I wonder whether examining recent historical, economic, biopolitical events (seismic shifts "outside" academic theory debates per se) might make some other kind of sense from Negri and Hardt's argument concerning deconstruction? Might theoretical discourses like deconstruction deploy historical force outside (or at least *in addition to*) the ins and outs of academic fashion? Is there something, for example, about the current socioeconomic situation—the end of the cold war, globalization, post-Fordism, the rise of so-called immaterial labor, or the intensifications of postmodern "finance capital"—that renders the tools and procedures of deconstruction problematic, in need of supplementation, or even maybe obsolete? Likewise, if Negri's work *has not* become the next big thing—nor Rancière, Agamben, Badiou—we might want to speculate concerning the reason.

To put the question slightly differently: Derrida consistently insisted that deconstruction is not a *method*, but much more a *situation*. As Derrida put it the late 1980s, for example, deconstruction "is what is happening today, in what they call society, politics, diplomacy, economics, historical reality, and so on and so forth. Deconstruction is the case" (1990b, 85). Here, I'm less interested in the status of deconstruction in such a statement than I am in using Negri's provocation as a wedge to do some thinking about "what is happening today"; and to think about how our "situation"—especially the *economics* of today—might or might not have changed substantially since the days when one could confidently say that "deconstruction is the case."

The Specter's Smirk

Despite *Empire's* incessant claims to everything "new," the book's sentiments concerning deconstruction's demise only intensify the critique of deconstruction launched by Negri in "The Specter's Smile," his response to Derrida's 1993 *Specters of Marx*. Here Negri suggests that "there's something exhausted" (1999, 10) in deconstruction, that Derrida's work is haunted by "an aura of nostalgia," saturated "with a regressive pause (the immersion in 'the work of mourning')" (8). In short, and at his most polemical, Negri insists that "deconstruction remains prisoner of an ineffectual and exhausted definition of ontology" (12), a neo-Heideggerian cocktail of flown gods and techno-phobia that's not particularly well suited to the productive complexities and capacities of the post-postmodern world of globalization.

Harsh as Negri's sentiments might sound, I'd argue that his is not so much a dismissal of deconstruction per se as it is a genealogical account of philosophical "critique" itself—or, more precisely, a genealogical account of the relations between philosophical critique and recent innovations within capitalism. In other words, Negri here questions the critical presuppositions of virtually all poststructuralist theory (negative critique, demystification, the demonstration of a necessary ambiguity, the breaking up of binary totalities, the freeing up of possibility, etc.)—presuppositions central to what he calls "the theoretical climate of the rue d'Ulm [École normale supérieure]" (5) in the 1950s. In other words, Negri's is as much a critique of contemporary Marxism and its Althusserian heritage as it is a critique of Derrida and deconstruction.

Tracing out Negri's *positive* claims concerning deconstruction may help to contextualize the *critical* ones. He writes, "The deconstructionist claim to a Marxian tradition and a Marxian spirit is even more valuable if . . . we take into consideration the rigorously critical direction that deconstruction embodies—a hermeneutic direction (in its own ontological manner) which takes part in capitalism's historical and conceptual world only to oppose itself to it from the first through demystification—demystification of its language, in the first place, and then by way of and behind language, demystification of a 'metaphysics of the proper' and a state of 'logocentrism' encapsulated in capitalism'" (6). For Negri, a certain unshaking commitment to demystification and difference (against the rule of binary normativity) is the most obvious link between Derrida and the "spirit of Marxism."[2]

From its inception, the project of deconstruction has shared with Marxism, however uneasily, the project of denaturalizing all the meta-theories of ideological totalization. While remaining very skeptical of the category "ideology critique," Derrida's deconstructive itinerary has never-theless set its sights on subverting the hierarchizing metaphysics of presence that grounds totalizing Western ideologies—privileged states that configure themselves only by abjecting their others in the constitution of a supposedly "pure" state of uncontaminated presence. The totalization of "the nation" abjects and canalizes the myriad possibilities of "the people"; the privilege of the masculine is bootstrapped on the abjection of the feminine; the privi-lege of whiteness is based upon a founding metaphysics of exclusion and purity that deconstruction can show to be completely incoherent. After deconstruction, all that's left of these founding metaphysical oppositions is the mystery of the desire for totalization itself, the trace of a founding al-lergy toward the other, the forgetting being's originary openness (*différance*), and the continued project of upsetting a techno-capitalist metaphysics of presence. In the end, Derrida reminds us, the conditions of totalization's possibility are simultaneously the conditions of its impossibility (1982, 328); and deconstruction, as another name for justice, stands always on guard against the totalizing dreams of ideologues, past and present (see, e.g., Der-rida 1990a). Wherever a claim to totalization rears its dominating, logocen-tric head, there deconstruction has a job to do. Even the most seemingly totalizing matrix of relations, Derrida shows us, "nevertheless opens, leaving room for the unanticipatable singularity of the event; it remains by essence, by force, nonsaturable, nonsuturable, invulnerable, therefore only extensible and transformable, always unfinished" (1993, 34).

However incredibly productive and oppositional this deconstructive insight has proven to be over the years, Negri points out that our contem-porary masters (corporations, media conglomerates, spin doctors, finance capitalists, post-Fordist outsourcers of all kinds) no longer dream of a kind of exclusionary, binary totalization and don't achieve their hegemonic ef-fects primarily through a normatively repressive logocentrism. What we've been calling post-postmodern capitalism is, as Negri and a host of others have argued, no longer exactly logocentric: it no longer primarily demands or seeks a kind of mass conformity, sameness, or totalization. Rather, to-day's cutting-edge capitalism celebrates and rewards singularity, differ-ence, and openness to new markets and products.

As a related example of Negri's argument concerning the anti-logo-centric theoretical climate of the Parisian Latin Quarter in the '50s, think for a moment of Foucault's work and its relation to the present. Foucault, of course, never could have envisioned, much less analyzed, what we call "globalization" as a mode of power. In fact, Foucault expended most of his political and theoretical energy smoking out the hidden indignities of a form of governmental power that's largely lost hegemony in the decades since his death: namely, the welfare state. One of the primary upshots of Foucault's mammoth studies of the madhouse, the prison, and sexuality is to show how the "helping hand" of modern welfare governments is a continuation and intensification of another mode of power (the chopping off of hands and the other "sovereign" modes of early modern power that so vividly open Foucault's *Discipline and Punish*). The vast panoptic society that Foucault envisions may or may not have come to full fruition in the so-called first world under the dictates of a global Fordism from the 1920s through the 1970s; but, one way or another, we'd have to admit that the totalizing, logocentric Fordist assembly line ("the factory") is no longer the dominant mechanism for explaining or harnessing social, economic, and cultural production in the West. Though one would have to admit with alacrity (and with Negri) that the Marshall Plan Keynesian Fordism of the 1950s, the petri dish in and against which École normale supérieure philosophy of the same period grew, *was* thoroughly logocentric.

As even deconstruction's proponents (people like me) will admit, not a whole lot has changed about the *methodological* aspects of Derrida's work since its inception in the early 1960s. Certainly the *topics* have changed considerably over the years, from the early double readings of philosophy proper, to a fascination with the powers of literature "before" philosophy, the Levinasian turn to ethics, an increasingly recognizable engagement with politics (apartheid, Marx, the New Europe, terrorism), to the later work's obsession with messianism and a "religion without religion." Of course, such periodizing is difficult for such a monumentally prolific and wide-ranging thinker (who's also made crucial interventions on autobiography, painting, video, gender studies, linguistics, and psychoanalysis, not to mention his reinvigoration of the epicedium as a postmodern form); and one could easily demonstrate that the supposedly "late" Derridean interests in politics, ethics, and religion are written all over the "early" work, and vice versa. In any case, there's a remarkable methodological consistency in Derrida's work, a consistency that is the hallmark of any

towering philosophical figure: the initial Derridean insistence on deconstructing binary oppositions (and emphasis on the necessarily cofounding
status of the so-called excluded term) has proven enormously productive
in its nomadic migrations from a neo-Saussurean point about the signified
and its reliance on the signifier, into politics, culture, ethics, sexuality, and
a thousand other varied sociophilosophical discourses.

Following Negri's line of inquiry, though, one could push a bit
harder on the historical fact that this emphasis on "binary oppositions"
is a figure native to the cold war and to the normative, Fordist economic
imperatives of the post-WWII nation-state that so negatively conditioned
the climate of 1950s and '60s French intellectuals. With the hindsight of
history, for example, one can easily see the influence of the cold war nation-state and its Fordist economic imperatives in Althusser's (1971) work
on ideological state apparatuses, where he argues that schools and other
superstructural or cultural apparatuses function largely as factories for the
Fordist reproduction of the dominant ideology. Likewise, Deleuze's work
on the incessant quality of escape and lines of flight seems clearly rooted
in resistance to "the present" of midcentury global Fordism and the norms
of the cold war nation-state. Trapped between American consumerism on
one side and Russian communism on the other, it's not surprising that
most continental political theory of the mid- to late twentieth century
found itself trying to find a kind of "third way" between the structuring
binary oppositions of the cold war: inside/outside, self/other, public/pri-
vate, system/lifeworld, aesthetics/politics, ethics/morality, writing/read-
ing, totalization/fragmentation, nature/culture, rationality/irrationality.

All of these oppositions in some sense boil down to this master binary: open/closed. Are there, in short, ways to keep "open" the inherently totalizing, exclusionary desires of sociopolitical power? There are, of
course, a lot of ways of dealing with this question within recent political
theory, but Negri's genealogical point is that there's also a great deal of
shared ground in mid- to late twentieth-century continental philosophy
on this topic. Consider, for example, Habermas and Derrida: on the one
hand is the Habermasian legacy of critical theory, which would want to
emphasize the importance of norms; on the other, a deconstructive emphasis on subversion of norms. But both Derrida's deconstruction and
Habermas's communicative rationality perform their political work in the

name of a greater openness, in the service of expanding the "open" end of the "open/closed" binary opposition. Whether openness is all about norms, or all about their subversion, both ends of this debate would seem to harness virtually all of their political energy from staving off the specter of "binary" or "instrumental" totalization: openness or possibility versus its dampening on a rigid, inflexible, univocal standard of value or right.[3] Put most simply, Negri's argument or critique is that a binary notion of "normalization" is not the primary problem with contemporary capitalist culture, or at least it's not the same problem it was at midcentury for someone like Adorno.

So, one might say, the *techniques* of poststructuralist critique have remained more or less similar from the 1950s to today: demonstrate the inevitable remainder—excess or lack—left by totalizing gestures. But the dominant socioeconomic suite of forces (one of the prime *targets* of that critique, the situation in which deconstruction hopes to intervene) has changed radically. As Negri sums up the economic changes of the past half century,

The juridico-constitutional system based on the Fordist compromise, strengthened by the constituent agreement between the national bourgeoisie and the industrial working class, and overdetermined by the conflict between the Soviet and US superpowers . . . has thus run out its time. There is no longer a long-term war between two power blocs at the international level, within which the civil war between classes might be cooled down by means of immersion in the Fordist constitution and/or in the organizations of the Welfare State. . . . The whole scenario is now radically changed. (Hardt and Negri 2000, 215)

In short, Negri's "historical" critique of deconstruction is that, like most poststructuralist theory, it "pushes against an open door" when it insists on the critical potential of openness, fluidity, and the hidden or uncharted possibilities buried within a binary or logocentric essentialism. "Global capitalism" is likewise a sworn enemy of essentialism, and a big backer of multiple ways of proceeding (the famous "flexible specialization"). Negri argues that the regimes of hyperflexible advanced finance capital are in fact immune from a certain kind of demystifying "deconstruction," precisely because these supple and mobile economic formulations don't primarily desire or produce binary totalizing effects. Contemporary global capitalism produces its effects—totalizing or otherwise—only through embracing the event of dispersion, differentiation, and singularization, rather than fighting endlessly against this open-ended state of affairs.

Post-postmodern materialism, of Negri's neo-Deleuzian variety, bases itself on an explicit critique of this whole postmodernist, "anti-totalization" mode of thinking. In other words, global capitalism of the advanced type doesn't want to totalize anything at all—other than this sense of fluid openness. So maybe the stake of considering Derrida around the topics of globalization or contemporary capitalism has less to do with seeing whether Derrida does or doesn't have anything helpful or compelling to say about these topics—of course he does, or he doesn't, depending on what you already bring to your reading of Derrida and how you feel about deconstruction. Nobody comes to deconstruction without an angle of approach. Maybe the most interesting question concerning deconstruction and the contemporary moment is less what deconstruction has to say about "today" (very interesting questions concerning how one might "deconstruct" the claims or ideologies of global capitalism, foremost among them right now the so-called War on Terror), but to look more obliquely at what "today" has to say to deconstruction. This is Negri's approach in "The Specter's Smile": "the question 'whither Marxism?' is inextricable from the question 'whither deconstruction?,' and both presuppose a 'whither capitalism'?" (1999, 6).

The historical project of deconstruction is perhaps most accurately described as the deconstruction of totalization, including (one might say, especially) capitalist totalization (the presence-fetishizing required by clock- and work-time, the reduction of all human and nonhuman relations to market relations, etc.). But with a mutation in the dominant mode of "totalization" in our world, whither deconstruction, a discourse dedicated to the exposure and overturning of an "essentialist" mode of power that's certainly not disappeared by any means, but is no longer dominant? What happens to the critical discourse "deconstruction" when capitalism in practice assumes the role of "deconstructor" par excellence? Capital may have fought the critical, norm-busting force of deconstruction throughout much of its history. "But now," Negri asks, "in the face of the total subsumption of society and the complete multi-nationalization of the productive processes, what alternative does it [capitalism] have left? Directly, today, the innovative process destructures, deconstructs capital. . . . Deconstruction is the broken line which leads across the transformations of the form of value" (1996, 159). To his credit, Derrida was fond of coining other historical names for deconstruction—recall that he was happy to rename deconstruction as "perestroika" in the early 1990s. Perhaps we should add "global capitalism" to the list of alternate names for deconstruction? I take this to be Negri's genealogical question.

The Theory Futures Market

As people invested in the discourses of theory today, are we to be encouraged or discouraged? Has deconstruction "won" or "lost" in relation to the armature of contemporary capitalism? Has deconstruction's triumph as a kind of capitalist *epistemology* ironically cost it the store in terms of its status as a *critical* discourse? In the end, there are an undecidable number of ways to grapple with the upshot of these events, but here I'd like to highlight two readings, both touching on the question of discouragement, obsolescence, or general exhaustion supposedly engulfing the discourses of theory today. On one reading, this is a very discouraging story indeed: deconstruction, the once-proud king of the critical discourses, now eaten alive, co-opted, by the inexorable machine that is capitalism. The deconstructed blazer was one thing, but how soon is it until we see Derrida on a billboard, parked in front of an Apple computer, or we're reminded that he, like Jack Kerouac, wore khakis? I'll call this one the "Borg" theory of reception ("resistance is futile"—they will co-opt everything); and while it seems to me that this isn't the most productive general reading of recent history, it is a plotline that's surprisingly prevalent on the US cultural left today (how else could a provincial know-nothing like Karl Rove remain situated as a Machiavellian genius within dominant political discourse)? Deconstruction here becomes a subgenre of a larger kind of lament about reception and contemporary capitalism: "They've stolen our icons again and drained them of all the cool libratory content." As my hipster friends lament, "Yeah, Zeppelin was still cool, until it played under a Cadillac commercial." And don't even get them started on the Flaming Lips' Hewlett-Packard commercial, or the indignity of our greatest bard of alienation, Iggy Pop, hawking luxury cruises (who knew that shuffleboard constituted a "Lust for

Life"?). Co-optation—it had to happen to deconstruction as well. Very discouraging.

On another reading, however, there really isn't anything to be discouraged about here. Negri's reading shows us that the "abstruse theorist" of the *Times* obituary was in fact *correct*: "Deconstruction is the case" under the rule of advanced global finance capital. Money, unmoored from any reference or gold standard, has arrived as the transversal conceptual machinery for constantly modulating "value" throughout the global *socius*. From the stock market to the corner market, it's all about floating rates of exchange: how much force does your currency deploy, and what kind? As anyone who lost a great deal of retirement savings in the 2008 market crash knows—or, for that matter, as anyone who's lost a great deal in the last ten seconds of an eBay auction knows—economic value at the edge of capitalism is in the process of being remade as an ongoing destruction of older norms in the name of producing, measuring, and evaluating "other" flows. Advanced global finance capital, one might say, is the most intense example of deconstruction (and vice versa). At some level, if this is correct (and I think it is), this should make us feel quite encouraged about theory's futures: Abstruse theorist was right—binary essentialist schemes are yesterday's news! As people interested in theory, this hardly leaves us without work to do.

We will of course have to redirect our efforts and stop worrying quite so much about "the next big thing" or spending quite so much time deconstructing particular artifacts. As I'll argue at more length in the next chapter, continuing to understand "theory" primarily as a series of methods for producing novel interpretations of cultural artifacts is, and to my mind always has been, the road to nowhere. Today, the "deconstructive" insight is not the purview of a single critical paradigm or hermeneutic method, but it is in fact what Derrida claimed it was: "the case, what is happening today." Deconstruction is not an esoteric knowledge to be lorded over by nerdy gurus like humanities professors. On the contrary: the necessary, structural openness of all systems is no longer so much an elite knowledge as it is what we might venture to call the "common."

So, in the end, I would have to agree with Negri when he intimates that deconstruction is obsolete as a critical or hermeneutic method for enacting what he calls "an exit from modernity." But, equally following from

Negri's account, we'd have to admit that deconstruction thus understood hasn't failed at all, but has in fact triumphed, insofar as it is or it names the ongoing enactment of that very flight. Deconstruction, then, is no longer an exit from where we are; but, just as important, deconstruction *is* where we are: deconstruction is the logic of value under late, later, or just-in-time capitalism. Freed from the restrictive job of having to show us again and again that we don't know the dancer from the dance, "theory" in this sense is hardly dead, but just being born.

CHAPTER 6

Interpretation

THE SWERVE AROUND P:
THEORY AFTER INTERPRETATION

Philosophy has not known until quite recently how to think in level terms with Capital, since it has left that field open, to its most intimate point, to vain nostalgia for the sacred, to obsession with Presence, to the obscure dominance of the poem, to doubt about its own legitimacy. . . . The true question remains: what has happened to philosophy for it to refuse with a shudder the liberty and strength a desacralizing epoch offered it?
—ALAIN BADIOU, *Manifesto for Philosophy*

Literature

Something odd (and a bit embarrassing) happened to me on a recent trip to the library to find an anthologized essay that a visiting speaker was going to talk about. I got the call number for the volume and beelined to the library's "P" shelves (the Library of Congress designation for language, literature, and literary criticism/theory). But I soon found that the entire section had been moved—students were working on laptops in the section where the literary criticism and theory used to be. I eventually found the volume I was looking for, along with some old friends like my own first book (a proud alum of PS 228, class of '93), relocated in the fifth-floor stacks. I later jokingly asked the humanities librarian, when I saw him at the talk, "Hey, when did the 'P' section get moved to the fifth floor?" "A couple years ago," he answered, a bit incredulously. I could see him wondering: this guy makes his living as an English professor, but he hasn't been in the literary criticism section of the building for years?

I guess it struck me as a bit puzzling as well. When I was in grad school—not *that* long ago—just about everything I needed to know was in the P section. I knew those shelves like the back of my hand. But I guess it is simply true that, in Library of Congress terms, for my work in recent years it's been all Bs, Hs, and Js (philosophy, social science, and politics), hardly any Ps—both in terms of the theory and criticism that I read, and in terms of the work I publish. At first I'd figured that this was simply an anomaly of my wacky research agendas; but an overwhelming number of colleagues I've since talked to about this experience have similar tales of the swerve around P. Others of course have different preferred Library of Congress designations for their research: the vast D through F shelves for the department historians, Q and R for the science studies folk, more H and J for the queer theorists and cultural studies people, as well as a healthy smattering of G and T (geography and technology). And even those whose work remains firmly on the language and literature shelves admit with alacrity that much of what goes into their books on literature is shot through with research from other places: history, sociology, social science, as well as the unclassifiable archival research that informs so much of the work on the P shelves. Even the scholarship on the language and literature shelves isn't "literary" in quite the same way it was even a decade ago. Plenty of superb "theory" and "criticism" is being produced in and around English departments, but the adjective "literary" seems oddly out of place when describing it—inapplicable as much to the work of historians ("don't call us *literary* historians," a colleague warns) as to theorists (editors at Rowman and Littlefield quickly wrenched the word "literary" out of the title of my coauthored textbook, *The Theory Toolbox*—marketing death, or so they said).

This swerve around P is probably something that most people reading this will recognize, in one way or another. And rather than coming before you in this chapter to celebrate or denounce the demise of the "literary" (the critical domain of P), I'd like to think a bit about how and why this situation came about, and how it may or may not be related to another story that's making the rounds in literature departments, the "death of theory." To anticipate, I'll suggest that research in and around language and literature is no longer literary most obviously in the sense that it's no longer primarily concerned with producing *interpretations* of existing or emerging literary artifacts. This—let's call it for now "anti-hermeneutic"—thrust is additionally the transversal line that connects the decline of the literary to the demise of "big theory." As Jane Tompkins had already pointed out in the heyday of theory, specifically in her 1980 collection *Reader-Response Criticism*, even as postmodern theorists fought seemingly life-and-death battles against new critical formalism, in the end those battles had the paradoxical effect of intensifying a crucial tenet of formalism: namely, what Tompkins calls "the triumph of interpretation" (219). Whether Wallace Stevens was all about organic unity or whether he was all about undecidability, either way it was interpretation all the way down.

Of course, there's a semantic confusion involved when one argues that literary theory was and is beholden to interpretation, insofar as big theory in North American literature departments got off the ground in the 1970s precisely through its *critique* of new critical notions of literary meaning. The attempt or desire to go "Beyond Interpretation," as Jonathan Culler names it in a 1976 essay, was part and parcel of the attempt to go beyond New Criticism. As Paul de Man writes, for example, with criticism's departure from the universe of new critical reading, "the entire question of meaning can be bracketed, thus freeing the critical discourse from the debilitating burden of paraphrase" (1973, 28)—from any mimetic or thematic notion of meaning—and thereby allowing new horizons of interpretive possibilities. That is, literary theory of the 1970s and '80s hardly abandons the project of interpretation wholesale—J. Hillis Miller famously insisted that "'deconstruction' is . . . simply interpretation as such" (1979, 230)—but the era of literary theory crucially shifts interpretation's emphasis from the "what" of meaning (New Criticism's "debilitating burden of paraphrase") to the "how" of meaning (the strangely "enabling" task of infinite interpretation). In retrospect, it seems clear that the era of postmodernism was characterized by a decisive intensification of attention to the process (rather than the product) of interpretation. This interpretive mutation from *what* to *how* constituted the state of affairs that Hillis Miller, in his 1986 MLA Presidential Address, dubbed "the triumph of theory."

However, as theory triumphed over the content- and theme-oriented criticism (as reading or interpretation becomes unmoored from older, new critical, or structuralist methodologies), it's important to recall that "meaning" nevertheless remained *the* privileged site of poststructuralist critical endeavor; in fact, literary "meaning," far from remaining a thematic unity hidden away within a rarified realm of dusty books, becomes in the poststructuralist theory era the slippery lure for "readings" of all kinds, the hermeneutic gesture exploded throughout the literary and social field. Despite the overt and constant critique of univocal meaning within literary theory (or more likely *because* of this critique's ubiquity), the insular or hermetic notion of univocal meaning remains the structuring other buried within postmodernist celebrations of interpretation's open-endedness, a kind of shadow passenger who must always be kept at bay by the vigilant rigors of interpretation. Interpretation becomes the enemy of univocal meaning in the theory era; but that old-fashioned sense of meaning still thereby remains a central concern, if only as that which is to be warded off by the critical act. (What, one might wonder, are the tasks or results of poststructuralist reading if they are not first and foremost the frustration of univocal meaning, and gesturing toward interpretation as an interminable enterprise?) As Culler writes in his 2006 defense of theory as poetics, *The Literary in Theory*, "One could say that literary studies in the American academy, precisely because of its commitment to the priority of interpretation as the goal of literary study, was quick to posit a 'poststructuralism' based on the impossibility or inappropriateness of the systematic projects of structuralism, so that interpretation, albeit of different kinds, might remain the task of literary studies" (10–11).

In other words, this decisive mutation from the *what* of hermeneutics to the *how*—from revealing meaning to performing readings—doesn't simply abandon the structural position of "meaning" in the hermeneutic enterprise. Far from fading into the background, the interpretive act here swallows up everything—even death (as de Man provocatively insisted) becomes a displaced name for a linguistic predicament. Meaning is reborn, even as it arrives stillborn in each and every reading. Interrupted, reading-as-interpretation nevertheless continues—and it lives on in fact even more strongly, in its newfound assurance that the text will never be totalized. Meaning remains the impossible lure, the absent center, the lack or excess that continues to drive the critical enterprise. And textual undecidability of this variety has been very, very good to literary criticism. Instead of opening a door to the nihilism and critical irrelevance that many traditionalists feared, the jettisoning of meaning-as-content was in retrospect absolutely necessary in order for postmodern, poststructuralist hermeneutics to really take off. Open-ended interpretation was the practice that launched a thousand successful tenure cases (including mine). In the era of big theory, the stakes among competing methodologies were high, but they remained *interpretive* stakes.

Indeed, we need to recall that the MLA "theory wars" were characterized not so much by disputes between interpreters of literature and those who held that there was some other thing or set of things that critics should be doing in and around the literary; rather, the theory wars were largely internecine battles among interpretive camps or methods. When we examine some of the larger methodological claims from the big theory era, perhaps the most striking thing about them is the way they feel now like clunky advertising campaigns, or the remnants of a marketing war in which various methodologies jockey for market share, often deploying slogans that would seem to us now to be hilariously "totalizing"—something akin to your local bar's claim to have "the best hot wings in the universe!" Perhaps the most infamous of these claims comes about in the aftermath of de Man's reading of Proustian metaphor and metonymy in 1973's "Semiology and Rhetoric": "The whole of literature," de Man writes, "would respond in similar fashion, although the techniques and patterns would have to vary considerably, of course, from author to author. But there is absolutely no reason why analyses of the kind suggested here for Proust would not be applicable, with proper modifications of technique, to Milton or to Dante or to Holderlin. This in fact will be the task of literary criticism in the coming years" (32). From the vantage point of the present, it's a little hard to believe that the "task of literary criticism in the coming years" could have been so earnestly and seriously (or perhaps winkingly and ironically?) presented as the application of one method among others.

Indeed, it's hard to imagine someone today arguing that we should dedicate ourselves to the task of rereading the canon according to the protocols of a particular interpretive approach (Geneva School phenomenology, Butler's gender performativity, Foucauldian biopower, or Shlovsky's

Russian Formalism), but such claims were ubiquitous in the era of big theory. Recall Fredric Jameson from *The Political Unconscious*: "My position here is that only Marxism offers a philosophically coherent and ideologically compelling resolution to the dilemma of historicism. . . . Only Marxism can give us an adequate account of the essential mystery of the cultural past" (1981, 19). Jameson thematizes his entire project in this book as the articulation of a "properly Marxist hermeneutic" (23), responding to the "demand for the construction of some new and more adequate, immanent or antitranscendent hermeneutic model" (23). One could go on multiplying these kinds of claims from the big theory era, recalling, for example, that the subtitle of Henry Louis Gates's *Signifying Monkey* (1988) is nothing less comprehensive than *A Theory of African-American Literary Criticism*, or recalling the claims made for certain kinds of interpreters—resisting or otherwise—in reader-response criticism.

My point here is not to underline the hubris of the North American theory era but to suggest that the big claims of big theory were underwritten by a disciplinary apparatus in and around literature departments that was completely beholden to interpretation (especially in terms of research publication). Whether it was deconstruction, Marxism, African American criticism, or most anything in between, the era of big theory was an era of interpretive models that fought for the status as the most powerful and universally applicable one—the "winner" being the critical method that could succeed in festooning the pages of the most journals with its inventive new readings of texts. As Josue Harari wrote in his hugely successful 1979 anthology *Textual Strategies*, "Method has become a strategy" (72). As Harari continues describing his anthology of strategic interpretive methods, "I have presented the various critical struggles at play among contemporary theorists. It remains to inscribe these strategies in a more global framework, to put them in a ring of criticism, as it were, and to determine how the rounds are to be scored" (68–69). And back in the day, scoring those rounds amounted to judging which was the most persuasive "new" interpretation of a given text. In short, the era of big theory constituted a decisive intensification, rather than a reversal or abandonment, of literary meaning and its discontents.

Though it's taken decades, contemporary criticism at this point seems to have fully heeded Tompkins's 1980 call for research to swerve away from interpretation and reconnect to what she calls "a long history of critical thought in which the specification of meaning is not a central concern" (201), a criticism based not so narrowly on the interior or formal relations among discourse and meaning, but focused instead on "the relations of discourse and power" (226). Tompkins's "break with formalism" (226) seems plausible enough as a description of recent history in literary criticism and theory (when was the last time you heard a junior job candidate do an actual close reading of a poem?), and one could at this point begin multiplying anti-hermeneutic references: critical theories invested in Deleuze and Guattari, Foucault, Gumbrecht, the later Jameson, Irigaray, Moretti's sociology of literary forms, evolutionary psychology, brain science, or Bourdieu's work on cultural capital; virtually the whole of fields like cultural studies, rhetoric, science studies, globalization studies, and a strongly resurgent (in fact, hegemonically dominant) "archival" historicism in literary studies; as well as the decidedly other-than-hermeneutic thrust of artistic formations like the "unreadable" postmodern novel, almost all contemporary American poetry (both the so-called workshop tradition—which relies almost completely on communicating subjective affect rather than verbal meaning—and more experimental traditions), contemporary painting, performance art, and so on.

While something like Tompkins's account of recent American literary critical history seems plausible enough to me (tracing a path from the hegemony of research questions concerning textual interpretation or meaning to the reign of questions about literature's inscription in history, discourse, power, or the everyday), I'd like to supplement or combine it here with a wholly different account of the swerve around the literary, Alain Badiou's in his first *Manifesto for Philosophy*. I'd like to do so not only because of the compelling quality of Badiou's account of continental philosophy's recent past, but also because hybridizing Tompkins's account with Badiou's may actually help resituate or reimagine a future for the literary. In short, it seems to me that on Tompkins's account (and others like it), the literary remains the marker for a kind of stale, apolitical formalism obsessed with questions of interpretive meaning and little else; if one accepts this rendering of recent critical history, it's hard to be concerned about the passing of the literary and/or equally hard to imagine any productive *research* future for the adjective "literary" in "literary criticism and theory."

The question of meaning is, and I think will remain, the bread and butter of classroom practice in literature departments; in particular, the undergraduate theory class will continue to function as an invaluable introduction to interpretive protocols for some time to come. On the other side of the podium, however, I think it's a different story: while faculty research surrounding the mechanics and production of meaning (and/or its flip side, undecidability) experienced a boom during the postmodern big theory years, it's almost impossible only a few years later to imagine a publishing future that consists of new and improved interpretations of Pynchon, Renaissance tragedies, or Melville. Contra much of the reactionary hope invested in the passing of big theory ("Finally, now we can go back to reading and appreciating literature, without all this jargon!"), I'd argue that the decisive conceptual difference separating the present from the era of big theory is not so much a loss of status for theoretical discourses (just look at any university press catalog and you'll be quickly disabused of that notion), but the waning of literary interpretation itself as a viable research (which is to say, publishing) agenda. As I suggest in the Excursus, the hermeneutics of suspicion has waned as an effective post-postmodern research agenda, for a whole host of social, political, institutional, and economic reasons. Or, to put it in language that I use throughout to discuss the text's methodology, the hermeneutics of meaning (or its impossibility) is no longer the code that overcodes all the others within literary research.

In other words, it is the taken-for-grantedness of literary interpretation's centrality, rather than a wholesale disciplinary rejection of something called theory, that separates our post-postmodern present from the era of postmodernism, the era of the hermeneutics of suspicion. And if there's no "next big thing" coming down the theory pike, it's precisely because such a notion of the "next big thing" (like feminism, deconstruction, or new historicism in their day) has tended to mean the arrival of a new interpretive paradigm. The primary reason there's no dominant post-postmodern interpretive paradigm on the horizon is not so much because of the exhaustion of theory itself (I can immediately think of a dozen underexplored interpretive models or theorists), but because the work of interpretation is no longer the primary research work of literature departments. There will be no Blanchot revolution, televised or otherwise; or, if there is a Blanchot renaissance on the horizon, it will likely be Blanchot's work on terror and terrorism, rather than his hermeneutic method, that will spearhead the revival.

To put the same problem somewhat differently, in the postmodern era of big literary theory, there was a certain unease at the perceived increasing distance between classroom practice and research publication— producing close readings in the classroom, deconstructing them in the journals. But in the present context, that seeming "gap" seems like a positive continuity, because back in the day, at least it was the same general operation—interpretation— at work both in the introduction to literature class and in *PMLA*. But if the work that we're publishing these days is increasingly driven by questions that seem foreign to interpretive classroom practice, that should give us pause—if for no other reason than to consider how the future of our discipline might be related to the practices that dominated its recent past. It is, in the end, precisely in the name of reimagining a post-postmodern future for the "literary" that I turn to Badiou's account of its demise in recent philosophy.

Philosophy

Though Badiou's work is becoming more well known in North America (the *Chronicle of Higher Education* tagged him as a potential "next big thing" in the theory world, surely the kiss of death; see Byrne 2006), perhaps a brief introduction to his thought is in order here. Against the thematics of the end or twilight of philosophy, and against all messianisms, Badiou calls for thinking's revitalization, primarily through an emphasis on what he calls a "positive," nonsacramental relation to infinity—a relation that, for Badiou, is on display most forcefully in the axiomatic thrust of mathematics. In returning to what he sees as the Greek origins of philosophy—he goes as far as to call his thinking a "Platonism of the multiple" (1999, 103)—Badiou locates four "conditions of philosophy": "the matheme, the poem, political invention, and love" (35). Western philosophy began in Greece with these four master topics (science, literature, politics, desire), and for Badiou "the lack of a single one gives rise to [philosophy's] dissipation" (35), which isn't to say its end. In other words, philosophical thinking is in danger whenever it becomes tied too closely and exclusively to one of its fourfold conditions. The danger, for Badiou, is "handing over the whole of thought to one generic procedure. . . . I call this type of situation a suture. Philosophy is placed in suspension every time it presents itself as being sutured to one of its conditions" (61). So, for example, Marxism has often been too sutured to the political condition— here Badiou even implicates his own earlier strident Maoism (76)—while analytic philosophy has on the whole sutured itself too closely to the scientism of the matheme. "Philosophy," in its simplest definition, is for Badiou "de-suturation" (67), the interruption of an exclusive thought-suture to either politics, science, love, or the literary. Hence, Badiou calls his a "subtractive" thinking, one that subtracts itself from constrictive sutures to reconnect with the multiple.

The most totalizing suture of recent philosophical times, Badiou polemically insists, is not the political or the scientific-mathematical, as we've perhaps come to expect our theorists to say, or even the suture of privatized "love," as cultural critics might argue; rather, the prime totalizer of our day is the poetic, the literary suture. As Badiou insists, today "it so happens that the main stake, the supreme difficulty, is to de-suture philosophy from its poetic condition" (67). Badiou rather cannily chooses Heidegger as his main foil in this argument. Even Heidegger's staunchest proponents would, I think, have to admit that the literary is in fact the ground of his thinking, and that he has relatively little overt or positive to say about politics, mathematics, or love for that matter—or, more precisely, anything compelling that he might have to say about those topics would have to be run through the poetic, as this suture is the ontological ground of the space of possibility in Heidegger's thinking. Anything that emerges does so in Heidegger through the structure of the literary opening, that privileged path to the meaning of Being.

Of course, my two example accounts of the literary's demise (Tompkins's and Badiou's) do not seamlessly map onto one another, for a host of disciplinary, historical, and geographical reasons. Most obviously, one might point out that the lion's share of American literary theory (or most continental philosophy, for that matter) isn't or never was so uniformly Heideggerian as Badiou's account would seem to suggest. However, much of the big theory era in literature departments did, I think, share the common bond that both Badiou and Tompkins point out: the questions of meaning or interpretation as the ultimate horizon of inquiry. This hermeneutic thrust was prominently on display in virtually all big theory in literature departments, even in the polemically new historicist work of folks like the *boundary 2* New Americanists, as well as much of the early new historicist work in English literature (think here of great books like Jonathan Dollimore's 1984 *Radical Tragedy*, which deploys its historical materialist mix of religion, ideology, and power primarily to produce startling new readings of Renaissance tragedies). Likewise, however anti-Heideggerian much *Tel Quel* thinking may have been, it did nonetheless protect the horizon of hermeneutics (the literary suture) as the royal road to larger philosophical and cultural questions. Like Tompkins's call for literary criticism to reconnect to a nonhermeneutic tradition, then, Badiou's critique of the poetic suture in philosophy is less a spring-green avant-gardism (calling for a radical new direction in thought) than it is an attempt to return critique to a series of other questions, ones not treated well within the poetic idiom. As Badiou reminds us, "Descartes, Leibnitz, Kant or Hegel might have been mathematicians, historians, or physicists; if there is one thing they were not, it was poets" (70).

*Un*like Tompkins's diagnosis of literary criticism circa 1980, however, Badiou's doesn't treat the poetic suture of neo-Heideggerian thought primarily as an ideological swerve away from the real or crucial questions of its day—politics, power, gender, sexuality, disability, and so on. For Badiou, the poetic suture is not primarily the offspring of a false or deluded consciousness concerning the centrality of literature: "there really was an age of poets" (70)—Badiou dates it from Holderlin to Celan, 1770–1970—when the central problems of philosophy were worked out most forcefully and concisely in poetic texts. Literary works, in other words, for a long time presented us with our most crucial philosophical enigmas: "the most open approach to the question of being," "the space of compossibility least caught up in the brutal sutures" of political coercion, "the enigma of time," (70), and of course the undulations of love and desire. Badiou, in other words, hardly seeks to dismiss the power of the poetic suture in philosophy: "Heidegger's thinking has owed its persuasive power to having been the only one to pick up what was at stake in the poem, namely the destitution of object fetishism, the opposition of truth and knowledge, and lastly the essential disorientation of our epoch" (74).

On Badiou's account the literary became central to an entire era of thought *not* primarily because of the ideological investments of its proponents (the general claim that's not too far below the surface of Tompkins's critique of formalist fetishizing of the poem), but precisely because the literary spoke most forcefully and succinctly to a whole set of crucial questions (political and otherwise): literature's critique of object and commodity fetishism (the poem's anti-instrumental resistance to appropriation), poetry's singular epistemological force (the impossibility of assigning it a single "objective" meaning), and the literary's testimony to the existential disorientation of the era. These were all crucial philosophical questions that could be accessed in their most intense manifestations primarily through the literary or hermeneutic suture—through the hermeneutics of suspicion, through the question of meaning and its discontents.

Badiou's concern is less in debunking the prestige, ideology, or inherent interest of the literary relation to philosophy than in exploring or emphasizing what we might call the "cost" of a primary suture onto the literary—how it recasts or downplays thinking's relations to what Badiou sees as its other properly philosophical themes (the political, love, and the mathematical-scientific). If, as Badiou (1994) insists, "Ultimately, being qua being is nothing but the multiple as such," then the literary suture can do little more than endlessly *demonstrate* or gesture toward this multiplicity, in what Badiou suggests is a primarily theological register. Poetry, he insists, functions largely as the "local maintenance of the sacred" (1999, 57), as repository of hidden meaning or the marker for infinite possibility. Badiou, however, takes his primary task to be the "secularization of infinity," which is the reason that for Badiou the mathematical language of set theory becomes a privileged one, precisely because it drains infinity or the multiple of its Barthesian *jouissance*: "That's the price of a deromanticization of infinity," he writes. Quite simply, "Mathematics secularizes infinity in the clearest way, by formalizing it" (1994). The project for Badiou is less guaranteeing or offering shelter to the openness of infinity (which was the primary job of the literary during the age of the poem) than it is mobilizing said infinity (the job that characterizes politics, science, love).

This, unfortunately, is also where Badiou's account begins to become unhelpful for rethinking a genealogy of recent developments in the history of literary criticism and/or philosophy, as his mathematical impulse is driven in large part by an attempt not to *connect* thinking to this or that transversal field, but to insist on philosophy's (absolute) autonomy as that discourse dedicated to the ahistorical "truth" best represented by mathematics: "I propose to tear philosophy away from this genealogical imperative" (1999, 115), he writes. "To forget history—this at first means to make decisions of thinking without returning to a supposed historical sense prescribed by these decisions. It is a question of breaking with historicism to enter, as someone like Descartes or Spinoza did, into an autonomous legitimating of discourse. Philosophy must take on axioms of thinking and draw consequences from them" (115). And for Badiou, this ahistorical thought must break with the poetic suture, precisely because the poetic comprises (as its inherent strength) a thinking "vis-à-vis," always in relation to the object or the world (rather than the ahistorical truth) as the bearer of the multiple.

Unfashionable as it surely is, Badiou's Platonism of the multiple is just that, Platonic fidelity to a "truth without object" (1999, 93): "The task of such a thinking is to produce a concept of the subject such that it is supported by no mention of the object, a subject, if I might say, *without vis-à-vis*. This locus has a bad reputation, for it envokes Bishop Berkeley's absolute idealism. As you have realized, it is, yet, to the task of occupying it that I am devoted" (93). As much as I appreciate (and to a large extent agree with) his sizing up of the "cost" of thinking's primary suture onto the literary, I have to say that this absolutist notion of the "subject" and ahistorical "fidelity" (to the originary "truth-procedure" or the founding "event" of truth) is where I get off the Badiou boat, desperately seeking again the literary *bateau ivre*. Badiou's thinking here seems to put us all somewhere in the vicinity of the quarterdeck of the *Pequod*, consistently menaced by a kind of dictatorial subjective decisionism masquerading (as it so often does) as absolute fidelity to the ahistorical truth. As Badiou (1994) writes, "There is no ethical imperative other than 'Continue!,' 'Continue in your fidelity!'" As the outline of a potential ethics, this notion of single-minded fidelity toward an ahistorical "truth without object" for me summons up the words of a great literary figure who himself most rigorously refused the world of relation (the vis-à-vis): as Bartleby puts it, "I would prefer not to."

Badiou's North American popularity, such as it is, comes I think from the sledgehammer critique of liberalism that his work comprises: in an American political world where the moniker "Democrat" is virtually synonymous with "sellout" or "flip-flopper," Badiou's self-founding subject and absolute political "fidelity" certainly do solve some of the problems that traditional liberalism creates for politics. If nothing else, Badiou's work is good for certain things: knowing what the truth is, or the only correct way to find it; tenacious commitment and fidelity to the cause; knowing which side you're on (an intensified version of Schmitt's friend/enemy distinction constitutes virtually the entire field of Badiou's "prescriptive politics");[1] as well as offering a virtual guarantee that what you're doing at any given point can be called "authentic resistance" (insofar as someone residing in the truth is by definition fighting the good fight against the enemy). Despite the guardrails that Badiou consistently throws up against a pure subjective decisionism (e.g., that truth procedures must be "generic," thereby open to all), one might argue that his thought remains not so much *haunted* as it is *grounded* by a decisionism or voluntarism.

The "plus" side of Badiou's Maoism is, ironically, that it seems a pretty good description of neoliberal biopower's best practices (the War on Terror is "without vis-à-vis" indeed!); but ultimately, one person's universal and ahistorical "truth-procedure" is—a thousand references to Plato, Leo Strauss, Hayek, the Federalist Papers, or the Koran notwithstanding—inexorably another person's doxa. This conceptual slippage (between the individual and the group, the universal and the particular, absolute truth and mere opinion) is, of course, the central problem around which liberalism configures itself; but as tempting or satisfying as it might be to jettison the inherent slipperiness of political events in the name of an absolute subjective and group commitment, this comes only at the cost of intensifying the fundamental problems of liberalism (and, indeed, the central problems of the contemporary economic and political world): fidelity toward those who share my commitment, and little but scorn for all the others. What we might call the "Badiou cocktail"—as Daniel Bensaïd has suggested, a potent mix of "theoretical elitism and practical moralism" (2004, 101)—hardly offers much of a hangover cure from liberal political theory's failures and historical disasters. While there are myriad problems with contemporary liberalism (or even more so neoliberalism), the most pressing among them is hardly that liberalism displays *too little* moralism, decisionism, or elitism.

So why be interested in Badiou's account at all? Or what can it offer us over and above something like Tompkins's swerve around the literary? It seems to me that Badiou, though he doesn't "go there" so to speak, offers us a way to think the literary again as one among a series of other crucial topics (love, science, politics, etc.), without literature having to carry the burden of being the privileged or necessary approach to those other questions. I think that Badiou is right when he suggests that literary interpretation has been the primary suture of our recent past, and that this suture has proven costly or ineffective when it's exported wholesale into other fields of inquiry. Politics, science, and love (one might add here most art forms in general) are hardly realms where "meaning" of a literary kind makes much difference, and it certainly can be a bit of a "disaster" (Badiou's word) to confuse political or mathematical questions with questions of literary interpretation. But, and this seems to be the most serious problem with Badiou's account, such an overreliance on the literary suture can hardly be rectified by absolutizing the mathematical or scientific suture: that "solution" seems to intensify the problem by insisting again on the autonomy of one suture over the others. (Indeed, the problem may be insisting that there are only four sutures, when in fact it seems that, mathematically speaking, there would have to be n sutures, an infinite number; just as there are n friends and n enemies within the political realm).[2] But in some ways Badiou remains right on target: we do at this point need to desacralize the interpretive, but without handing over the whole operation to Badiou's solutions: the matheme, the self-grounding subject, the ahistorical truth, a prescriptive "with us or against us" politics. This kind of hesitation or critique undoubtedly makes me a Badiouean enemy, a liberal accommodationist sap. So be it. When it comes to the friend/enemy distinction, I think Foucault critiques it best: "Who fights against whom? We all fight each other. And there is always within each of us something that fights something else . . . [at the level of] individuals, or even sub-individuals" (1980, 208).[3]

Literature and Philosophy, Again

While I subscribe fully to neither of the general accounts that I have just sketched, it seems to me that Badiou's philosophical account of the literary's demise, cross-hybridized with Tompkins's literary critical one, offers us some provocative ways to think through the present and future of the literary, and to begin retheorizing its possible future relations to philosophy. First, while these two accounts diverge in significant ways, they both suggest that the hegemony of the "literary" in recent theory is in fact better understood as the hegemony of "meaning" (and its flip side, undecidability); likewise, both accounts agree that the hermeneutics of suspicion doesn't and shouldn't saturate the category of the "literary." The first time around, in the postmodern era of big theory, the disciplinary relationship between literature and philosophy was pretty clear: literary studies needed interpretive paradigms, which it found in philosophy; and philosophy needed some real-world application, a place to show examples of what it could do, and it found this oftentimes in literature. Either way, the relation between philosophy and literature in the era of postmodernism was almost wholly a narrow hermeneutic one, one having to do with the mechanics, production and (im)possibility of meaning (much more on this in Chapter 7).

Against this narrowly interpretive sense of literature, I'd suggest that the literary can, in a more robust sense, comprise a thinking "vis-à-vis *without* meaning." While this probably sounds a little odd—what's literature without the ultimate question of meaning?—it always seemed equally strange to me that literary studies found itself in the recent past so completely territorialized on this question of meaning, when virtually no other art form or art criticism is as obsessed by it. "What does it mean?" seems like the wrong question to ask, for example, about music or sculpture, not to mention performance art or postimpressionist painting. And it's always seemed to me likewise a puzzling (and, finally, zero-sum) question to put to Joyce's texts or Shakespeare's.

Indeed, the strength of literature, contra Badiou, lies in its constitution of a strong—infinitely molecular—brand of a thinking the vis-à-vis, of thinking about and through the world of infinite relation. The mistake or Achilles' heel of the literary suture, though, was that in the era of postmodern literary theory, this inherently positive, multiple, machinic, and molecular thinking was templated or overthrown by questions of meaning—questions about the play of presence and absence. Such a hermeneutic thinking of the multiple is always and necessarily tied to the lack or absence of a kind of neo-objectivist one (multiple interpretations being thought in hermeneutics primarily through a founding absence, multiplicity only possible in the wake of the flown god or the death of the author). In short, the "presence" of this thing called meaning in poststructuralist theory is always already made possible by the chiasmic "absence" of some thing or things (the spectral materiality of the signifier, the haunting of other interpretations, the originary dispensation of being, etc.). The hermeneutic suture's primary Achilles' heel, is that it commits you to showing first and foremost what literature *can't* do (it can't mean univocally), rather than what it *can* do (a thousand other things).

In other words, for an entire generation of postmodern theoreticians, the use- or cash-value of literature was constituted by a kind of spoiling move. Literature demonstrated the ultimate frustration of objective knowledge or totalizing thought, through a series of crucial philosophical maneuvers, all of them touching on the (im)possibility of "meaning." First of all, literature shows how texts or other systems don't contain a meaning, but how such meaning is always multiple and always generated by a performative reading process. Meaning, for virtually the whole of what we know as literary theory, is, as I have argued, a question of "how" rather than "what," and such an emphasis on the how (the mechanics of meaning) inexorably keeps open the text, without having to posit an overflowing organic richness (e.g., the genius of the author) as the ground of all interpretations. In addition, literature models a systematicity that functions only in and through generating such multiple meanings—that is, the lack of a single meaning is an *enabling* function for the literary theorist, rather than a philosophical disaster. There are as many meaningful "whats" as there are methodological "hows," so seeming obstacles to figuring out what a text means—lacks, gaps, lacunae, and fissures, the high-value targets of literary reading since structuralism—are hardly philosophical obstacles to interpretation, but instead became the very conditions of (im)possibility for meaning(s).[4]

Either way, my point here is this: such hermeneutic literary theory is inexorably a thinking based on a notion of *lack*. Find the gaps, fissures, or absences, and there you'll find either a secret trace of lost or impossible plenitude (the hidden subtext of meaning) or a hollowing out of the text so as to render it multiply undecidable. And, as much as it pains me to say this, it is those, strictly speaking, interpretive questions (that painstaking tracing of the chiasmic reversals of presence and absence of meaning in a text) that are at this point research dead ends in literary study. Don't believe it? Try deconstructing the hell out of an Emily Dickinson poem, and send the results to *PMLA*—see what happens.

By way of a caveat or disclaimer, it seems to me that the future of the literary is not at all a matter of finding ways simply to abandon the theoretical discussion of literature that was inaugurated by New Criticism and intensified in the era of postmodern theory. To my mind, that would be a huge mistake because, after all, new critical interpretation was the thing that took the backyard conversation that was "literature" and made it into a research profession, for better or worse. My provocation here, if I have one at all, is simply asking theoreticians to rethink the possible sets of relation among literature and philosophy, *other than in the key of interpretation.* This is a call that has already been well heeded by our literature department colleagues: historicists, environmental critics, public intellectuals, and myriad others are producing vital and interesting work in and around literature, outside the mechanics of meaning. However, the department theorists seem these days to be mired in a kind of funk, too many of us driven by a sense that our heyday has passed, leaving us stuck with a hard drive full of Heideggerian readings of *The Anglo-Saxon Chronicle* (I actually have such an essay, should anyone ever care to read it), or bereft of journals interested in our inventive uses of Agamben to reinterpret *The Scarlet Letter.*

But enough mourning for big theory. So much does, in fact, depend on something like William Carlos Williams's "red wheel / barrow / glazed with rain / water / beside the white / chickens"—so much *more than meaning* depends on the sense of irreducibly multiple relation that *is* this thing called literature. And as Badiou suggests, at this point in the history of the literary, a release from the hermeneutic suture may in fact be what poetry "wants": its primary job should, perhaps, no longer be to provide exemplary fodder for interpretive methods or to offer examples of philosophical truths.

I can already feel a kind of query or invitation coming from the reader: "Yes, I've had it with bland historicist job talks concerning novels written by pirates, or tracking what Frederick Douglass did on the weekend, and would love to think theoretically about the literary again. How about an example of the kind of reading you're talking about—using, say, *Heart of Darkness* as a sample text? Show us what your paradigm can do—take it out for a test drive on Conrad." While I'll try to do some of this in the next chapter, on the whole I'm suspicious of that kind of invitation: the whole sense of offering an example reading or a critical template is, as I've argued previously, itself a relic of the postmodern era that I'm asking theorists to consider fleeing. I'm not interested in founding a new interpretive school here, or prescribing hot new topics for critique. I'm simply insisting that, despite claims to the contrary, the literary—and with it literary theory—is or should be alive and well; but, I'd add, it can remain so only if we abandon our nostalgia for the primary suture of the interpretive itself and turn literature and literary theory back to the multiplicity of uses and questions that characterize our engagements with other forms of expression—to reinvigorate the myriad transversal theoretical connections among literature and philosophy, outside the interpretive suture. It's already happening in a widespread way: just look at the table of contents for any recent "good" journal and you'll see plenty of theoretically inflected work, but very little of it begins or ends with the question of literary meaning.

Maybe the current post-postmodern state of affairs—the swerve around P—commits theorists to revisiting the critique of "interpretation" that got postmodern literary theory off the ground in the first place, and trying to locate there a series of roads less traveled. I think here of moments like Michel Foucault's call, at the beginning of 1969's *Archaeology of Knowledge*, to treat historical monuments and archives not primarily as documents (delving ever more into the question of the past's meaning), but to reverse the polarity: to treat documents and archives as monuments, to remain at the descriptive level of the document itself rather than attempt to ventriloquize archives or render texts "meaningful" through an interpretive method of some kind. Or one could recall Deleuze and Guattari's provocations in *A Thousand Plateaus*, where "the triumph of theory" goes by the much less grandiose name "interpretosis . . . humankind's fundamental neurosis" (1987, 114). Their symptomology of this malady goes like this:

Every sign refers to another sign, and only to another sign, ad infinitum. . . . The world begins to signify before anyone knows what it signifies; the signifier is given without being known. Your wife looked at you with a funny expression. And this morning the mailman handed you a letter from the IRS and crossed his fingers. Then you stepped in a pile of dog shit. You saw two sticks positioned on the sidewalk like the hands of a watch. They were whispering behind your back when you arrived at the office. It doesn't matter what it means, it's still signifying. The sign that refers to other signs is struck with a strange impotence and uncertainty, but mighty is the signifier that constitutes the chain. (112)

There remains, in Deleuze and Guattari's world, much interesting that can be said about stepping in a pile of dog shit or being summoned by the IRS; but what those events *mean*—inside or outside the context of a novel—is hardly the only place to begin or end a theoretical inquiry. In the search for lines of flight, one could even return to Culler's "Beyond Interpretation" and its proleptic response to those who still today yearn for the "next big thing" in literary theory: "There are many tasks that confront contemporary criticism, many things that we need if we are to advance our understanding of literature, but if there is one thing we do not need it is more interpretations of literary works" (1976, 246). In fact, Culler's 1976 diagnosis of "The Prospects of Contemporary Criticism" seems a fitting (if largely unheard) caveat for the decades of literary theory that would follow: "The principle of interpretation is so strong an unexamined postulate of American criticism that it subsumes and neutralizes even the most forceful and intelligent acts of revolt" (253).[5]

I fear that many of us in the theory world—people in literature departments who "do theory" for a living—have been slow to engage fully with changing research practices in literature departments. Nobody in music theory, architecture theory, or art theory ever really asks what the work of Beethoven, Brunelleschi, or Jackson Pollock *means*. These days, maybe that question doesn't make much sense for literary theorists either.

CHAPTER 7

Literature

CAN LITERATURE BE EQUIPMENT
FOR POST-POSTMODERN LIVING?

Users don't read.   —WEB DESIGN TRUISM[1]

It's not much of an exaggeration to say that literature was king during the academic postmodern revolution of the late twentieth century. Taking "the linguistic turn" as its central premise, postmodern theorizing in myriad disciplines turned to avant-garde poetics and narrative as models for what the world feels like if it's structured like a language, if indeed "there is nothing outside the text." In short, the linguistic turn of postmodernism made textual skills—reading and interpretation—central to discourses and disciplines that formerly had very little overt traffic with the ins and outs of language. From the study of history and philosophy, through the workings of the unconscious and subjective identity, even as far afield as economics and the life sciences, a Saussurean version of language (that socially constructed place where there are no positive terms, only differences) was the postmodern paradigm that overcoded all the others.

Insofar as literature was, to steal a phrase from Kenneth Burke (1973), "equipment for living" in the postmodern era, it specifically served as equipment for making your way through this world saturated with the lacks or gaps so characteristic of the literary hermeneutics that I discussed at length in the previous chapter—undecidable meanings, undecipherable codes, unconscious desires, uncertain values, unforeseen plot twists. The postmodern world was a world where reading or interpretation (specifically understood as the art of inhabiting and maybe suturing such narrative gaps or aporias) was the primary pivot: the referential guarantees of essentialism (the "positive terms") were dead in all the academic disciplines, so meaning throughout the humanities had to be *made* rather than *found*. And what better laboratory than postmodern literature for studying those anti-essentialist, meaning-making operations?

But over the past fifteen years or so, there's been a slow but decisive turn away from the linguistic turn in the North American academic world. This has perhaps been most obvious in literary studies, which (as I argue in Chapter 6) has swerved away from interpreting texts—from pivoting on questions about textual meaning and its discontents—to examining the historical, archival, scientific, biological, and political contexts of literary production. Likewise, other humanities and social sciences discourses have quietly abandoned the linguistic turn—economics has almost completely reterritorialized on mathemes, and if you told anyone working in contemporary academic psychology departments or in language acquisition research that "the unconscious is structured like a language," the person would think you were crazy. Likewise, academic sex and gender studies were during the 1980s and '90s nearly synonymous with the "performative identity" linguistic theories of Judith Butler and Eve Sedgwick, just as postcolonial theory was for a long time taken with Homi Bhabha's language-based theories of "dessemi/nation" and "hybridity," but not so much anymore.

Even in continental philosophy, arguably the home of the linguistic turn, it seems that the deconstructive phase of axiomatic linguistic mediation has been eclipsed. Deleuze is the thinker du jour; and Deleuze's wide-ranging corpus is, one might argue, held together primarily by his consistent and harsh critique of the linguistic turn. Nowadays even sympathetic Derrideans like Catherine Malabou suggest that if deconstruction is to "live on," it needs to move beyond its myopic focus on the literary suture of écriture.[2] Finally, one might note that in recent biological research (where Malabou suggests we turn our attention), life itself is no longer primarily understood on the genomic analogy of the book (where life contains a hidden code, requiring the scientist's interpretation), but on a model of the microscopic or molecular, the smallest particles that might be manipulated by researchers. So, with an ironic nod to Marx, one might say that contemporary biology is not merely interested in *interpreting* genes, but in *changing* (and thereby potentially *financializing*) them.[3]

And this is maybe what biology has most decisively in common with its various sibling academic fields who are fleeing the linguistic turn: they participate in a general movement away from the postmodern metaphorics of socially constructed mediation (the literary problem par excellence, filling gaps and working through undecidabilities), to examining more direct modes of biopolitical and economic manipulation. From a focus on *understanding* something to a concern with *manipulating* it—from (postmodern) *meaning* to (post-postmodern) *usage*, one might say. And as any Web designer or technical writer will tell you, "Users don't read."

Maybe a linchpin for all these disparate anti-hermeneutic maneuvers is found in Foucault's work on biopower, which Foucault diagnoses as a form of power that works on bodies differently than the institutional mediations of disciplinary training. Rather than see it function as a series of linked practices in play at scattered disciplinary sites (hospital, family, school, workplace, and so on), Foucault sees biopower as a new type of power that works on bodies "really and directly" (*réellement et directement*) at every point in the power-saturated *socius*.[4] So, for example, your disciplinary identity as a soldier or a student is mediated through training in a specific institution, the army or the school; on the other hand, your biopolitical identity—your sexuality, for example—is under constant construction at all times, everywhere, inside and outside the training grounds of institutions. What Randy Martin (2002) calls "the financialization of daily life" over the past several decades is probably one of the most widespread markers of this smear of power into places where it previously didn't travel, but the infiltration of subjective identity questions into the spaces of work (the idea that your job is or should be a self-actualization technique, rather than a means to garner the free time to practice self-actualization) is likewise an intense and emergent smear of biopolitical identity questions—which have mutated from previously rarified realms like literature into the office cubicle and the factory floor.

To put it another way, if you understand social power as working inexorably through institutional mediation, then language is a key methodological tool, insofar as language is a figure for social mediation in its most widespread and inescapable form. However, if mediation at privileged institutional sites has given way to direct access of various kinds (if your whole life, public and private, is the surface area of biopower rather than the discrete parts of your life that discipline worked on one at a time), then language will also, it seems, be displaced as the primary grid of intelligibility. When power is at work literally and figuratively everywhere, on the surface of "life" itself, then the spaces of mediation (between the subject and the *socius*, the body and the state, science and literature, and so on) are no longer the privileged fields where the agon of social power and resistance is worked out in its most intense manner.

Language and literature were king in the postmodern era precisely because they were the most economical markers for the experience of a social world where essentialism had lost its explanatory focus, and the mediations of social construction were the questions du jour. And if understanding an anti-essentialist world of endless mediation is the problem, then language and literature constitute the most obvious place to begin looking for a solution (or at least a grid for understanding the problem). If not, probably not. In other words, maybe this post-postmodern (anti-language or anti-hermeneutic) set of stances is not exactly a return to essentialism (as some have charged),[5] but rather a recognition that not all deployments of force (social, biological, historical, unconscious, etc.) can easily or satisfactorily be modeled on a Saussurean understanding of linguistics—that we're looking at a mutation or evolution of paradigms rather than a simple return to the essentialist past. Indeed, fifty years hence, one imagines that people will puzzle over why so many people in the twentieth century thought that language was *the* privileged paradigm for understanding literally everything else.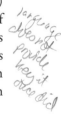

In a slightly different lingo, one might say that if "fragmentation" (the anti-essentialist necessity to put disparate things together) was the watchword of postmodernism, then, of course, reading follows as post-modernism's linchpin practice, largely through synecdoche: the hermeneutic conundrums of literature (especially avant-garde literature) functioned as the *part* that stood in for the *whole* postmodern world of piecing together undecidables. Post-postmodernism, on the other hand, seems to take "intensification" (an increased spread and penetration) as its paradigmatic ethos, with globalization as its primary practice—all access all the time. And this historical shift of focus or orientation inverts (and maybe destroys) literature's privileged synecdochic role. In short, in our critical work throughout the humanities we no longer tend to go to the revelatory "part" in hopes of grasping the larger "whole" (arguing, for example, that reading *Gravity's Rainbow* gives us a window into the workings of the world at large, the contradictory logic of everyday life); rather, we now tend to start with the larger, post-postmodern whole (e.g., globalization), of which any particular part (say, postmodern literature) is a functioning piece. To repurpose a quote from *Gravity's Rainbow*, it may be that post-postmodernism "is not a disentanglement from, but a progressive knotting-into" (Pynchon 1972, 3); and if that's the case, the "disentanglement" function of literature (the interruptive, hermeneutic power of reading's hesitating slowness—its questioning of "meaning") becomes increasingly less useful as a way to engage the superfast post-postmodern world.

To put it crudely, in a world of economic globalization (flat, though unevenly so to say the least), it's not clear that mediated representations or signs matter as much as direct flows of various kinds—money, goods, people, images. And the question posed by this historical novelty to literary research is obvious: whither poetics in a world where language and its workings are no longer the privileged pivots? What's the role of literature in a world where language is no longer seen as *the* central humanities concern, as it was throughout the second half of the twentieth century? How do we move, as I've asked previously, from the postmodern hermeneutics of suspicion to a post-postmodern hermeneutics of situation?

W(h)ither Poetics?

Unfortunately, much of the literary world's response to this colonization of everyday life by an emergent post-postmodernism has relied on a kind of linguistic nostalgia, clinging to the life raft of the hermeneutics of suspicion. If literature has any "use-value" or offers us equipment for living after postmodernism, that value remains primarily thematized as a kind of spoiling move, an antiquarian slowing down of all the superfast flows that characterize the post-postmodern world. Recently I heard a Pulitzer Prize–winning contemporary author say just this on (where else?) National Public Radio: "The world is so insanely complex and fast and distracting, and one of the things I think a good book can do is slow the reader's attention down a little bit and give them [*sic*] a chance to think through some of the consequences of these changes which otherwise are so quick that all you can do is react."[6] This kind of sentiment is unfortunately not far from seemingly more sophisticated or "radical" attempts within contemporary theory to reinvigorate an ethics of close reading, or to rekindle various other high-modernist theoretical nostrums concerning the autonomous, resistant importance of reading or interpretation. If we continue the line of reasoning laid out in modern and postmodern meditations on literature of the twentieth century, most contemporary gambits concerning poetics as "equipment for living" continue to suggest that literature's real use-value is . . . that it has none. Literature functions as a mode of inexorable slowness, maybe interruption on a good day, in a too-fast world of capital; and as such it indexes the old dream of poetics as the last remaining realm that's semi-autonomous from the world of getting and spending.

A primal scene for this kind of critical investment in postmodern literature is, arguably, constituted by the response of poets and critics to Fredric Jameson's notorious use of Bob Perelman's poem "China" in Jameson's famous "Postmodernism" essay. According to the critical response offered by those interested in "defending" avant-garde poetics from Jameson's positioning of it, Jameson is perhaps right when he says that postmodern architecture or robust markets in museum art are synonymous with late capitalism and the structural position it affords to a formerly autonomous aesthetic notion of "innovation"; but not so avant-garde poetics. In other words, contemporary avant-garde poetry is not really another *symptom* of late capitalism's saturation, as Jameson suggests; rather, its defenders argue, such linguistically ambitious literature constitutes a *critique* of said capitalism, in terms of both its form (parataxis is hard to consume, so a certain Brechtian V-effect morphs the reader into something other than a mere consumer) and content (even the most successful poetry, avant-garde or otherwise, is hardly a meaningful niche market on the spreadsheets of multinational capital).

Charles Bernstein nicely sums up this skeptical response to Jameson's discussion of "schizophrenic fragmentation" (1993, 73) as the trace of
late capitalism within language poetry:

The "same" artistic technique has a radically different meaning depending on
when and where it is used. . . . Juxtaposition of logically unconnected sentences or
sentence fragments can be used to theatricalize the limits of conventional narrative
development, to suggest the impossibility of communication, to represent speech,
or as part of a prosodic mosaic constituting a newly emerging (or then again, traditional but neglected) meaning formation; these uses need have nothing in common. . . . Nor is the little-known painter who uses a neo-Hellenic motif in her
work necessarily doing something comparable to the architect who incorporates
Greek columns into a multi-million dollar office tower. But it is just this type of
mishmashing that is the negative horizon of those discussions of postmodernism
that attempt to describe it in unitary socioeconomic terms. (91–92)

Like many poets and critics who respond to cultural studies work on the
economies of poetics, Bernstein here tries to highlight what we might call
a certain semi-autonomy for the literary—insisting on the fact that the
poet's work, like the cultural production of her friend the "little-known
painter," in fact can't be discussed in the same vocabulary as multi-mil-
lion-dollar skyscrapers, at least not without mangling the work of poetry
by wrenching it into a foreign idiom and context.

However, it's just this critical move—harnessing literature as an
"other" to the dictates of late capitalism—that I want to wonder about,
after postmodernism, after the linguistic turn. If everything's modeled on
language or the mediating workings of language, then paratactic interruption has a crucially important job to do—interrupting all the too-
hasty conclusions and too-easy consensus of "totalization," that thing to
be avoided at all costs in the world of postmodern literary and cultural
theory. But if the binary pairs of fragmentation and totalization, meaning
or chiasmus, are no longer the structuring tropes of post-postmodern life,
how to reposition the literary, away from its (now unfortunately comfortable) deconstructive posture as the subordinated, supposedly subversive
term in any opposition (the literary as the constant reminder of the meaning's impossibility, its inability to be totalized or "whole")?

As I have argued earlier concerning Jameson's *Postmodernism*, it
doesn't help much to follow Bernstein's path of critique and isolate one

of Jameson's postmodern cultural modes—avant-garde poetry, video art, painting, the novel, architecture—in order to suggest that he's gotten its connection to socioeconomic phenomena wrong (that X phenomenon resists late capitalism, rather than is merely a symptom of it), because that's to make the very "modernist" mistake that the essay suggests is no longer available to us. Everything does in fact exist on the same flat surface of culture; or, as Jameson provocatively puts it, "Postmodernism is what you have when the modernization process is complete and nature is gone for good . . . 'culture' has become a veritable 'second nature'" (1991, ix). If, as everyone in the theory game seemingly agrees, there is no transhistorical "human nature" existing somehow "outside" contemporary capitalism, then the question necessarily becomes, How are these modes of cultural production related; how do they configure a kind of odd open totality (what one might call, in another lingo, a poem)? And how can one kind of cultural production process usefully overcode another, insofar as what formations "mean" is of as little relevance for contemporary poetics as it is for economics or cultural studies? *What, we may want to ask, can poetics tell us about the workings of economics and culture, rather than vice versa? What roles can literature play, other than "the other"?*

To take a question and make it into a statement, I'm trying to follow out the methodological gambit of this book (the language of overcoding, from a postmodern hermeneutics of suspicion to a post-postmodern hermeneutics of situation) by suggesting here that the socioeconomic questions of culture can quite fruitfully be explored by deploying the tools and languages of poetics—so skilled at the creation of discontinuous, open entities—"at" seemingly unrelated cultural and economic formations, rather than strictly the other way round (deploying the cultural/economic theory "at" the literature, which tends to yield not much more than the tautological conclusion that, like everything else, contemporary literary production bears traces of the economic system in which it's produced). In short, if poetics wants to have any substantial traction in contemporary debates about culture, literature will in fact have to be discussed in the same socioeconomic terms as downtown office towers, museum art, or hip hotels—with the important caveat that literature being *discussed* in those terms doesn't mean literature being *determined* by them. In fact, the practices of economics are these days becoming more overcoded by the language of poetics than the other way round (as many of us learned painfully in recent years, even the value of your home is a bardic "performative" rather than an objective "constative" entity); so this historical situation should, if nothing else, give another directionality to engaging the debate between literature and economics.

Baldly stated, it seems to me that the general line of reasoning concerning the uselessness and/or semi-autonomy of literature is all but exhausted at this point in our economic and cultural history—and not so much because we're all inexorably forced to work through the omnivorous leveling logic of "the market" (a defensible position), but because the notion of aesthetic semi-autonomy implied by this kind of argument is more a hindrance than a help in harnessing the singular critical potential of poetics in the contemporary world. This suggests that what remains culturally singular and potentially critical about "ambitious" literature at this historical juncture is not some negative notion of its contentlessness, or its inexorable frustration of meaning—literature as something like Adorno's noncommodity par excellence. Rather, the "equipmental" (sorry, Heideggerians) force of literature at this historical juncture may precisely lie in intensifying and expanding our sense of "the poetic" as a robust form of cultural engagement or analysis, whose force is enabled not by its *distance from* dominant culture, but its *imbrication with* contemporary socioeconomic forces. Within such a rethinking, even literature's seeming uselessness could be recoded from a stoic, prophylactic avoidance to a positive (maybe even joyful) form of critical engagement with contemporary biopolitical and economic life. Is there literary life after the hermeneutics of suspicion?

Negatory

Without such a refashioned notion of literature's engagement with the superfast world of capital, about all you have left is a kind of saddened nostalgia for days gone by—all you've got left is the negative pole of a dialectical thought, one might say. For example, this is overtly the function of literature that Don DeLillo lays out in his (both ironic and prescient) novels *Mao II* (1991) and *White Noise* (1985). As Bill Gray, the writer-protagonist of *Mao II*, is quoted by his assistant: "The novel used to feed our search for meaning. . . . It was the great secular transcendence. The Latin mass of language, character, occasional new truth. But our desperation has led us toward something larger and darker. So we turn to the news, which provides an unremitting mood of catastrophe. This is where we find emotional experience not available elsewhere. We don't need the novel" (73). Gray, who is portrayed as the postmodern author-function writ large (Pynchonian genius recluse), sees the visceral visuality of terrorism and its manipulation of the news media (all the screens and moving images of visual culture) as having taken over the hermeneutic identity-shaping functions of literature. As he puts it in his meditation on "novelists and terrorists," "Years ago, I used to think it was possible for a novelist to alter the inner life of the culture. Now bomb-makers and gunmen have taken that territory" (41). He continues and clarifies later in the novel: "Beckett is the last writer to shape the way we think and see. After him, the major work involves midair collisions and crumbling buildings. This is the new tragic narrative" (157).

There has, of course, been a lot of ink spilled over these passages since 9/11, and surely DeLillo was on to the importance of media saturation, globalization, and terrorism long before the academic world caught up with it—not to mention his various tutorials, in *Mao II* and *Underworld* (2000), on the importance of the World Trade Center as a global symbol, and his foreseeing (in *White Noise*) commercial airplanes being used as missiles by terrorists (146). While that prescience is all very interesting, and seems maybe to argue against Bill Gray's entire line of reasoning on the obsolescence of literature, the thing to focus on for our purposes is less the argument about literature's centrality (or not) in an image-saturated world, but the implied reasons why DeLillo's character suggests that literature is no longer central to such a mediatized *socius*. Literature is outmoded, on this reading, not so much because it's prisoned by old-fashioned sentences and language rather than visual images, and thereby can't produce anything relevant or "new"; but the problem is much more that literature can't produce interruption of the same (anymore).

In a world of lightning-quick turnaround in news cycles, capital flows, and images, only the spectacular excess of terrorism, DeLillo's characters conclude, can overtake literature's traditional job and slow us down, show us a glimpse of the outside: "What terrorists gain novelists lose.

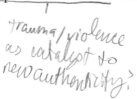

trauma/violence as catalyst to new authenticity?

The degree to which they influence mass consciousness is the extent of our decline as shapers of sensibility and thought. The danger they represent equals our own failure to be dangerous. . . . In societies reduced to blur and glut, terror is the only meaningful act. . . . Only the terrorist stands outside. The culture hasn't figured out how to assimilate him" (157). This sense of literature's obsolescence is importantly different from the usual canards concerning literature's demise: it's not so much that people don't read anymore, or that a combination of the Internet, ubiquitous TV screens, and rampant smartphone use has shortened our collective attention spans to the point where we can no longer engage productively with literature's unique temporality. DeLillo is not, in other words, playing the subjective depth of literature off against the mass delusions of image-saturated culture; rather, I take the point to be that media images have taken over the very resistant, interruptive power of the "thought from outside" that for so long was the privileged territory of literary language. The value of poetics—indeed, the value of art itself—on such a rendering remains the unthematizable contact with the outside that has made literature a privileged ethical discourse within modernism and postmodernism. Which is to say, artistic value remains thematized in DeLillo as interruption, plain and simple.

However, given not so much its temporality but its privatizing form (the book and private time of reading), literature is forced to pursue its interruptive work on what we might call the "retail" level of the individual consciousness; and if that's to be the case, it would seem literature is gone forever as a generator (or even as a reflector) of meaningful levels of widespread cognitive dissonance. The inscribed page is simply not a mass phenomenon in the way that the dancing screens of visual culture (television, Internet, even film) inherently are.

Given DeLillo's characters' rendering, one might say that writers have become the last believers—not in any positive content or anything as predictable as "meaning," but writers are the last believers in language's ability to be the primary driver in the interruption and reshaping of subjectivity (which is also to say, the resisting and disrupting of so-called normative subjectivity). It may, in fact, be that writers are among the last to hold faith in the linguistic-turn creeds of postmodernism itself. And in the process of morphing into those last believers, writers in *Mao II* become figures almost identical to the nuns in DeLillo's *White Noise*, who explain to Jack Gladney that they don't actually believe in anything so silly as God, but their job is to continue to act as if they still did: "It is our task in the world to believe things no one else takes seriously. To abandon such beliefs completely, the human race would die. This is why we are here. A tiny minority. To embody old things, old beliefs. The devil, angels, heaven, hell. If we did not pretend to believe these things, the world would collapse. . . . We surrender our lives to make your nonbelief possible" (1985, 318–19). Perhaps surprisingly (perhaps not), this sentiment is iterated in *Mao II* by Brita, the obsessive photographer of writers: "I want others to believe, you see. Many believers everywhere. I feel the enormous importance of this. . . . I need these people to believe for me. I cling to believers. Many, everywhere. Without them, the planet grows cold" (1991, 69). Initially here, Brita is talking about her attractions to writers—those who still believe in the power of the word to change the world. But of course the passage is also the linchpin for her post-postmodern abandonment of writers at novel's end, in order to photograph terrorists: those who really are, as Bill Gray insists, involved in the project of radical cultural disruption and change, bulwarked by strong beliefs.

On DeLillo's account, one might say that the contemporary author-function has ironically become one not with the terrorist-function, but with the nun-function: in the present, a professional class of intense "believers" comprises both nuns and authors, a "tiny minority" upholding and venerating tradition of consciousness raising in a world where most people don't have time or inclination to care about preserving the past or mulling over the questions of what it all means for the future. And this version of literature's future provides an even less appealing subject position for literary critics, who could be said to share their worldview less with the savvy, doubting clergy than with the credulous, pious churchgoers—those who still believe in officially sanctioned believers.

Two Powers of the False

Rather than see literature's power emerging primarily through its status as the bearer of old truths (even if they're essentially negative modernist or postmodernist hermeneutics of suspicion verities concerning the falseness of all totalizing truths), one might directly focus on literature's powers of the false, its post-postmodern abilities to create other, virtual worlds. The "powers of the false" is a phrase most immediately associated with Gilles Deleuze's use of it as the title of chapter 6 in his *Cinema 2: The Time Image.*[7] There Deleuze presents the "time image" as a direct mode of manipulating filmic time (a general kind of maneuver we've been calling "post-postmodern"), in contradistinction to the montage-laden "movement image" and its necessarily mediated relation to temporality. (In its insistence on mediation, the movement image is then more symptomatically "postmodern," though this is not a terminology that Deleuze uses.) As Deleuze explains, time images "are direct presentations of time. We no longer have an indirect image of time which derives from movement, but a direct time-image from which movement derives. We no longer have a chronological time which can be overturned by movements which are contingently abnormal; we have a chronic non-chronological time which produces movements necessarily 'abnormal,' essentially 'false'" (1989, 129). For example, one sees the movement image's mediating powers of the false on display in ideology critique: the power of the false as that which unmasks the exclusions or illegitimacy of the totalizing "truth" by showing it to be beholden to multiple mediating viewpoints—think the montage as the most intense form of movement image, the extension and contraction of chronological time in Eisenstein's "Odessa Steps" sequence. In contradistinction, the time image's direct power of the false does not work through mediation by the true (by interrupting, deconstructing, or questioning the objectivist truth), but gives another account of the real altogether, one that's beyond the current regimes of true and false. Deleuze here draws on examples from American film noir, which is clearly driven not by movements that reestablish norms but by the navigation of virtual worlds created by packs of falsehoods. Likewise, Deleuze leans very heavily on Orson Welles's final film, *F for Fake*, which equates whatever creative power cinema possesses not with being true to the auteur's individual vision, but with the collective powers of error and the false.[8]

To articulate the same point somewhat differently, one of the primary things falsified by this second power of the false is the idea that art or language primarily strives (and inexorably fails) to be "true." In fact, Deleuze's work with Guattari on language constitutes a decisive swerve around the despotic nature of signification or representation—the idea that language is primarily made for communicating truth or meaning; they insist on "the unimportance of [the question] 'What does it mean?'" (1983, 180). "Interpretation is our modern way of believing and being pious" (171), Deleuze and Guattari write, because signification is consistently territorialized on tautological questions about meaning, truth and its absence, "the symbolic lack of the dead father, or the Great Signifier" (171). Because every signifier fails adequately to represent its signified (attesting to the *absence* of the signified, not its presence), then every interpretation always already lacks—it inevitably fails to do justice to the text at hand. As I argued previously, such an assured interpretive failure (and its symmetrically inverse flip side, the postmodern infinity of interpretation) inexorably defines meanings and subjects not in terms of what they *can* do, but in terms of what they *can't do*: they can't be complete, "true" in an objective manner. However, such a subverting hermeneutics of suspicion discourse is also oddly totalizing or "despotic," because each and every term in the field shares the same fate, an unfulfilled destiny doled out by the central logic of the signifier. This "weak" power of the false, represented most succinctly by the logic of the signifier, performs the relentless work of the negative, always and everywhere hollowing out the true (the signified).

"There are," then, "great differences between . . . a linguistics of flows and a linguistics of the signifier" (Deleuze and Guattari 1983, 241), insofar as a linguistics of the signifier remains territorialized on tautological questions of representation (on the question, What does it mean?), rather than on axiomatic determinations of force or command (the question, What does it do?). For Deleuze and Guattari, "Language no longer signifies something that must be believed; it indicates rather what is going to be done" (250): "No problem of meaning, but only of usage" (77–78). As they argue in *A Thousand Plateaus*, "The elementary unit of language— the statement—is the order-word. Rather than common sense, a faculty for the centralization of information, we must define an abominable faculty consisting in emitting, receiving, and transmitting order-words" (1987, 76). Language is better treated as a direct form of interpellation than it is as a mediating form of communication, information, or signification. Language directly commands and configures—"'I' is an order-word"

Power

Political

(84)—and hence it is not treated productively as the trace of an absent or future meaning. In short, Deleuze and Guattari teach us that language is not primarily meant for interpretation, but obedience and resistance: "Writing has nothing to do with signifying. It has to do with surveying, mapping, even realms that are yet to come" (4–5). One might say that the performative in Deleuze doesn't succeed by failing to be a constative; rather, it succeeds the old-fashioned way—as a direct deployment of force, as a provocation. The cash-value of truth or representation is beholden to a prior deployment of force—the power of the false as *production* (of something, not necessarily the "new") rather than as *interruption* of the same.

As odd as it sounds, this strong or positive sense of the power of the false is actually a linchpin of twentieth-century French thinking, most obviously within Georges Canguilhem's work on truth and normativity in the life sciences. All discourses are essentially games or regimes of truth, Canguilhem points out, so any new discovery will, within the truth procedures of these existing games, simply have to be received as an error or a falsehood. Given, for example, a scientific consensus concerning how photosynthesis works, any new discovery that challenges this dominant understanding will, by definition, be rendered "false" in terms of the existing paradigm. Error, then, is not the thing that scientific discourse works ceaselessly to eliminate (merely the "other" of the true), but error is in fact that which science thrives on, what science actually seeks to produce.

The emergence of "truth" is largely an effect not of a sudden triumph over the darkness of falsity, but of the slow evolution of "true" practices that consistently work to normalize the effects of new discoveries, finding ways to account for (rather than simply dismiss or exclude) emergent falsehoods. As Foucault explains in his work on Canguilhem, "Error is not eliminated by the blunt force of a truth that would gradually emerge form the shadows but by the formation of a new way of truth-telling" (1998, 471), the emergence of what the late Foucault calls a new "mode of veridiction." There is, in other words, a "strong" power of the false that lies in its direct ability to create the new, understood specifically as the abnormal or the error—rather than (or at least in addition to) the false's traditional philosophical, "weak" job of subverting the true.

Following the course laid out for the false in Plato's dialogues, this weak (mediating or interruptive, what I'm calling "postmodern") power of the false is inevitably to be found in the designed-to-be-overcome arguments of the minor characters, who function not as generators of new knowledge, but as the (Socratic) true's other or its bungling interlocutor. Thereby this weak power of the false is simply a momentary sidekick, serving as adjunct or enabler along the path to a higher truth. And, of course, literature has for a long time played this Platonic part as the dialectical rival, the subverting other, of philosophical thought. Indeed, even in the high-flying, anti-Platonic realm of postmodern theory, this job of interrupting the true remained the primary job laid out for literature.

However, it's this more robust, direct, post-postmodern, or "strong" power of the false that I'd like to try to reconnect with as the power of literature. As Foucault argues in his essay "Lives of Infamous Men," as early modern sovereign power began to break down, practices of power became more invested in "everyday life." In other words, sovereign practices of the "true and false" began to pay attention to things they'd never seen as important before: the comings and goings of "infamous," everyday people. The lives of the not-famous—of everyday people and their relations to family, health, sexual matters, diet, and so on—increasingly became places for the dominant mode of power to look for truth. But precisely because of this increasing spread or saturation of power, the dramas of everyday life likewise became intense sites for a certain kind of resistance within the emergent *dispositif* of power. Among the names for this early modern resistance was "literature." As Foucault writes,

Just as an apparatus [*dispositif*] was being installed for forcing people to tell the "insignificant"—that which isn't told, which doesn't merit any glory, therefore, the "infamous"—a new imperative was forming that would constitute what could be called the "immanent ethic" of Western literary discourse. Its ceremonial functions would gradually fade; it would no longer have the task of manifesting in a tangible way the all too visible radiance of force, grace, heroism, and might [*puissance*], but rather of searching for the things hardest to perceive—the most hidden, hardest to tell and to show, and lastly most forbidden and scandalous. A kind of injunction to ferret out the most nocturnal and most quotidian elements of existence . . . would mark out the course that literature would follow from the seventeenth century onward, from the time it began to be literature in the modern sense of the word. . . . Whence [literature's] dual relation to truth and to power. Whereas the fabulous [*le fabuleux*] could function only in an indecision [*une indécision*] between true and false, literature based itself, rather, on a decision of nontruth [*une décision de non-vérité*]; it explicitly presented itself as artifice while promising to produce effects of truth that were recognizable as such. (2003, 292–93)

Here, Foucault explicitly ties a direct or strong power of the false—"a decision of nontruth"—to whatever "resistant" function literature may deploy under the *dispositif* of an emergent modern practice of power. While it's not immediately clear what the positive content of such a claim might be (which is not surprising, as the emergent or resistant can hardly be circumscribed in advance), I think it's very clear what Foucault is avoiding or critiquing in this passage, concerning the powers of literature and their relation to the powers of the false. Foucault here subtly but decisively upends or "falsifies" the *Tel Quel* faith that literature primarily functions to subvert the totalizing claims of philosophical or social truth.

Foucault lays out here in a very economical fashion the two literary powers of the false that I've been discussing: first, there's the "fabulous"—or "fabulating" (*fabuleux*)—"weak" or "postmodern" power of the false, which consists in subverting the true, thereby bringing about a neodeconstructive "indecision between true and false." Further down the literary continuum, however, there is a "strong" power of the false in literature (the one I'd like to harness to post-postmodernism), based on "a decision of nontruth" that nevertheless "produces effects of truth" in an alternative fashion. And this decision of nontruth indexes the emergent power of error, the intensification of the power of the false as the engine for the emergence of another, different mode of speaking the truth. No longer merely serving as the interruptive or indecisive "other" of philosophical or social power, literature here takes on a productive function of its own within the *dispositif* of an "everyday" biopower.

Those of us who lived and worked through the years of big theory in academia know all about the weak or interruptive power of the false, which was the job that literature was explicitly given throughout the postmodern linguistic-turn years: what, for example, would deconstructive literary criticism be without its breathless claims to literature's resistance to philosophy, consistently interrupting the sinister dream of reified, completed meaning?[9] And this assault on reification is likewise the kindred thread that connects deconstruction with other postmodern critical discourses that may have seemed hostile toward deconstruction in its day—for example, Marxist ideology critique or new historicist work on politics. All that literary critical work was territorialized on the power of literature as the power of interrupting totalization, a certain weak power of the false. And for interruption to function plausibly as a mode of resistance to truth, the primary social and theoretical "problem" logically has to rest in a social system that does whatever sinister work it does through the desire for totalization.

In the end, what's "subverted" in virtually all postmodern notions of "subversion" is the desire for totalized "meaning." Hence the great thematics of literature as an interruptive mode of what de Man called "negative assurance"—the literary as the primary guarantee of Adorno's negative-dialectical catchphrase, "the whole is false"; thereby for many modern and postmodern theorists, literature and language have also functioned as powerful models of resistance to the exclusions and closures characteristic of fascism, racism, sexism, and the mutually assured destruction of the cold war nation-state. To put it bluntly, all the potential functions of literature and language got overcoded, in the postmodern years, by literature's ability to interrupt something like singular truth. Literature carried a certain power of the false, but one that was characterized almost wholly by the negative—literature's power was simply in displaying the inability of its binary partner, philosophical "truth" or totalized "meaning." Thereby that interruptive power of the false under postmodernism remained parasitic on falsification's relation to what remains necessarily a primary mode, the dominant power of the true. This weak or postmodern power of the false, then, has no power of its own, one that's not already understood in terms of truth (and its discontents).

But what of this "other other" power of the false, the power not to interrupt existing truths, but to create objects or posit different ways of separating out the true and the false? What of those powers of the false that are directly related to its ability to create error (rather than primarily to reify or subvert truth)—the affirmative powers of the false, rather than the primarily negative ones? When I think about this strong power of the false in literature, where it's on display in a most intense version, I tend to think first of the work done by so-called language poet Bruce Andrews, whose composition method consists of writing down phrases and sentences on small rectangles of paper and editing them together into discontinuous onslaughts of phrasing.[10] The result looks something like this, the better part of a more or less randomly chosen chunk from the opening section of his *I Don't Have Any Paper so Shut Up*:

Brandish something clean—there is no more reason to limit
ourselves to the customary rhetorical confinement. White
commission, piss shall triumph.
Get busy looking at immaculate doves; I *couldn't* stab
myself . . . you want subgum?—fuck your kitchen. Gandhi
becomes handsome cholo. I hate scenes.

And palpitating! Candle suckers, don't react to the given.
Dignity for resale ankle be sister farm fear swallows the
unwary unison feeble heart such me mug
sauce plenitude preservatives; spores,
variable halvah. Thinking about genocide all the time make
me hopeful. Catholics fly to the lips & smoke out the sting,
you can poop my duck, mastery of craft; turquoise makes the I
dumb stick.
Buckets of chicken urine in the blue gauzy non-urban sounds
apocryphal. Brood of drum majors to cause their trouble.
Once bread got that staff of life crap attached to it, it became
Inedible. Wasn't it Solzhenitsyn that pardoned Patty Hearst? (1992, 10)

In Andrews's work, it's as if the entirety of poetic meter wants to be reduced to spondee—the desire at least is for all stressed syllables all the time. And literature is thereby reduced, like a watery sauce is reduced, to its stronger version: not the job of meaning or edification ("Get busy looking at immaculate doves . . ."), or even the job of pleasure (" . . . there is no more reason to limit / ourselves to the customary rhetorical confinement . . ."), but the austere task of relentless provocation: "fuck your kitchen."

Literature gets repurposed, in Andrews's work, precisely because of its too-easy links to the sacred trace of meaning: "Once bread got that staff of life crap attached to it, it became / Inedible. . . ." Of course, there's a certain kind of "interruption" here, parataxis in its perhaps strongest form, but the focus is not so much on deforming wholeness (where would totalization rest in the force field that is this page?), but obsessively on production of all kinds, all the myriad productive powers of the false: reflexive or "critical" statements, nonsense, insults, porn lingo, slightly changed "ad-buster" style slogans, hate speech, bureaucratic discourse and its evil of banality, religion, cults of personality, and so forth. Andrews speeds up language as a series of creative practices, rather than primarily slows it down and territorializes it on one function, language's meaning (or lack thereof). It's the confrontation of performative or inventive force that you see on every line; in every "gap" there's not meaning waiting to burst forth (or not), but a kind of hinge, linkage, movement, intensification—what Andrews calls "torque." And this torque returns to poetry a series of other jobs, the functions it had years, even millennia, before poetics became linked inexorably to the question of meaning and its discontents: here, we see poetry function as discourse that's ceremonial, aggressive, passive, communal, seductive, repulsive, humorous, persuasive, insulting, praising, performative, and lots more. But one thing it doesn't do—or even really attempt—is to "mean" something. What you get in Andrews's texts is precisely a kind of massive overcoding operation, this schizoid "dialectic," mishmashed all at once. Reading is less a hermeneutic operation than the kind of performance that Andrews sometimes does with dancers and musician improvisers—they respond to his words with their own riffs, do their own "readings" of these provocations as body and sound gestures, movements, translations.

Perhaps an even sharper example of a post-postmodern writing practice is found in the work of so-called Conceptual Writers. The leading practitioner and theorist of the movement, Kenneth Goldsmith, suggests that he doesn't so much write (in the sense of innovating new forms or expressing anything in particular) as he does transcribe, quite literally. His magnum opus trilogy, *The Weather, Sports*, and *Traffic*, consists of straight transcriptions of eleven o'clock news weather reports (a year), a baseball game (every word of a single Yankee game radio broadcast), and traffic reports (a full day of traffic reports, "on the 1s")—as well as works that consist of retyping every single word in the *New York Times* for a single day (which becomes the nine hundred–page book *Day*), every movement made by the author over a thirteen-hour period (*Fidget*), every utterance for a week (*Soliloquy*), and what is to my mind his masterpiece, *Head Citations*, a list of more than eight hundred misheard popular song lyrics (like "Killing me softly with Islam," or "This is clown control to Mao-Tse-Tung"). The point of all this, you ask? Goldsmith (2004) thematizes his writing practice like this:

In 1969, the conceptual artist Douglas Huebler wrote, "The world is full of objects, more or less interesting; I do not wish to add any more." I've come to embrace Huebler's ideas, though it might be retooled as, "The world is full of texts, more or less interesting; I do not wish to add any more." It seems an appropriate response to a new condition in writing today: faced with an unprecedented amount of available text, the problem is not needing to write more of it; instead, we must learn to negotiate the vast quantity that exists. I've transformed from a writer into an information manager, adept at the skills of replicating, organizing, mirroring, archiving, hoarding, storing, reprinting, bootlegging, plundering, and transferring.

Goldsmith's poetics puts him squarely within an Internet age—what does "writing" look like when a searchable database of nearly everything ever written is easily within reach of anyone with an Internet connection? If postmodernism played to an end game the thematics of innovation born in modernism (can you really "make it newer" in the twenty-first century?), then the problems of writing shift to negotiating through the vast archive of the powers of the false, the creative powers in combining preexisting language, rather than hoping through force of creative will to add something novel to that archive. As Goldsmith (2009) puts it succinctly, referring both to the Conceptual Writing he's aligned with and Flarf, a rival but related movement dedicated to writing poems through Internet searches: "With so much available language, does anyone really need to write more? Instead, let's just process what exists. Language as matter; language as material."

When pressed to explain further, Goldsmith likes to quote Brion Gysin's mid-twentieth-century observation that writing is fifty years behind painting, and certainly his project owes much to the Burroughsean cut-up and the antisubjectivist collage and splatter methods of modernist visual art: What do sculptors do but take blocks of given material and carve something out of them? What does Jackson Pollock foreground but the basic stuff of painting—movement and oil paint, that's all there is. Ditto someone like Rothko—color and shape—not inventing anything new in terms of what art "is" on a traditional register, but inventing new questions, juxtapositions, modes of provocation (which is, of course, what art has *become*: a series of discourses and practices as much as it is a series of discrete objects). The midcentury conundrums that forced painting into the abstract expressionist and pop art realms (i.e., the economic and technological truism that photography had by that point completely taken over figuration) have for a long time now hung over literature as well, even more so poetry: if advertising and the greeting card industry have completely territorialized short, pithy expressions of "authentic" sentiment, showing us how to reenchant even the most mundane corners of everyday life (everything's an opportunity for self-actualization, even doing the laundry, doing your job, or driving your car), then what's left for poetry to do in a post-postmodern world?

On someone like Andrews's account, what's left for poetry is relentlessly to avoid those very structures of "meaning," to reinvent or reemphasize alternative uses for poetry—for intense language usage—that have long since been forgotten as the lyric became the safe repository for our authentic, "true feelings" or affects. And Goldsmith's project is certainly related to Andrews's—deploy language's powers of the false—but goes in a slightly different direction. As Goldsmith (2001) writes about work like Andrews's, "Language Poetry has fulfilled the trajectory of modernist writing and as such, has succeeded in pulverizing syntax and meaning into a handful of dust. At this point in time, to grind the sand any finer would be futile." For Goldsmith, the critique (if there is to be one) is not to be found so much within the work, but in what might come after it—the discourses, acts, and further appropriations that surround, circumscribe, and respond to the work. As Goldsmith (2004) writes, "The simple act of moving information from one place to another today constitutes a significant cultural act in and of itself." This post-postmodern project constitutes a decisive turn away from the linguistic turn of resistant, infinite meaning (from all the powers of the true—even the critical ones), and returns a different kind of density (a new set of everyday concerns regarding how one manages language overload) to the complexities of contemporary language use. If everyone's a poet in this sense, the reason is that everyone has to sculpt his or her linguistic identity out of a vast sea of available, iterable text.

Of course, this anti-originalist performativity was surely the project or home terrain of postmodernism and deconstruction as well, although it's hard to imagine either of those discourses working without some sense of linguistic meaning, if only negatively; so perhaps, as I suggest throughout, the practice of something like Conceptual Writing is less "other than postmodern" (wholly foreign to it or simply beyond it) than it is post-postmodern—intensifying certain strains within postmodernism in order to render it not so much a "new" postmodernism, but a kind of intense, hyper-postmodernism of positive usage—a power of the false not derived from the powers of the true, but one that remains the ground of any truth-effects. The performance of poetry sparks other types of performance, provokes other powers of falsification, rather than primarily calls for contemplation or understanding of the truisms contained therein. This sentiment is, of course, as old as the hills—or, in poetic terms, at least as old as Jack Spicer's 1959 pronouncement, "No / One listens to poetry" (2008, 373), which is to say, *no one* listens to poetry—harkens after or obeys its hidden truths. No, one *listens* to poetry—responds to it.

In the end, though, the positive pole of the powers of the false is hardly "contained" in a particular literary work or even kind of work (it doesn't need to be as relentlessly avant-garde as Andrews's or Goldsmith's work is); but their work is instructive precisely in its relentlessness and the way that its intense deployment of the powers of the false models a mode of engagement, with the text or the world. Though one might be tempted at this point to begin putting together a list of operative texts that foreground this strong power of the false, on the "eat this, not that" template of contemporary weight-management pseudoscience: Pynchon, not Foster Wallace; poets Lyn Hejinian or Charles Bernstein, not most of the stuff Garrison Keillor reads on the radio; Brian Evenson, not William T. Vollman; Dashiell Hammett, not Raymond Chandler; Gertrude Stein, not Virginia Woolf; the Flaming Lips, not emo bands; Appadauri, not Bhabha; Nietzsche, not Hegel; Shakespeare, not Spenser; Irigaray, not Kristeva. Negri, not Agamben; Adorno, not Benjamin. Steven Shaviro, not Bernard Stiegler. The Derrida of force and provocation, not the Derrida of prayers and tears. Or Jameson, not Jameson—depending on how you read him, and what you emphasize within your reading.

Of course, these last two quite deliberately suggest the utter nonsense of pretending to have located privileged texts that "contain" more of the strong power of the false (and less of the weak). Maybe at the end of the day, thinking about literature as equipment for post-postmodern living is less a plea to "read this, not that" than it is "read this way, not that": sure, literature and cultural theory have a powerful conceptual resource in meaning, memory, and nostalgia, and as such can be a wedge against the present, in memory of a day gone by, or a series of roads not taken. Likewise, on the sentence level of literature or on the theoretical plane of language, the linguistic turn can continue to mirror that kind of recovery project by slowing thought down, the weight of the signifier always forcing us to turn things over in our minds—to hesitate, own the connections we make, all that other "ethics of reading" stuff. All that remains crucial to the arsenal of reading, of making sense (rather than making meaning) of the present.

But by itself, the linguistic turn of hesitating slowness does not constitute an effective arsenal against the present and its ubiquitous post-postmodernism of speed and production. So now maybe I'm back to where I began this book, looking closely at Jamesonian critique as a mode of engagement with the present and trying to affirm or intensify its positive modes. This is not necessarily to exclude the negative modes of dialectical critique, but to suggest that they can't do all the work (even most of it, really). If the Jamesonian dialectic is an operation primarily of overcoding—of rewriting one sense with another—then one can't dispense with the weak power of the false; but it may be more a matter of trying to overcode the weak power with the strong power, rather than the opposite operation that was so characteristic of the postmodern, big theory years—where it was all lack all the time, literature hollowing out the positive claims of this or that totalizing discourse.

So, the post-postmodern call is not simply to abandon slowness, the work of the negative, or even nostalgia as a mode of literature's engagement with the globalized world; but it is rather a call to reinvigorate those more "positive" powers of the false and modes of engagement with that world, and with literature's myriad positive critical connections to it, outside the purely negative suture of undecidability. From the hermeneutics of suspicion to the hermeneutics of situation. So, for example, it may be less a matter of abandoning literature's privileged relation to subjectivity, memory, and identity than it is reemphasizing literature's roles not in provoking us to become otherwise. Literature could again be a key component in the project that Foucault lays out for us in his late work: "Maybe the project nowadays is not to discover who we are," he writes, "but to refuse who we are" (2003b, 134).

too aware
of its
role in
human
psyche –
too
confident

In the end, this is perhaps less a call to innovate "new" roles of jobs for literature, new modes of equipment, than to recall that literature was equipment for a lot of becomings before it somewhat myopically became equipment tailor-made to interrupt the totalizing claims of philosophy. And literature can be a lot of things again in a future that seems sure to be festooned with spam messages, texts, and tweets so enigmatic as to make the most difficult postmodern novels or avant-garde poetries seem recognizable and usable in new ways. Literature, of course, didn't choose the job of totalization-interrupter par excellence—it was the job given to literature in the postmodern era of big theory (and, hey, academic jobs have long been hard to come by). But for thousands of years before (in fact, for virtually all of its existence), literature was equipment for living in myriad ways, not just as a provider and/or frustrator of "meaning." Hopefully, a more robust sense of the literary can make it crucial, or at least useful, equipment again for post-postmodern living.

Liberal Arts

NOT YOUR FATHER'S LIBERAL ARTS:
OR, HUMANITIES THEORY IN THE
POST-POST FUTURE

Where Keynesian economics attempts to safeguard the productive economy against the fluctuations of financial capital, neoliberalism installs speculation at the very core of production. —MELINDA COOPER, *Life as Surplus*

Any attempt to wrap up this book by thinking about future relations among cultural production, cultural theory, and economics probably requires just a bit more genealogical work on those relations in the past— at least partially because, on the face of it, the glory years for humanities theory in North America coincided with economic neoliberalism's rise. Both theory and neoliberal economics really took off in the US during the Reagan '80s and had their full-blown years of flower in the Bush-Clinton-Bush 1990s to early 2000s; likewise, both have begun to struggle somewhat as dominant paradigms in the present. And while there was no Black Friday for theory (no single event where it decisively crashed, as there was for neoliberal finance capital in October 2008), I think it's safe to say that "theory" is no longer the roost-ruling discourse that it once was in and around the humanities. Of course, the sense with which I open this book (that neoliberalism's death has been greatly exaggerated) should probably also be extended to humanities theory: just look at the current catalog for any top-tier university press, and you'll be very quickly disabused of the notion that the era of theory is over. Though theory is, unlike neoliberalism, no longer the only game in town—no longer the "cultural dominant" in whose terms everything else has to position itself.

But what exactly has been the genealogical relationship between the rise of these two formations, literary-cultural theory and neoliberal economics? When we think about the relations among literary theory and political economy over the last generation or two, the picture not surprisingly seems clearer the farther you get from the present. For example, there has for many years now been a consensus that midcentury New Criticism was, socioeconomically speaking, a cold war discourse par excellence—focusing as it did on the organic values of literature as a kind of reservoir of fullness, and on the creative punch and power of the individual against the backdrop of Soviet-style collective consensus.[1] Additionally, it's worth noting in retrospect that part of New Criticism's cold war appeal was its nascent neoliberalism, its insistence on individual modes of creative effort ("the text itself" and "close reading") as the skeleton keys to a "make it new" modernism. In short, New Criticism portends our own era of neoliberal biopower, wherein a mode of consumption (reading) becomes intensified to the point where it becomes a mode of production (interpretation).

Look again at the theoretical texts of New Criticism: while their native historical moment (amid the 1940s–60s manufacturing boom in the US) is positively soaking in the postwar disciplinary imperatives of factory Fordism, new critical dogma is as anti-Fordist as anything you'll read. Despite what Brooks and Warren do with the *pedagogical* aspects of New Criticism (essentially making it into a factory classroom practice to process GIs after the war), the high end of new critical speculation (its insistence on autonomy and the individual work and the individual interpreter) was already in the cold war leaning neoliberal, if neoliberal means first and foremost a critique of the normalizing, disciplinary collectivist state apparatus. In fact, those who are today nostalgic for the humanities as a kind of citizenship training tend not to recall this genealogical legacy. The model of the humanities as citizenship training (emphasizing deliberation, critical thinking, open debate, and rational individualism) is not really a classical idyll held over from Plato's Academy, but a cold war invention of the American academy, and one that—as Geoffrey Harpham has persuasively argued—was overtly sculpted on the scaffolding of I. A. Richards's New Criticism. Richards was among the principal architects of the very influential Harvard 1944 "red book" (*General Education in a Free Society*) that charted out the course and purpose of the postwar humanities in the US.[2]

But what of North American postmodern theory's relation to its native historical moment? Here, the air is a little thinner, because it's closer to our own historical present, and the consensus is far from clear. Of course, to circle around again to where we began this book, one might note that the codependent relation between humanities theory and late capitalism is already part and parcel of Jameson's analysis of postmodernism: Jameson argues that as much as the architecture of downtown office towers or the diamond-dust paintings of Warhol, the rise of theory itself has been of a piece with the economics of postmodernism all the way down. As postmodernism reoriented the disciplines of economics, art, or architecture around speculation, and not-knowing (more specifically, about not-knowing what really counts as value, art, or good design), so too has "theory" remade literary and cultural studies as that thing dedicated to the open-endedness of interpretation, undecidability, and living primarily through the wages or wagers of futurity. Neoliberalism, in Melinda Cooper's words, is consumed with an "ambition to overcome the ecological and economic limits to growth associated with the end of industrial production, through a speculative reinvention of the future" (2008, 11). Indeed, there's probably no better description of the notoriously complex financial device known as the "derivative" than what Derrida called, after Benjamin, a "messianism without messianism."

Of course, this isn't to suggest that theory ruined your 401k or foreclosed on your mortgage, but it is to insist that the dominant logic of economics in the neoliberal revolution years has in many ways been isomorphic—how could it not be?—with the cultural logic of the humanities and the rise of theory. As undecidability came to reorganize the larger cultural field, stock portfolios as well as tenure files became structured around the wildest kind of speculation—the humanities in particular made a decisive transformation away from the heavy, Fordist enterprise of teaching and researching a set canon of "great texts" and building citizens, toward an innovation-based economy of "flexibly specialized symbolic analysis." Indeed, as I argue in Chapter 3, on one reading the economy at large over the past thirty years has come more to look like a humanities discipline than vice versa: long before they became business concepts, not-knowing, resisting consensus, the importance of information/interpretation, and unfettered speculation were the coin of our realm. And while the rewards and bonuses in the academic profession—tenure and promotion—are criticized by right-wing pundits as the last bastion of socialism, they have for a long time in practice been doled out on grounds that are wholly privatized—tenure decisions are almost entirely based (ideologically, at least) on "brilliant" individual accomplishment in research and teaching rather than collective measures like teamwork, service, or community building. If you want to get promoted, don't become director of undergraduate studies—finish the book instead.

In short, we literary and cultural theorists are, and have been, neoliberal postmoderns; but I think that's just to say that we swim in the same sea as everything else that's been economically "successful" over the past thirty years—theory is neoliberal, Microsoft is neoliberal, anti-retroviral drugs are neoliberal, even anti-globalization protests against neoliberalism are neoliberal in their own way. Unless you're a theologian or a certain kind of orthodox neo-Kantian, there's no space of pure autonomy outside the dominant form of global economic organization. Insofar as neoliberalism is this dominant economic logic in our era, one cannot merely escape it through an act of will or fiat.[3] And this mantra of "there is no outside" was, I think, the major content overlap of most humanities theory from the beginning in the 1970s and '80s: as much as, say, Derrida, Jameson, and Foucault would have their differences, they all agree on a kind of social truism that's maybe best summed up by the slogan, "The only way out is through." That is, there is no "place" outside power, capitalism, metaphysics, the social. So, *of course* humanities theory is related in myriad complicated ways to neoliberalism, just as Jameson reminded us decades ago that museum art, rock music, independent cinema, and even avant-garde poetry (in other words, even those things that seek to resist the dominant or normative economic mode) have to find their way through a relation to that dominant economic discourse: postmodern cultural production has had to go through the dominant mode of economic production, and vice versa, through a Möbius-style overcoding mechanism. And that socioeconomic overcoding of culture and economics has only intensified since the dawn of neoliberalism a generation ago.

Now let me be very clear here—I have no interest in denouncing theory as having been, from before the fact, just another wing of the neoliberal economic takeover of just about everything. In fact, I am wholly uninterested in performing a moralist exercise of point scoring by making surface connections between theory's commitments and neoliberalism's—something like the critique of Steven Greenblatt offered in Tobin Siebers's *Cold War Criticism and the Politics of Skepticism*, wherein Siebers writes, "Greenblatt's theatre, like Reagan's vision of America, attempts to take the government off the backs of the people. [The notion of 'social energy'] deregulates the system as it has existed, claiming that rules are unnecessary because the economy of the system has its own laws" (1993, 62). Siebers argues that "it is clear that Greenblatt has little but contempt for Reagan and yet seems to have adopted wholesale the major metaphors of his presidency" (63).

One would never want to deny that there are connections between the rise of the new historicism and the rise of Reaganite neoliberalism in the 1980s—again, on a, strictly speaking, historicist account (old or new), there would have to be some positive connections between them, by definition. New historicism no more lived in an autonomous, ahistorical bubble than did Reagan's budding neoliberalism. But the fact that they deployed the same metaphoric universe or work according to a similar cultural logic, and as a consequence theory is simply a handmaid or manservant to economics—this seems to me a far cry from a persuasive or illuminating historical account. Such moralism is wholly beside the point in an economic or historical analysis.

Here is where we can profitably circle back to Jameson's work on late capitalism, to relearn one of its primary lessons. The dominant reading of Jameson's work on postmodernism thematizes it as remaining squarely in the kind of orbit laid out by Siebers—most people continue to understand Jameson's work as a kind of moral outrage, interested primarily in pointing out the homology between postmodern economic production and postmodern cultural production (Warhol, language poetry, the Bonaventure Hotel), and thereby somehow denouncing *cultural* postmodernism as merely another regressive symptom of what we'd now simply call neoliberal *economics.*

However, the fact that cultural production shares a "logic" with neoliberal economic production is, from Jameson's point of view, simply axiomatic—the collapse of cultural production into the logic of economic production is not the conclusion of his late analyses, but their starting point. As I argue throughout, the stake of the continuing "economics and culture" discussion for Jameson is certainly *not* occupying the finger-wagging moral high ground: as he insists in *Representing Capital,* "Capitalism is good and bad all at once and simultaneously" (2011, 8). In fact, I take the Jamesonian reason that we need a new cognitive map to be that our old maps (most crucially, the map of ideology critique) could depend on pointing out a homology between cultural production and economic production, and having thereby done some politically or ethically useful work. Under prior dominant modes of economic production, if you could reveal a homology between modes of cultural production and economic production, you could seriously call into question the value of that cultural production—as, for example, someone like Adorno tirelessly demonstrates concerning the culture industry. Those supposed escapes from the workaday world of midcentury—the movies, the radio, and pop music—are for Adorno simply a displaced version of the dominant factory Fordism, over and over and over again. "Real life is becoming indistinguishable from the movies" (Adorno and Horkheimer 1993, 126) for Adorno in 1944 not because reality is becoming an unreal fantasy, but because for Adorno the movies are saturated with the same Fordist imperatives as the factory floor: "The whole world is made to pass through the filter of the culture industry" (126). And like a factory, the culture industry produces one product—subjects—on a mass scale.

Under postmodernism and post-postmodernism, the collapse of the economic and the cultural that Adorno sees dimly on the horizon has decisively arrived (cue Baudrillard's *Simulations*—where reality isn't *becoming* indistinguishable from the movies; it *has become* indistinguishable): we arrive at that postmodern place where economic production is cultural production, and vice versa. And I take that historical and theoretical axiom to be the (largely unmet and continuing) provocation of Jameson's work: if ideology critique depends on a cultural outside to the dominant economic logics, where does cultural critique go now that there is no such outside, no dependable measuring stick to celebrate a work's resistance or to denounce its ideological complicity? If we forgot this Jamesonian provocation, I think it would be very tempting for us to say "insofar as the logic of neoliberalism is isomorphic with the logic of theory, good riddance to both of them"—or insofar as we can easily point out a structural homology between the theory era's logic, thereby we should be "worried" or "troubled" by the connections.

Ultimately, the idea that value does not refer to a preexisting gold standard of plenitude—it's free floating, determined by material practices rather than by metaphysical or theological reference—no more "belongs" to contemporary economics than it does to contemporary humanities theory. Of course, the practices implied by the idea of free-floating value and radical openness, as a piece of dominant cultural logic, certainly do have (widely varying) consequences for both economics and cultural criticism; however, as I have suggested, it seems unhelpfully abstract to suggest that the disastrous economic havoc wreaked on Latin America by the Chicago boys has any serious homological value when examining the influence of Yale's so-called hermeneutic mafia.[4] A radically open text doesn't have the same consequences as a radically open market—though both of them do owe a founding debt to a cultural logic of some kind.

Genealogy of the Future?

If Jameson's name for postmodern neoliberalism is a "dominant" sociocultural logic, we could note that there's a similar set of practices at work in what Foucault calls the "historical a priori"—an odd phrase that imbricates an ahistorical a priori with a strict historicism in a way perhaps even more striking than Jameson's famous chiasmic slogan, "always historicize." For Foucault, the historical a priori names a theoretical mechanism by which one can describe how certain practices are able to saturate domains seemingly far removed from them. So, for example, he famously argues in *The Order of Things* that the nineteenth-century triumvirate of life, labor, and language—the discourses of biology, Marxism, and linguistics—all emerge in the context of the same historical a priori: the search for new practices of analysis in the wake of the epistemic breakdown of representation (which is partially to say, stable reference) in the early modern period. So, as linguistics turns away from Adamic understandings of language (the sense that things are represented by their original names), so too economics gradually turns away from discussions of ground rent (as natural, representational value) to discussions of money and credit, while biology abandons the plant (fully representable from root to stem) as the primary marker of life and slowly adopts the unrepresentable vitalism of animality to model this thing called "life" (see Foucault 1973, 187–304).

Despite their many political and ideological differences, perhaps what Jameson and Foucault most obviously have in common is a thoroughgoing commitment to historical emergence and the difference it makes: what they have in common is that both are willing to play the risky (and at times, theoretically expensive) speculative game of historical periodization.

If we turn back to our present and recent past with that sense of periodization in mind, it seems clear whole series of new practices rushed to the speculative forefront over the past thirty years, some of them creating progressive cultural and economic effects, some regressive, some we're still not so sure; but at the end of the day, it's not the animating or overarching logic within the practices themselves that predicts or conditions their effects. Humanities theory and neoliberal economics today both run on speculation, undecidability, and the impossible wager on the future—just as Foucault shows us that Marxism, biology, and linguistics in the nineteenth century all emerged out of a larger cultural breakdown of representation as value. That's the axiomatic universe presented to us by a Jamesonian dominant cultural logic or a Foucauldian historical a priori—it's not a game you get to choose to accept or reject at the wholesale level.[5]

However, this kind of analysis either begs or reveals one of the primary questions for theory at the present moment and going forward: at that level of generality—there is no outside of any era's dominant mode of power, and socioeconomic power at this point is primarily neoliberal—what good are periodizing insights like Foucault's or Jameson's? Well, not much, I guess—but the level of generality is obviously not where the primary action happens in Jameson's work (think of the laundry list of examples in his postmodernism essay) or in Foucault's work (I counted them, and in the entirety of his books, there are no more than about a dozen pages on the general question of power). In Foucault as in Jameson, all the heavy lifting is done in the performance of analyses. Because Foucauldian power is a "how," not a "what," he doesn't spend a lot of time describing the "what" of power, until he's forced to do so in interviews and occasional essays; at the same time, the infiltrating level of generality (saturation and spread of practices) is important, if not crucial, to what Foucault's doing when he periodizes these dominant modes of power throughout history. I think Foucault insists on power's mobile changes not so much for what the insight "there is no outside of power" *gives* us, but for what it *takes away from* us: the easy sense that, prior to an analysis of a concrete situation, we know beforehand what formation occupies what position in any power relation. In addition to committing us to doing an analysis, "there is no outside of power" takes away from us any primarily *moral* conclusions or starting points.

Maybe Foucault himself says it best, when he asks,

> What did Marx do when in his analysis of capital he encountered the problem of working-class misery? He refused the usual explanation of this misery as the effect of a rare natural cause or of a concerted theft. And he said in effect: given what capitalist production is in its fundamental laws, it can't help but to produce misery. Capitalism's reason for being is not to starve the workers, but it cannot develop without starving them. Marx substituted the analysis of production for the denunciation of theft. (1996, 140)

This emphasis on trading an "analysis of production for the denunciation of theft" is important for the contemporary situation of theory in the academy primarily because people on the left still believe they own this vocabulary of openness-as-resistance—that one can point out or denounce stifling norms, call for resistance to them, and have done some progressive work by definition. This, it seems to me, is no longer the case under the intensified neoliberal global capitalism we've seen flourish in the decades since Foucault's death—a cultural dominant whose very mantras turn on the celebration of the new, the resistance to norms and regulations. And even if one could locate in theory a certain native resistance to dominant economic imperatives, that's no necessary indication of any kind of politically progressive effect: New Criticism certainly seems "resistant" to a midcentury factory Fordism, but that resistance doesn't necessarily translate into any kind of effective critique of the cold war nation-state. Like Jameson's, Foucault's work on the subject of neoliberalism is first and foremost an "analysis of production," a diagnosis or a genealogy of the present.

However, many Foucauldians want his 1979 lecture course on *The Birth of Biopolitics* to function as a full-blown critical condemnation of the neoliberal present, but I'm not so sure that can work. Certainly, the late '70s were the historical infancy of the highly intensified neoliberal revolution that we've seen in the decades since, and the Milton Friedman– or Gary Becker–style, market-take-all stuff that might have seemed shocking in 1979 (Foucault calls Becker's work "isolated" from mainstream economics; see 2010, 270), has more than a decade into the twenty-first century simply become orthodoxy, standard operating procedure for American pundits, politicians, and certainly for economists. Since the end of the cold war, the truisms of neoliberal capitalism have intensified beyond anyone's wildest dreams (or nightmares), and economics has become the default setting for understanding virtually everything in our world. The best-selling airport literature of "freakonomics" is particularly full of such stuff: here, economics can explain to us everything from the efficacy of abortion and drug policy, to why there's rampant cheating in sumo wrestling, and how real estate agents are like the KKK (it's not the uniforms—the white sheet and the gold jacket—but that they both make a proprietary and necessary commodity out of secrecy). My point is not that any of this does or does not make sense; it's rather that today, it's ubiquitously familiar to us that economics is a—if not *the*—privileged discourse for explaining our world. This is the general conclusion that Foucault was at some pains to point out in 1979: neoliberalism extends the practices and rationality of the market to a series of hitherto "noneconomic" realms.

Many commentators, though, want to see Foucault as being here engaged in a full-blown (if not high-minded) critique of the likes of Gary Becker—in, for example, his pointing out how the theory of human capital represents one striking example of economic analysis into a previously unexplored domain (see, e.g., Hamman 2009). Foucault in this context specifically discusses the mother-child relationship: a neoliberal economic analysis would treat the time the mother spends with the child, as well as the quality of the care she gives, as an investment (2010, 243–46). Well, this insight hardly strikes me as a critique in Foucault, and more as a diagnosis—one that turns out to be quite prescient. Any parent will, I think, not find this to be a particularly "striking" or shocking example at all. You've got only so much of this thing called time, and you do need to invest it in some way—you have to manage your employer, your relationship with your partner (should you be lucky enough to have one to help out), child care, the household duties (which feminism importantly reminds us is a job!); we could in addition note that *Freakonomics* ends with a helpful chapter on what economics teaches us about good parenting and education (a waste of time—children who do well in school don't necessarily get good parenting at home), and an analysis of the economics of children's names (why there are so few CEOs named "Che" or "Sunshine"). In short, economics has, at this point, positively saturated our family relationships, for better or worse. That was a barely visible emerging trend as Foucault delivered his biopolitics lectures in 1979, and a banal everyday reality thirty years later.

As readers of Foucault, though, I'm not sure how or why this mutation of economics into the confines of the family should surprise or shock us. Sovereign power, social power, and discipline all had and continue to have substantial (and substantially differing) investments in the parent-child relation—from the disciplinary policing of the pregnant body (no one will serve you alcohol, no smoking, constant checkups) to the social canalization of reproduction (more or less childbirth has been touted as patriotic, depending on where and when you lived—more children for the Nazis, more for today's Christian fundamentalists, fewer for the Chinese Cultural Revolution); from the heavily saturated medicalization of infants (mandatory immunization, campaigns against breast-feeding to formula and back again, sleep on their back, sleep on their stomach, in tight-fitting flame-retardant sleepwear) to the encroachment of law enforcement into the realm of infancy (kids sit in the back, in car seats, facing backward until they're twenty-two pounds, then forward thereafter, with a booster seat for toddlers, it's the law). Anyone who's been around kids recognizes this immediately—the disciplinary apparatuses of government, the medical establishment, and law enforcement have for a long time now been all over the parent-child relation. So the idea that we "invest" time in our children, following the highly intensified finance capital of our day, should hardly shock or surprise us. (And as we ubiquitously use the economic metaphor of "investing" in our children, we would do well to remember that the prior dominant metaphors for family life—"taking care" of or "protecting" our children, for example—came just as surely from discourses of political and medical discipline.)

This is finally to say that the practices of our economic present begin where Foucault's *Birth of Biopolitics* leaves off—with the sense that our lives have become supersaturated with a new form of power. And that power—which, like the forms of power before it, is neither good nor bad, but dangerous—and how we respond to it are largely dependent on our analysis of how it works, what effects it produces, and how it might produce effects otherwise. The Foucauldian point is not to denounce neoliberalism (any more than an analysis like the *Birth of the Clinic* rejected medicalization or that *History of Madness* suggested the mad should simply be left alone). The point is to work through the limits, procedures, and costs of dominant procedures, how they intensify as they migrate from their original, bounded domain into other ones—helping us to map the process by which "what was an islet, a privileged place, a circumstantial measure, or a singular model, became a general formula" (Foucault 1979, 209). And insofar as Foucault's is a diagnostic discourse rather than a primarily prescriptive one, I think it's very hard indeed to say that the saturation of the market into family relations is "better" or "worse" than the saturation of the state or the medical establishment within them—though it certainly is *different*, requiring different tools and different angles of analysis.

And this may help to explain some of theory's falloff in recent years: the diagnostic project just isn't as sexy as the kind of vanguard resistance to totalization that you used to be able to count on from any concluding paragraph of virtually any essay in the era of big theory—including several written by yours truly in the late '80s and early '90s: "My interpretation of X," the triumphant conclusion announces, "shows that meaning is an open question, value is undecidable and always has to be (re)configured in a particular context." Well, thanks for the hard-won insight, one might respond, but my mortgage banker told me that this morning, when he foreclosed on my condo.

Surely, as literary and cultural theorists, we should today be able to tell our students, the public, maybe even ourselves something more trenchant or useful than the fact that cultural texts, like your stock portfolio, contain a lot of interpretive possibilities—true as that insight is, it no longer seems much of a wedge against what we might call the fierce banality of now. At the same time, I would want to insist that this confluence or proximity with neoliberalism isn't the *death* of theory, but precisely its *strength* for the future, for talking about why the humanities matter in a just-in-time world.

Axiomatics: Overcoding the Humanities Future

To end, then, with a syllogism, of sorts:

1. Post-postmodern economics is cultural to the core.
2. Cultural production is the purview of the humanities.
3. So, the humanities are (or at least should be) central to post-postmodern economics?

Or, maybe more directly, the inference is that cultural capital is real and has real economic consequence and value. Remember Robert Reich's (1992) "flexibly specialized symbolic analysts"? That's the humanities, what we teach and do research on.

But in my experience, people in the humanities back off from this economic isomorphism immediately, sometimes recoiling in horror that their mode of cultural production can be talked about in dirty (some call it "evil") capitalist terms.[6] For example, at a recent meeting of English department chairpersons (which I attended because our department chair had the good sense to be in Rome at the time), there was to my mind a surprising amount of hand wringing over the identity of the discipline, conditioned by the ubiquity of shrinking budgets. Is there a coherent English curriculum anymore? Is the discipline still driven by some notion of content? How are we training graduate students, if we can't even define what it is *we* do? These are, I suppose, perennial liberal arts questions, and they make for spirited conversation over wine and cheese. But in an academic world of increasing scarcity, these questions are increasingly being posed not only at disciplinary conventions (MLA, AHA, APA), but by state legislatures, university boards of directors, the general public, deans, provosts, donors, parents, and students. Before they invest their time and/

or shrinking resources in a humanities discipline like English, they want to know some specifics: Who are we? What do we do presently? And what are the prospects for the future?

This imperative to define the proper terrain of any humanities discipline is, of course, where the trouble begins, because not only department chairs but most faculty and students within these departments experience them as a kind of chaotic mess—a loose assemblage of fiefdoms that have little or nothing in common: under the umbrella "English," for example, you've got medieval studies, history of the book, science studies, creative writing, drama, performance studies, film and video, theory, American studies, historicisms old and new, disability studies, visual culture, new media studies, comix and the graphic novel, various Marxisms, early modern studies, the long eighteenth century, myriad ethnic, racial, and sexual-orientation studies (queer studies, Chicano/a studies, Asian American studies, African American studies, women's studies, whiteness studies), girl studies, temporality studies, cultural studies, oceanic studies, Anglo-Saxon studies, animal studies, trauma studies, rhetoric and composition, linguistics, and so on. Each of these subfields has its own more-or-less distinct sets of concerns and methodologies, many of which aren't directly related to other subfields, much less to the traditional "literary history" taught in English departments. And we could of course multiply this multiplicity even further: there are dozens of fields I've neglected to mention, and even within those subfields hastily listed, there's a vast variety of approach and content: rhetoric and composition or African American studies are themselves widely varying fields of inquiry, as are the seemingly more recognizable fields of literary history. Medieval literature covers a whole lot of historical, linguistic, methodological, and theoretical turf. But I trust the point I'm trying to make here is relatively uncontroversial: these days, the discipline of English doesn't possess what used to be called "thematic coherence." And while English is routinely the biggest and messiest department in the liberal arts, most other humanities disciplines enjoy (or suffer, as the case may be) similarly diverse self-understandings: continental philosophers don't share a common understanding of the discipline (its key figures, methods, and questions) with analytical philosophers, any more than cultural and biological anthropologists see eye to eye, or qualitative and quantitative scholars in various disciplines (political science, psychology, sociology, or language and linguistics departments) agree on disciplinary identity markers.

Friends and colleagues of mine routinely narrate this state of affairs as a "crisis" for the humanities, especially in articulating what humanities departments *do*, what we *should* be doing, or what we *want*. A kind of panic sets in when we have to talk to "outsiders," insofar as we're hard pressed to say what it is that unites all this "stuff" that people do in the humanities. Hardened by years of reading and responding to student essays, we assume that what looks like disorganization—having multiple, sometimes contradictory trajectories and styles of engagement—is a recipe for shoddy work and intellectual incoherence. So at moments that seem to call for disciplinary coherence—when responding to the question, "What is it you do in your humanities department, and why should we continue to support you?"—it inevitably seems to be retrenchment time. As Stanley Fish (1995) and others have argued, in a corporatized academic world of shrinking resources, we'd better be able to articulate—very exactly and narrowly—what it is that we in departments like English do, or they're destined to be steamrolled by the sciences and engineering. As a potential return on your investment, the hard sciences can offer better roads or cures for cancer, while we can't even seem to deliver kids who can write a decent e-mail.

Not surprisingly, this "humanities-in-crisis" narrative inevitably leads to some sort of "downsizing" or "rightsizing" solution. In times of economic crisis, portfolio managers and department heads alike are advised to stick with the blue chips, the proven "core business" winners. For example, Fish suggests we'd best start articulating our uniqueness by performing some elementary disciplinary hygiene, saying to some scholars, "That's *not* the kind of thing we do around here." In Fish's view, "The 'kind of thing we do around here' . . . comes into view against a background of the practices it is *not*"—that is, a discipline like English can be shown as unique and worthy only if we can prove that it exists in profound "contrast with the kind of thing done by members of other enterprises (history, sociology, statistics)" (1995, 16). If we can't even articulate the uniqueness of what we do, he suggests, why would anyone invest his or her time and money in a liberal arts discipline, and not somewhere else? Ironically, here the student essay comes full circle, reemerging in a most unlikely place—the liberal arts department's report to the dean: "Since the beginning of time," we intone, "the humanities have always been about reading and writing about classic texts. This is even more true in today's modern world." In a brainstorming session, someone adds helpfully: "Don't forget the importance of 'critical thinking.'" "Yeah, that's a *great* idea! They're gonna eat this up." Disciplinary identities saved. Crisis averted.

In the name of disciplinary coherence and clear articulation of what makes us unique, humanities departments seem in danger of retreating into just such a narrow articulation of their work. In the face of pressure to give the liberal arts coherence, it's tempting to respond—as Fish does—that reading texts (or even classic texts) and writing about them is our primary product line. I think that such a retrenchment—when asked what you do, cry "old-school humanism"—is a poor strategy. Even if it's true, the futures market on this skill set—producing the well-rounded person—is pretty weak. In terms of funding, the humanities on this model would become akin to the little park or open space that the engineers and architects agree to fund so they can secure the rights to build a huge skyscraper on a plot of downtown land. If we're going to be content to be the little park—the aesthetic oasis in the big, cold corporate university—then we'd best resign ourselves in the future to working with piddling funding streams of what amounts to intellectual hush money.

We need to find ways to combat the scenario that talk-poet david antin narrates as his entry into the university in *what it means to be avant-garde*:

they brought me in to add a certain
cultural respectability   because you cant let scientists
all alone by themselves theres no telling what they might
do so what you do is bring in people from the arts and
humanities so they might feel ashamed
or they might feel
gratified and flattered and beneficent   so that you would
stand in the corner of their nuclear reactor and they would
feel better and then they would make gifts to you and
you could make art and art would go on the walls of the
nuclear reactor or whatever else they were constructing (1993, 137)

The feel-good obsolescence that antin so powerfully conjures is, it seems to me, the inevitable cost of articulating the work of the humanities *solely* in terms of preserving or transmitting a narrow idea of culture. It's just a bad idea. Also, let's remember that this humanist or historicist line of argument—endorsed by Fish as a kind of savvy *realpolitik* maneuver—has already proven to be an utter loser in the corporate university. Talked to anyone in a classics department lately? Probably not, as classics is being savagely downsized nationwide. This line of reasoning ("what we do is read and write about the great texts") didn't work for classics' futures prospectus in the corporate university, so it seems unlikely to save other humanities departments either. The past isn't the future.

The other obvious way to articulate the humanities' future value is to play up the commitment to communication skills that one sees throughout the humanities. For example, Cathy Davidson writes in the *Associated Departments of English Bulletin* (2000), "If we spend too much of our energy lamenting the decline in the number of positions for our doctoral students, . . . we are giving up the single most compelling argument we have for our existence": the fact that we "teach sophisticated techniques for reading, writing, and sorting information into a coherent argument." "Reading, writing, evaluating and organizing information have probably never been more central to everyday life," Davidson points out, so—by analogy—the humanities have never been so central to the curriculum and the society at large. This seems a compelling enough line of reasoning—and donors, politicians, students, and administrators love anything that smacks of a training program.

But, precisely because of that fact, I think there's reason to be suspicious of teaching critical-thinking skills as the humanities' *primary* reason for being. The last thing you want to be in the new economy is an anachronism, but the second-to-last thing you want to be is the "training" wing of an organization. And not because training is unnecessary or old line, far from it; rather, you want to avoid becoming a training facility because training is as outsourceable as the day is long: English department "writing" courses, along with many other introductory skills courses throughout the humanities, are already taught on a mass scale through distance education, bypassing the bricks-and-mortar university's (not-for-profit) futures altogether, and becoming a funding stream for distance ed's (for-profit) virtual futures. Tying our future exclusively to skills training is tantamount to admitting that the humanities are a series of service departments—confirming our future status as corporate trainers. And, given the fact that student writing and communication skills are second only to the weather as a perennial source of complaint among those who employ our graduates, I don't think we want to wager our futures solely on that.

I want to stress that I'm all for the great texts and great ideas, and for teaching people to write clearly and effectively about them. I traffic in these crucial areas every single day. But my point here is that it's poor strategy to articulate the humanities' future *solely* in those terms. As satisfying as it may be, such thematic coherence—"Our core business is X and only X"—is more a trap than it is a liberation or future direction.

That having been said, let me try to finish with a positive model for describing how the humanities disciplines might talk about what they do for the university and the culture at large, in an age of neoliberalism. First and foremost, I think we need to revisit the "identity crisis" narrative of the humanities. Only in the inverted bizarro world of academics can the centrifugal forces that make up "the humanities" be thematized as a crisis or fall from a golden age. In contemporary business-speak, we're an operation with astonishing flexible specialization among its workforce of highly trained (yet hilariously underpaid) symbolic analysts, boasting multiple successful product lines (American history, government, literature, and politics, as well as Plato, ethnic and gender studies, *and* Shakespeare), and a broad-based constituency of loyal customers (no shortage of majors in the liberal arts). As for the golden past of intellectual coherence, rest assured that no credible voice in business literature says, "If only GE had stuck with light bulbs and not gotten into finance, transportation, entertainment, research, global capital services, and all this other newfangled crap." Of course, this is not to say that any old kind of diversifying is simply good, but I think we too often fall for the "diversification = chaos" narrative; and, it should be noted, we are virtually alone in falling for it. No one in the corporate world thinks this way. (As a passing example, consider diversified corporate giant GE's recruiting slogan: "Why join one great company when you can join many?")

The English department, routinely the biggest department in the humanities, is the prime example here, because it's already organized as a kind of highly diversified corporate entity, akin to the way mega-enterprises like GE are corporate entities: today, English is diversified all over the place, more like a mutual fund than like a '50s-style, bricks-and-mortar, single-product "company." And, like any good mutual fund, English's investments are highly diversified. It still does the things that alums remember from their undergraduate education: Shakespeare and Chaucer are still paying great returns—as is an emphasis on writing, critical thinking, and all the other stuff that made "English" the formidable brand-name that it is.

Like any good mutual fund or new economy company, English still has a large amount of holdings in its core businesses: literary history and teaching writing. But the discipline has also made a shrewd series of diversified investments that tap it into new markets and help to round out core investments in the past, present, and future. Importantly, these newer programs aren't divorced from the core business of disciplinary history. In fact, this is where these new movements came from: people working on gender in the nineteenth-century novel, or the representations of otherness in Shakespeare, are the pivotal figures in many of these "studies" areas. (Recall that Fish, for example, didn't exactly practice the disciplinary hygiene that he preached: he's a well-known Miltonist, as well as a scholar of literary theory, critical legal studies, pragmatist philosophy, and myriad other humanities subfields—and has roles as public intellectual, newspaper columnist, and university administrator.) The "new" diversified programs grew in the English department's portfolio through what the biz folks call the "synergy" of literary history with the English department's R&D wing: theory, feminism, new historicism, race and class studies, and so on.

So, while English has large investment holdings in reading literary history and teaching writing, it simultaneously has investments in a lot of other diversified markets. This is not chaos or intellectual incoherence, but a diversified investment strategy, with each investment intimately connected to all the others: the humanities' writing emphasis, for example, wouldn't make any sense if students weren't writing about cultural and artistic events of importance; and our reading and writing pedagogy—call it "mapping" if you want sexier language—wouldn't make a lot of sense or work very well if it were completely divorced from the institutional history of our disciplines.

In the end, in articulating "what it is we do around here" and why people should invest in our futures, I see a tripartite map of the humanities' investments: we have about a third of our holdings in disciplinary histories, upholding and passing along the base cultural formations of the humanities—Aristotle, Jane Austen, Durkheim, Eisenstein, Frederick Douglass; about a third of our portfolio is tied to skills markets—writing, cultural literacy, critical thinking; and about a third of our investments are in R&D—the new "studies" programs. Again, it seems important to emphasize within this structure that these are *not* distinct, unrelated segments of any given department: all three of these operations are at work in any given course, and in any given faculty member's research itinerary. The Kant course isn't just about some transhistorical "Kant," but about how changes in research methods and topics have changed our understanding of Kant's thought. Likewise, the skills emphasis of our investment is peppered all throughout the portfolio: the whole point of interdisciplinary cultural studies or feminism, one might say, is to construct a social ability to respond to the past, present, and future.

When it comes to articulating what we do, I'm arguing that we need to emphasize and insist on the literal futures component of the humanities—that is, our R&D or research emphasis. In a panic, it's too easy to fall back on the transmission of a tried-and-true humanistic canon or a communicative rationality model of humanities disciplines. In fact, this characterization of the humanities is (ironically) what often secretly connects the proponents of the humanities and their critics: oftentimes, they both agree that humanities disciplines and methods are "useless" to most contemporary profit-making economic enterprises. The only question becomes whether one lauds the humanities because of this fact or condemns them (or, more commonly, unwittingly condemns them precisely by lauding them as "useless"). For example, in *Not for Profit: Why Democracy Needs the Humanities*, Martha Nussbaum sums up the opposition that structures much of this "crisis" discourse: "What we might call the humanistic aspects of science and social science—the imaginative, creative aspect, and the aspect of rigorous critical thought—are . . . losing ground as nations prefer to pursue short-term profit by the cultivation of the useful and highly applied skills suited to profitmaking" (2010, 2). The opposition before us is starkly rendered here: imagination, creativity, and rigorous thought versus short-term profiteering and what that mode presumably values above all else in university education, the increasing vocationalization of "useful and highly applied skills." Whatever one may say about this kind of opposition, it's certainly familiar: as technical skills and profit motives take over education, we're in danger of losing, in Nussbaum's words, all those precious skills "associated with the humanities and the arts: the ability to think critically; the ability to transcend local loyalties and to approach world problems as a 'citizen of the world'; and, finally, the ability to imagine sympathetically the predicament of another person" (7).

As a thought experiment, just forget about assessing the logic of this argument for a moment, and consider instead the performative truism that following Nussbaum's verbs here tells you all you need to know about the humanities: to think, to transcend, to approach, to imagine. Great stuff, and stuff that is as venerable as its other—the dead end of economic rationality—is soul stealing. Indeed, Nussbaum's choice is stark: "between an education for profit-making and an education for a more inclusive type of citizenship" (7). And in the abstract, nearly everyone thinks that the critical-thinking skills of the humanities are laudable; it's just that they're too expensive and that outcomes of such liberal education are a little hard to measure: how much imagination, transcendence, sympathy, and critical thinking is enough? There's no standardized test for these virtues, as there is for math and science knowledge. In fact, buried in many unsympathetic stances toward the humanities is the sense that they're not knowledge at all, but merely ideological approaches to knowledge: the humanities are dedicated to *how* one learns; the sciences are dedicated to bottom-line *what* one learns. And for a bean-counting rationality of profit motive, only a "what" (things or skills one can immediately sell for a profit) has economic value.

Of course, this way of structuring the debate depends on a slightly dated version of political economy and how it functions (or what it requires from higher education to function) in the twenty-first century. Or at least it's a description that conjures a kind of Fordist world of factories and commodity production that doesn't seem to exhaust the global cyber-capitalism in which universities are ostensibly training students to participate. The world of factories and commodity production has hardly disappeared altogether, but one assumes that not too many students see themselves as seeking training for that world at American research universities. The jobs that American universities are ostensibly training people for, one assumes, are in the cutting-edge sectors of the global knowledge economy, where these humanities core values (imagination and thinking outside the box and outside your own national boundaries—innovation) are not opposed to economic valuation, but are in fact virtually identical to the measures of value within the ideological universe of post-postmodern capitalism. For example, the 2010–11 report of the Global Economic Forum (the Davos people) shows that the United States is quickly losing its global hegemony as an economic powerhouse, slipping to number four in the Global Competitiveness Index. In fact, the United States remains a notable powerhouse in only two of the economists' myriad categories— consumption (little surprise there, though hoarding Hello Kitty accessories manufactured elsewhere is not much of an accomplishment) and a quite coveted category in the report's universe, "innovation."

As the World Economic Forum Global Competitiveness Report, 2010–11 puts it,

The United States continues the decline that began last year, falling two more places to 4th position. While many structural features that make its economy extremely productive [*sic*], a number of escalating weaknesses have lowered the US ranking over the past two years. US companies are highly sophisticated and innovative, supported by an excellent university system that collaborates strongly with the business sector in R&D. Combined with the scale opportunities afforded by the sheer size of its domestic economy—the largest in the world by far—these qualities continue to make the United States very competitive. (27)

If innovation is key to any kind of economic competitiveness, then so too should the R&D wing of the humanities. Innovation—it's what the humanities do. And if the prized economic value of "thinking outside the box" is another name for our R&D focus, then it's not so much the transmission-of-culture (teachers of citizenship) focus that makes the humanities central to the cultural and economic future, but the research profile—combining and intensifying existing cultural formations in ways that open up different ways of thinking about them.

"OK," you say, "as a way of repackaging the cultural-economic work of the humanities, deans and other 'insiders' may go for this line of reasoning, as they're already invested in humanities research. But donors,

alums, and the general public will balk at this entire line of reasoning—
they don't want to hear anything about innovative paradigms; they want
the humanities to be exactly what they were when alums were in school." I
think this is patently untrue. No matter what her job, anyone in a position
to care about and contribute to the life of the humanities will have worked
in a business environment that's been completely transformed since her
college days. It would be irresponsible—an intellectual travesty—to teach
engineering or biology based on a fifty-year-old curriculum; research has
inexorably transformed these fields. So why would donors, savvy businesspeople that they ostensibly are, be interested in funding an antiquated
humanities curriculum? They're *precisely* interested in futures—whether
we are or not.

Indeed, as robotic technology increasingly takes over most vocational brands of "skills" work—beware MLA, robots are even teaching
English in South Korea[7]—the virtual, seemingly misty and ethereal abilities that the humanities trade in (thinking, innovating, problem solving)
look like they will in fact be the only economically viable human commodity of the future. Now, in other words, is precisely the wrong time to
vocationalize any curriculum. But such calls are especially disastrous for
the humanities—and not only because we'll lose some precious (though
economically "useless") legacy of what's made us human in the past, but
precisely because of what one might call the economic and cultural futures market on the humanities. Marina Gorbis, president of the RAND
Corporation offshoot the Institute for the Future, puts it succinctly: in the
future, "well-paid work will demand more skills than it does today. And it
will be the sort of creative work that machines can't do." In short, Gorbis
argues that the economically viable human job skills of the future will be
comprised not by measurable tasks or testable knowledge, but rather by
"everything that cannot be defined, that's novel, improvisational, where
you need to quickly adapt on the spot. Anything related to kind of abstract, high-level thinking."[8] And, to repurpose a slogan, the office supply store Staples "*don't* got that"; rather, the humanities got that. And in
particular the "theory" aisle at the humanities superstore, far from being
home to the bruised and reduced bin within a remaindered sector of the
university, is or should be the place most brimming with the cultural and
economic commodity of the future: "abstract, high-level thinking."

And in the end, this perhaps brings us back to where we began, with Jameson, for whom one must "always historicize" precisely in the name of the future: one must do a genealogy of the past in the name of an as-yet-impossible genealogy of the future. As Jameson writes, "There is so far no term as useful for the construction of the future as 'genealogy' is for such a construction of the past. . . . The operation [of analysis] itself, however, consists in a prodigious effort to change the valences on phenomena which so far exist only in our own present; and experimentally to declare positive things which are clearly negative in our own world" (2009, 434). At present, it seems that most of the valences of post-postmodern hyper-capitalism in our world are and probably should be coded as "negative," and recent developments in the corporate university leave little doubt that the humanities are under fire. But post-postmodern thought additionally and importantly has to take on the job of looking positively toward the intensifications and transformations of the present that might offer escape lines for the future. In that spirit, we might insist that the humanities and their highly diversified and abstract intellectual investments—the commitments to theory—are not signs of irrelevance, chaos, or incoherence, but precisely the humanities' cultural and economic power and future. We offer a post-postmodern version of innovation not as spring-green creation ex nihilo, but precisely through the kind of mishmashing, overcoding operation that I've been trying to thematize and enact throughout this book. Innovation these days consists of putting existing things together in stark and productive "new" ways; and the humanities are (or should be) a key laboratory for such a transformed practice of innovation. The humanities offer a hermeneutics of (the) situation, tools for producing a kind of cartography that can diagnose and respond to the post-postmodern present. We're really *not* your father's liberal arts, and maybe it's time we started embracing and foregrounding that fact, rather than apologizing for it.

Notes

1. See also, in the literary critical context, the essays collected in a 2007 special issue of *Twentieth Century Literature*, "After Postmodernism," which essentially try to draw a series of distinctions between the "high" postmodern novels of, say, Thomas Pynchon, and whatever a newer generation of "ambitious" writers is doing (Dave Eggers, Jonathan Safran Foer, Zadie Smith, and the like); in architecture, see Turner's 1996 *City as Landscape*. Those working specifically in the wake of Jameson's analyses (and other economic analyses, like David Harvey's) tend to stick to the phrase "late postmodernism": see especially Wegner's fine book, *Life between Two Deaths* (2009).

In the *New York Times*, the adjective "post-postmodern" functions, just like "postmodern" did in its day, as a synonym for tragically hip. Just to take the fate of the word in 2010–11 as an example, "post-postmodern" was used to describe the March 2010 Fashion Week in Paris, to name composers in the wake of Philip Glass (January 24, 2010), and to characterize a modern dance work in which there's no dancing (April 16, 2010). In addition, "post-postmodern" in the *Times* has modified everything from the experimental music of Jim O'Rourke (November 23, 2010) to the portraits in a Connecticut art show (April 30, 2011) and even the Hollywood blockbuster *Captain America* (July 21, 2011).

1. Though the numbers were kept secret during the actual bailouts of 2008, the staggering numbers finally came out, as the result of regulatory reform on disclosures. See *Bloomberg News* for August 22, 2011, "Wall Street Aristocracy Got $1.2 Trillion from Fed," http://www.bloomberg.com/news/2011-08-21/wall-street-aristocracy-got-1-2-trillion-in-fed-s-secret-loans.html.

2. On the question of style, see especially Jameson (1961, 1990).

3. "Transcoding" is a word that Jameson initially borrows from Greimas; see Jameson (1972), where he offers this gloss: "Truth as transcoding, translation from one code to another. . . . The truth-effect involves or results from just such

a conceptual operation" (216). Such an operation opens the way for a hermeneutics not of narrow textual meaning, but a more robust mode of interpretation that takes into account the historical situation, what Jameson calls a "genuine hermeneutics" that would "reopen text and analytic process alike to all the winds of history" (ibid.).

4. This non- or antimoralistic nature of Jameson's project is, it seems to me, the most misunderstood aspect of his work. To this day, most people think of his work on postmodernism as arguing that there's something "bad" about it—that the negative valence of his work always overcodes the affirmative. And while Jameson is clearly no booster for capitalism in any of its guises, he's just as clear that one can't injure or resist said capitalism (at least anymore) simply by denouncing it.

CHAPTER 2

1. Of course, commodity production, direct exploitation, and the labor theory of value don't merely disappear—but my point is that they don't appear as major players in the transactional logic of finance capital. Under the global hegemony of finance capital, the work of direct exploitation certainly continues—in fact, it seems to become even more vicious as it's outsourced or displaced from the so-called first world toward the so-called third.

2. On the Deleuzian terminology, see Massumi (1992): "To every actual intensity corresponds a virtual one. Actual intensity has extension (form and substance), virtual intensity does not: it is a *pure intensity*. The virtual has only *intension*" (66).

3. On this base-superstructure question, see Williams (1980): "There is a difficult passage in the *Grundrisse* where [Marx] argues that while the man who makes the piano is a productive worker, there is a real question whether the man who distributes the piano is also a productive worker; but he probably is, since he contributes to the realization of surplus value. Yet when it comes to the man who plays the piano, whether to himself or to others, there is no question: he is not a productive worker at all. So piano-maker is base, but pianist superstructure. As a way of considering cultural activity, this is very clearly a dead-end" (34–35).

4. This collapsing of the cultural and the economic is in fact why Las Vegas *works* so effectively in separating people from their money. In your "regular" economic life, you'll routinely go all the way across town to save $2 on a bottle of vodka. But when you're at the casino, surrounded by the cultural signifiers of risk and privilege, you'll just as routinely stake hundreds more than you can afford or tip someone $25 for bringing you a "free" drink.

5. I steal this phrase from a conversation with my friend Rich Doyle.

6. In the Forum, this special brand of intensive consumerism is linked everywhere to *water*, the condition for life as we know it. This ubiquity of water symbolism also functions as a recurring auto-tribute to the founding of Las Vegas itself, the intensive eruption of life in the godforsaken desert. Following the Romans, who sealed the hegemony of empire with the flow of aqueducts, what could be more unquestionably forceful than controlling water in the middle of a desert? Caesar's is an empire that finds its considerable thirst slaked only by resources—water and money—brought in from elsewhere and endlessly circulated.

7. On the risk society, see especially Beck (1992).

8. In Dostoevsky's *The Gambler*, a true gambler plies his trade against (feminine) abstractions and gambles solely to overcome them, thereby hoping to secure a kind of masculine nobility in an otherwise absurd universe. As the unrepentant gambler holds near the end of the novel, "As long as I am around [roulette], I have a chance to be a man" (1977, 171).

9. In fact, Mother Russia has come to Las Vegas in the form of the "Red Square" restaurant, complete with a headless Lenin statue guarding its entrance inside the Mandalay Bay Casino. The original pitch: "Welcome to the warmer half of Moscow. By that we mean Red Square, an original restaurant where you'll discover vodka and caviar fit for a Czar. So forget everything you thought you knew about the frigid Siberian tundra, and enjoy the particular comforts that only the Motherland provides." The phone message reminds you to "avoid bread lines" by making reservations early.

Here one might also argue that terrorism represents the "other" left for casino capitalism to conquer, but the very logic and practice of terrorism is less extensive than it is intensive. (We are reminded time and again that terrorists have no homeland—they are everywhere and nowhere; terrorism is, in Derrida's parlance, not so much an external threat as it is an "auto-immune disorder" generated internally by contradictions and exclusions in the current ruling world order. See Derrida (2005).

10. Parallels to Ronald Reagan and Margaret Thatcher are hard to resist here, or at least the broad ideological sense that after the era of the cold warriors, political leadership has given way to media showmanship—with Bill Clinton and Boris Yeltsin blazing a public relations trail that's been well trod by Tony Blair, George W. Bush, Barack Obama, Nicolas Sarkozy, and the like.

11. Even if the strategy is in essence doomed, as it is in *Spartacus*: in the end, slaves are crucified as far as the eye can see along the Appian Way. But that failure is part and parcel of the film's ruling existentialist ethos: one gains authenticity only by facing up to certain death, refusing its power, acting honorably in an absurd universe. Several times Spartacus reminds his followers that "a free man only dies once, but a slave dies every day." As Hardt and Negri write in *Empire*, such modernist "refusal certainly is the beginning of a liberatory politics, but it

is only a beginning. The refusal in itself is empty. . . . In political terms, . . . refusal in itself (of work, authority, and voluntary servitude) leads only to a kind of social suicide. . . . What we need is to create a new social body, which is a project that goes well beyond refusal" (2000, 204). Note also that Kubrick's film—true to its existentialist ethos of authenticity—closely follows actual historical events, so the film has to end with the revolt's failure and the mass crucifixion.

Scott's *Gladiator* is not so hamstrung by historical "facts." There is no Maximus in the historical record; and while Marcus's son Commodus did in fact succeed him (and by nearly all accounts Commodus was a disaster as an emperor), Commodus was not killed by a gladiator, nor did he seem to experience substantial friction with his father. The historical Commodus was in fact elevated to the status of co-emperor during the last years of Marcus's life and reign.

12. Baseball was once euphemistically known as "the American pastime," but today almost twice as many Americans visit a casino each year as attend a baseball game (Cooper 1997, 28). On the staggering growth of the prison industry and its ties to other sectors of the American economy, see Parenti (2000); and Davis (2000).

CHAPTER 3

1. See Hoffman (2008) for an extensive overview and chronology of twentieth-century popular music.

2. For recent work on the continuing (even structural) role of "authenticity" in popular music consumption, see Moore (2002), Shumway (2007), and C. Williams (2001); for an argument that authenticity no longer matters, see Grossberg (2002).

3. In addition to the canonical background provided in Frith (1998), Grossberg (2002), and Marcus (1990), see Hebdige (1981), the source text for most subsequent cultural studies writing about music of whatever type. One might note in passing that there's a hidden "cost" to Hebdige's approach to studying punk— namely, that music is taken unambiguously to be the expression of a "subculture," and hence it doesn't leave much for music critics to say about "dominant culture" (other than that subcultures exist in opposition to it).

Though one starts to wonder when Grossberg writes, "I do not think that writing about popular music has significantly changed (to say nothing of 'progressed') in forty years" (2002, 29), I might urge the reader toward Dettmar's (2005) insightful book on the structuring trope of rock's "death" and Lipsitz's (2007) recent work on the globalization of music. For my money, the most interesting recent work on rock music is Keightley's (2004), concerning mid-twentieth-century technology (the birth of the LP) and popular music consumption patterns of the past and present. In short, Keightley argues against the grain that the classic rock era was a continuation of, rather than a revolt against, the dominant recording and distribution practices of the midcentury music business (386–88).

4. As Keightley puts it, in a more scholarly idiom, "the ideology of rock itself consistently disavows rock's commercial status" (2004, 376).

5. See Densmore (2002), who is in fact the only remaining member of the Doors who's holding out against selling their songbook to advertisers.

6. For an insightful overview and critical analysis of this "indie rock" dust-up about race and class (and the obvious missing terms, "gender" and "sexual orientation"), see Kheshti (2008). To extrapolate from Keightley's thesis about continuities in the distribution and format of popular music from the 1950s to 1980s (in short, the absolute hegemony of the LP), the "crisis" in contemporary music would be less one of sonic or social content than one of distribution, with iTunes and other Internet downloading and file-sharing technologies breaking the hegemony of the music industry's preferred model—the store-bought album. Therefore, it's hardly a coincidence that the biggest news in recent indie rock is the return of the concept album—by Radiohead, Mars Volta, Magnetic Fields, Belle and Sebastian, and the Decemberists, just to name a few. The point in producing a full-blown concept album in the new millennium is both to recall the cultural capital of '70s classic rock's concept albums (*The Lamb Lies Down on Broadway, Dark Side of the Moon,* or *Quadrophenia*), but perhaps more important, to try to ensure that listeners actually buy an entire album and don't cherry-pick songs they like for ninety-nine cents apiece.

7. One could very quickly be disabused of this notion by watching the "throngs sitting around listening" to the Rolling Stones' free 1969 concert at Altamont, captured in the Maysles brothers and Zwerin's film *Gimme Shelter.* The Hell's Angels, who were hired for security, beat up zoned-out hippies by the dozen, and one of the few African Americans in evidence in the crowd is stabbed to death by an Angel. As we watch scores of burned-out kids staring pathetically at Mick Jagger to get him to stop the violence, it's a bit hard to see how classic rock functions as a harmonious cultural past. As Bangs (who was actually there) writes, watching Jagger try to calm the crowd was a bit "like Betty Boop trying to quell a race riot" (2002, 144). Bangs concludes, "Death of Innocence in Woodstock Nation my ass, Altamont was the *facing up*" (145).

8. It's hard to see, just using Brooks's (2007) list of canonical roots rock as an example, what would be lost for American culture, race relations, authenticity, or common identity if the Allman Brothers simply dropped off the musical face of the planet—though I guess they are the Southern rock gateway to Lynyrd Skynyrd, 38 Special, Molly Hatchet, and the "rock" sound of much contemporary country music.

9. In classic rock terms, think of the genre's lyrical allergy to stagnation: Kansas's "Dust in the Wind," Zep's "The Song Remains the Same," Aerosmith's "Same Old Song and Dance," the Who's "The Music Must Change," and so on. In the secondary literature, Reynolds (2011) represents the most full-throated recent rendition of this durable modernist lament concerning pop music's inability to "make it new" anymore. Odd how someone who is blatantly recycling aesthetic truisms from a century ago can accuse pop music of being too enamored of its own past.

10. This kind of move is endlessly on display, for example, in Zizek's (2003) "critiques" of Deleuze: because Deleuze's work is committed to smoothing striated space, becoming, and multiplicity, and these are the very values of transnational capitalism (!), then Deleuze is logically an apologist for (and ideologist of) late capitalism.

11. See Mehdi (2008) for a general overview of Iranian youth culture.

12. As Hardt and Negri put it quite succinctly, the powers of our time "produce not only commodities but subjectivities. . . . They produce needs, social relations, bodies, and minds—which is to say, they produce producers" (2000, 32). This, I think, is the most economical way to state the difference between Adorno and Horkheimer's (1993) work of the mid-twentieth century and work on our present. For Adorno and Horkheimer, the *socius* is a Fordist factory that produces, in the end, only one product: consumers. Hence the constant sense of theft or swindle in their work. Like the pornography that is one of their primary examples, the culture industry consistently works on a bait-and-switch logic: it forces you to be satisfied by consuming rather than doing. The culture industry, to use the Deleuzian parlance, always separates the subject from what it can do, and in the process it levels all potential action onto the plane of consumption. The post-Fordist (or post-postmodern) imperatives that Hardt and Negri describe are slightly different: they precisely ask you to produce yourself through consumption, which doesn't separate you from who you are "authentically," but is your only means to make yourself, period. Precisely because *Empire* begins with the realization that there is nothing "outside" commodification—"nothing escapes money" (2000, 32)—it is only to that immanence of consumption or commodification that the dominant system (as well as those trying to resist it) can look for innovation or production.

CHAPTER 4

1. The best general overviews of "the corporate university," its history, and practices, can be found in Bousquet (2009), as well as Slaughter and Leslie (1997) and Slaughter and Rhodes (2004); though perhaps the most widely cited book on the general crisis is Readings (1996), discussed in the text. There's a vast critical

literature on "the crisis of the corporate university," and it's probably best understood as a general term for a series of related subissues. For example, for a specific history and critique of technology transfer (the making of the American university into an R&D wing of industry), see Miyoshi (2000a, 2000b). On the part-time and contingent labor situation, see especially Bousquet (2009); as well as Nelson and Watt (2004); and the collections in Martin (1998); Johnson, Kavanagh, and Mattson (2003); and Bousquet, Scott, and Parascondola (2004). On the general relation between academic labor and the recent changes in other US labor markets, see Watkins (1989, 2009). On the culture wars and their relation to the university, see Bérubé and Nelson (1995); and Bérubé (2006). On the academic star system, see Williams (2001).

2. In the era of development, when the university endowment is king, this nonprofit status is becoming increasingly suspect. In this context, one wonders about Harvard's decision to appoint former Treasury secretary Lawrence Summers as its president (2001–6)—insofar as it gave the impression that Harvard is nothing other than its endowment (valued at $32 billion as of June 2011). In other words, Summers's appointment risked exposing Harvard as a mutual fund that's found the ultimate tax loophole—nonprofit university status; in fact, Harvard's, like many university's endowments, is a mutual fund that looks increasingly like a Ponzi scheme—getting donors to pay in money at the "bottom," which is then disgorged in multi-million-dollar salaries to those running the fund at the "top." In 2003, the height of the madness, the highest-paid people in all of academia were the top two investment managers at the Harvard Management Company, who earned $69 million ($35.1 and $34 million, respectively) in fiscal year 2003 (Basinger 2004). The number-three man at Harvard Management had to settle for a paltry $17.3 million for the year.

3. Quoted in Gordon (1996, 51). Gordon's book questions whether there ever was any substantive downsizing within the management ranks of American business in the wake of the 1980s. Among other things, he points out that American business was so "fat" with managers going into the 1980s, downsizing would have had to go a long way indeed to make it "lean." He points out that American businesses average *three times* more "managerial and administrative employees" than German or Japanese firms (in 1989, 13% of all employees for US firms; 4.2% for Japan; and 3.9% for Germany) (43). Given this initial managerial heft, even substantial downsizing wouldn't necessarily make an organization svelte: "A fat corporation would still be a fat corporation" (51). Likewise, he points out that many of those targeted by the high-profile downsizings of the 1980s and '90s found similar jobs in smaller firms—spreading management obesity throughout the economy, even as it thinned within some large corporations (55). Depending upon how one understands the numbers, then, it may be that the increasing manage-

ment hiring in academia actually follows—rather than contradicts—a certain "fattening" of management in American business.

4. These are full-time employment numbers taken from the NEA's *Update* publication (4.3–4, May and September 1998). If we delve into the numbers a bit more, the NEA points out that "executive and administrative hiring" is the only sector of academic employment to experience *any increase at all* in "newly hired full-time staff" for the past twenty years: "Overall, the number of newly hired full-time employees decreased by 35% from 95,939 in 1977 to 62,091 in 1995. . . . The number of new hires increased only in executive and administrative and other professional jobs" (*Update* 4.3, 5). By comparison, faculty full-time new hires are down 17% over that time period, with physical plant and clerical staffs both off more than 50% in full-time new hires since 1977.

5. And regarding salary, NEA *Update* 9.4 (2003) states: "Over a 30-year period, the average salaries (in constant 2002–03 dollars) for fulltime faculty on 9/10-month contracts increased a dismal 4.6%, with professors and instructors accounting for the increase. Nonranking faculty, assistant and associate professors showed a decrease in spending power by as much as 13.8%. The average salary for women still remains lower than men." This over a time span when presidents and provosts saw their pay rates climb to CEO-like heights (see Basinger 2004), and the hiring boom in the academic administration ranks brought higher salaries there as well. According to the 2004–5 salary numbers reported by the *Chronicle of Higher Education* (2005), about 90% of all job titles classified as "Executive" and "Academic Administration" have a median salary higher than the nationwide average faculty salary, $68,505 (see Smallwood 2005).

6. Given the intensification of fund-raising by presidents and provosts, it's easy to forget the extent to which "quelling internal dissent" remains a key function in the corporate university. In 2004, for example, there were high-profile firings of a tenured professor at Penn State Altoona and two professors at the University of Southern Mississippi. The reason given? Faculty members were critical and unsupportive of their programs: the Penn State professor of sixteen years, named "an excellent classroom teacher who is quite popular with her students" (Ward 2004) by the very committee who fired her, dared to question whether her Altoona campus theater program was in fact "Your Ticket to Broadway," as the program was supposedly sold to students. For their part, the tenured professors from Southern Miss conspired, among other sins, to question the credentials of an administrator: they (truthfully) pointed out that a dean at Southern Miss claimed in her CV and on the university Web site to have formerly been a tenured professor at the University of Kentucky. She had in fact never worked there, but at Ashland Community College in Ashland, Kentucky (same difference, the administrator says, and she goes on to have the accusers' e-mail monitored, while any faculty member would be summarily dismissed for such misrepresentation).

On the Penn State situation, see Fogg (2004) and Ward (2004); re the Southern Miss case, see Smallwood (2004).

7. This line of reasoning is developed more fully in Burgan's *Whatever Happened to the Faculty?* (2006).

8. This argument is advanced most persuasively in my own discipline by David Laurence, the director of Associated Departments of English, to whom I owe the pithy phrase "fewer seats in a more comfortable boat." See Laurence (2002) for his take on the disciplinary "crisis" supposedly brought about by the death of a "coherent" core curriculum in English.

9. One finds a bit of a numbers problem when turning back to Nelson and Watt's (2004) critique. If, as they write, "for every person earning $50,000 to $100,000 or more for teaching a course there are hundreds more earning about $1000 or $2000," it's hard to see how taking down the tenured fat cats would make things substantially better. Rhetorically inflated though their numbers may be, let's simply take them at face value—for every $100,000 per course star, let's say that there are 200 part-timers making $1,000 per course. So, we'll simply pool the money and split it evenly: that's $300,000 for every 201 teachers, around $1,500 per person. Crisis not averted.

This blame-faculty-first line of reasoning also mirrors a bill of goods consistently offered by crackpot politicians and right-wing ideologues: someone somewhere is in fact making this mythical $100,000 primarily for *teaching* an arduous three—or six, nine, even twenty—hours a week, when K–12 teachers do it fifty hours a week for half the pay (and these are hardworking folks who don't teach courses on music videos and porn). As Watkins (1989) definitively demonstrates in *Work Time*, academic "work" and its socioeconomic effects extend far, far beyond the hours spent in the classroom, but these kinds and sites of work often remain invisible in debates surrounding the university, just as the economic costs of obtaining a PhD (an additional decade of debt-ridden apprenticeship taken out of your working life—not to mention the heavy psychic tolls paid along the way) too often remain equally invisible in discussions of "exorbitant" faculty pay rates.

10. See Nelson's indispensable *No University Is an Island* (2010).

11. See, for example, the sentiments of Richard T. Ingram, president of the Association of Governing Boards of Universities and Colleges (AGB), responding to faculty concerns (expressed by James T. Richardson, president of AAUP, and Cary Nelson) over AGB's mission statement: "It underscores the need for the board, the chief executive, and appropriate stakeholders to clarify the authority delegated to the faculty and other participants in the governance process. . . . It calls on boards and chief executives to be certain to include appropriate stakeholders in discussions when their participation is relevant. . . . Its principles and standards can help restore the voice of faculty members in their areas of expertise

and primary professional concern" (1999, 10). So, if the board of trustees ever finds itself discussing Adorno, I suppose we can expect a call. But in the meanwhile, we can only take such language as a not-too-subtle invitation for faculty to butt out of the university's governance.

12. In the end, it may well be that a robust faculty union movement will be the only way to perform this revitalization of faculty sovereignty in the university. And while I am certainly sympathetic to calls for faculty unionization as the fix for the corporate university—who doesn't love sentiments like Nelson and Watt's "Keep on Truckin' and Fighting the Good Fight" (2004, 136)—here I'm trying, as a kind of thought experiment, to think *within* the (admittedly cramped) space of contemporary corporatization, rather than primarily *against* or *outside* it. While unionization presently lies far outside the thinkable spectrum for the theory and practice of corporatization, I should note that there is a growing literature in mainstream economics showing faculty tenure (often criticized as the ultimate in union-style job entitlement) to be "good" (which is to say, rational and maximizing) for the corporate university. For an overview of mainstream work on the positive economic effects of tenure, and a specific "proof" of tenure's maximizing worth to the university, see Chatterjee and Marshall (2005).

EXCURSUS

1. Most persuasively, see the chapters on Nietzsche and Adorno in Terada (2009).

2. Claiming ill health, Nietzsche resigned his professorship at Basel in 1879 at age thirty-five and obtained a pension. He never held a steady job again.

3. Goux then goes on to question what he calls "Nietzsche's *regressive materialism*, which denounces conceptual abstraction in order to revert to the original image" (1990, 106).

4. Terada uses this same quotation as the titling epigraph for *Looking Away*, wherein she discusses at some length Nietzsche's "looking away" as a kind of self-thwarting gesture, a "moralization of arguments about appearance and reality" (2009, 1). Her chapter on Nietzsche is called "No Right: Phenomenality and Self-Denial in Nietzsche" and reads Nietzsche as a hermeneutician of suspicion par excellence, a thinker agonized by his own inabilities to think past the fact/value distinction, unable to find a truth that's not at another level a lie: "The implosion of Nietzsche's contradictory self-exhortation is black comedy, for Nietzsche really is in agony" (146). In the end, Nietzsche can't solve this problem of hermeneutic suspicion run amok, so he must look away. Compelling as this may be, as I have suggested, I'm trying to construct a very different, more affirmative, Nietzsche here.

5. For more on chiasmus and Adorno's style, see Jameson (1990, 5–12); Rose (2006, 11–26); and Jay (1984, 56–81).

6. Adorno, of course, has much to say about "Hegel, whose method schooled that of *Minima Moralia*" (1974, 16). According to Adorno, however, dialectic "is distorted in Hegel: with serene indifference he opts once again for liquidation of the particular. Nowhere in his work is the primacy of the whole doubted" (17). Hence, "the whole is false" (50).

7. See, for example, Culler's *On Deconstruction*: "Attempts to reverse and thus displace major hierarchical oppositions of Western thought open possibilities of change that are incalculable" (1982, 158).

8. See, for example, Zizek: "Lacan's point is not that full self-consciousness is impossible since something always eludes the grasp of my conscious ego. Instead, it is the far more paradoxical thesis that this decentered hard kernel which eludes my grasp is ultimately self-consciousness itself" (1993, 66).

9. Most cultural studies analyses fit within this rubric—attempting to move away from a base-superstructure model of capital's relation to culture. As Larry Grossberg writes in *Bringing It All Back Home*, cultural studies "rejects analyses that . . . operate as if capital determines [culture] in a mechanical way from start to finish" (1998, 10–11).

10. A potential link, which will remain unexplored here: Melancholia is certainly about loss, but it's *unacknowledged* loss in Freud—precisely its distinction from mourning, which has a more defined (lost) object. So melancholia, as Judith Butler points out (1993, 233–36), has a privileged link to performativity as rage—it can be seen as an "acting out" over a loss that can't even really be named. To paraphrase Leonard Cohen, the melancholic can't forget, but doesn't remember what.

11. Adorno insists that the bad dialectician is like the bad musician—using the dialectic instead of working through it: "The harm is done by the *thema probandum:* the thinker uses the dialectic instead of giving himself up to it. In this way thought, masterfully dialectical, reverts to the pre-dialectical stage: the serene demonstration that there are two sides to everything" (1974, 247).

12. Again, one learns this from Hegel, who insists in the *Phenomenology* that "philosophy must beware of the wish to be edifying" (1977, 6).

13. Slowness, we might note, is already a particular modality of speed, though not vice versa.

14. This quotation is William Burroughs's rewriting or inversion of T. S. Eliot's famous line from "The Waste Land." Eliot suggests a kind of passive, apocalyptic waiting: Eliot's line, "HURRY UP PLEASE ITS TIME," longs for some mystical force to hurry up the time of this "IT," a coming revelation. Burroughs's rewriting, "Hurry up please. It's time" (1987, 258) suggests a much more positive sense of deployment or praxis—now is the time to do something. In addition, Burroughs's active rewriting of Eliot comprises the final words of "the old writer who couldn't write anymore because he had reached the end of words" (258) in

Burroughs's final novel, *The Western Lands*; and as such these words are a kind of Burroughsian farewell to words, a final and always-resonating call for action. See Murphy (1997, 200) for more on this Burroughsian rewriting.

CHAPTER 5

1. See "Transgressing the Boundaries" (2005), Hitchens's inane review of the *Johns Hopkins Guide to Literary Theory*. (Full disclosure: I am the author of the "effusively respectful entry for Judith Butler" that Hitchens beats up on in his review.) See also the more straightforward journalistic account of theory's demise by Howard (2005), as well as memoirs by Lloyd (1997) and Metcalf (2005).

2. For a slightly different version of this refrain, we could see also the de Manian wing of American deconstruction, for whom the "materiality of the signifier" is the link between deconstruction and ideology critique par excellence: all ideological totalizations of the signified are based on the material negotiations of the signifier, and hence those totalizations are from the beginning ideological concepts subject to slippage, undecidability, future renegotiation. Close reading itself becomes ideology critique in works like Hillis Miller's *The Ethics of Reading* (1987).

3. For the points of agreement and disagreement between Derrida and Habermas, see the interviews in Borradori (2004).

CHAPTER 6

1. As Hallward writes, Badiou's "problem with Schmitt's concept of the political, in other words, is that it is not prescriptive *enough*. Politics divides, but not between friends and enemies (via the mediation of the state). Politics divides the adherents of a prescription against its opponents" (2005, 774). That's right, the official political theorist of the Third Reich was too soft—"not prescriptive *enough*"—in his thinking of the friend/enemy distinction.

2. Infinity, at the end of the Badiouean day, is akin to the *il y a* of Levinas, the given multiplicity of the world that we have to "evade" if we are to be ethical subjects (see Nealon 1998, 53–72). For his part, Badiou (1994) writes in "Being by Numbers" that "most of the time, the great majority of us live outside ethics. We live in the living multiplicity of the situation." In other words, for Badiou, like Levinas, infinity or multiplicity is something that has to be escaped rather than deployed otherwise (à la Deleuze) or mapped (à la Foucault): "The set of a situation's various bodies of knowledge I call 'the encyclopedia' of the situation. Insofar as it refers only to itself, however, the situation is organically without truth" (ibid.). All claims to radicality notwithstanding, this is the profoundly conservative heart of Badiou's thought: Truth either has to be autonomous and absolute, or there's nothing but the chaos of the bad infinite. That sentiment is,

it seems to me, the driver not of philosophy, but of philosophy's (eternal?) enemy: dogmatism.

Unlike Levinas's, Badiou's ethics is (literally) not for everyone. In "Being by Numbers," Badiou is asked by an interviewer about the ethics of the ordinary person, who doesn't care much for universal "truth": "But can one seriously confide and confine ethics to mathematicians, political activists, lovers, and artists? Is the ordinary person, by definition, excluded from the ethical field?" He responds not in a Foucauldian sense (with the sense that we are all hailed by literal encyclopedias of truth procedures), but with this: "Why should we think that ethics convokes us all? The idea of ethics' universal convocation supposes the assignment of universality. I maintain that the only immanent universality is found in the truth procedure. We are seized by the really ethical dimension only inside a truth procedure. Does this mean that the encounter of ethical situations or propositions is restricted to the actors of a truth procedure? I understand that this point is debatable." It's "debatable" whether most people are capable of ethics or truth? That really *is* Platonism for a new age.

It seems equally clear that Badiouian "events," those drivers of change in the historical and political world, are exceedingly rare and addressed narrowly to certain quite unique individuals—people like Badiou, one would assume, folks who are long on smarts and short on modesty: "Actually, I would submit that my system is the most rigorously materialist in ambition that we've seen since Lucretius" (ibid.).

3. Badiou is, of course, no fan of Foucault, though given sentiments like the following in "Being by Numbers" (1994), it's hard to imagine he's read Foucault closely or sympathetically: "Foucault is a theoretician of encyclopedias. He was never really interested in the question of knowing whether, within situations, anything existed that might deserve to be called a 'truth.' With his usual corrosiveness, he would say that he didn't have to deal with this kind of thing. He wasn't interested in the protocol of either the appearance or the disappearance of a given epistemic organization." Foucault was of course obsessed by nothing other than the appearance and disappearance of epistemic organizations (sovereign power, social power, discipline, biopower), which he called "ways of speaking the truth." Though of course the only "truth" worth the name in Badiou is ahistorical and subjective, and here Foucault can be "corrosive" indeed: "Truth is a thing of this world: it is induced only by virtue of multiple forms of constraint. And it induces regular effects of power. . . . The problem is not changing people's consciousness—or what's in their heads—but the political, economic, institutional regime of the production of truth" (1980, 131, 133).

4. I take this to be the primary line of reasoning in Foucault's "What Is an Author?" As he explains in a subsequent interview, "We have seen a certain number of themes of Blanchot and Barthes used for a kind of exaltation, at once

ultra-lyrical and ultra-rationalizing, of literature as a structure of language sus-
ceptible to analysis only in itself and in its own terms. . . . Political implications
were not absent from this exaltation. Thanks to it, one succeeded in saying that
literature in itself was at this point freed from all determinations, that the fact of
writing was in itself subversive. . . . Consequently, the writer was a revolutionary,
and the more the writing was Writing, the more it plunged into intransitivity,
the more it produced in doing so the revolution! You know that these things were
unfortunately said. . . . In order to know what is literature, I would not want to
study internal structures. I would rather grasp the movement, the small process
through which a non-literary type of discourse, neglected, forgotten as soon as
it is spoken, enters the literary domain. What happens here? What is released?
How is this discourse modified in its efforts by the fact that it is recognized as
literary?" (1996, 116–17).

5. Among the many proleptically insightful moments in Culler's 1976 essay
is his account of Northrop Frye's work as it became institutionalized in the US:
"Though it began as a plea for a systematic poetics, Frye's work has done less to
promote work in poetics than to stimulate a mode of interpretation which has
come to be known as 'myth-criticism' or archetypal criticism. The assumption
that the critic's task is to interpret individual works remains unchanged, only
now . . . the deepest meanings of a work are to be sought in the archetypal symbols or patterns which it deploys" (249). This seems an excellent (if somewhat
ironic) general description of what would later happen to deconstruction, and
then to new historicism in its turn.

CHAPTER 7

1. See, for example, Krug (2005), especially chap. 2.

2. See especially Malabou (2007, 2009). One could in fact take Malabou's
work on plasticity (which, unlike Derridean writing, directly forms entities—it
does not "mediate" and leaves no "trace") to be another paradigmatically post-
postmodern discourse, though she has no use for any trendy "post-" terminology (see 2009, 8). Though she does put in a late bid for the "next big thing." Just
one word, plastics: "Today, the concept of plasticity tends to become at once the
dominant motif of interpretation and the most productive exegetic and heuristic
tool of our time" (2007, 439).

3. On this point, see Doyle (1996); and Rose (2006).

4. The wording is used in the first volume of the *History of Sexuality* (Foucault 1996, 47–48). On why "really and directly" might be important beyond the
rhetorical level, see Nealon (2008, 45–48).

5. See, for example, Briadotti 's "A Critical Cartography of Post-Postmodern Feminism," where she writes: "At the end of postmodernism, in an era that

experts fail to define in any meaningful manner because it swings between nostalgia and euphoria, in a political economy of fear and frenzy, new master-narratives have taken over. They look rather familiar: on the one hand the inevitability of market economies as the historically dominant form of human progress, and on the other biological essentialism, under the cover of 'the selfish gene' and new evolutionary biology and psychology" (2005, 1).

6. The author is Adam Haslett; http://www.npr.org/templates/story/story.php?storyId=123542128.

7. For more on the Deleuzian powers of the false, see Lambert's (2002) definitive *Non-Philosophy of Gilles Deleuze*, especially 73–151.

8. The linchpin of Welles's film comes during a visit to Chartres Cathedral, which might seem a bit odd in a film about the strange power of contemporary art fakes and forgeries. But of course, part of that power of the false is its ability to injure the supposed authenticity and truth of the original. Chartres was built by thousands of faceless artisans, over hundreds of years—not slavishly following some original master plan, but cobbling together error and experiment on top of error and experiment. Hence, it becomes a monument to the collective power of the false, rather than the individual power of the true, in the production of art. Welles himself narrates: "Ours, the scientists keep telling us, is a universe which is disposable. You know it might be just this one anonymous glory of all things, this rich stone forest, this epic chant, this gaiety, this grand choiring shout of affirmation, which we choose when all our cities are dust; to stand intact, to mark where we have been, to testify to what we had it in us to accomplish. Our works in stone, in paint, in print are spared, some of them for a few decades, or a millennium or two, but everything must fall in war or wear away into the ultimate and universal ash: the triumphs and the frauds, the treasures and the fakes. A fact of life . . . we're going to die. 'Be of good heart,' cry the dead artists out of the living past. Our songs will all be silenced—but what of it? Go on singing. Maybe a man's name doesn't matter all that much" (transcribed from *F for Fake*, 1973).

9. Though I don't want to dwell on it here, this seems to me another point of serious divergence between Derrida and American deconstructive literary criticism. First, we need perhaps to recall the definition of "literature" at work in Derrida's texts. Contrary to the understanding of literature that many people carry into their reading of deconstruction (literature as the transhistorical binary opposite and "other" to the literalist dreams of philosophy—literature as the name for any indeterminate, highly metaphorical language usage), Derrida has a quite precise and historically bounded version of the concept. When asked by Derek Attridge what he means by literature, or what it meant to him to be invested in literature as a young man, Derrida answers: "Literature seemed to me, in a confused way, to be the institution which allows one to say everything, in every way. . . . The institution of literature in the West, in its relatively modern form,

is linked to an authorization to say everything, and doubtless too to the coming about of the modern idea of democracy" (1991, 37). A couple of things we notice right away here about Derrida's sense of literature: first, and most surprisingly, we see that for Derrida, literature is not the long-suffering "other" of philosophy (its oldest enemy, literature as the proper name for the undecidability that always and everywhere haunts the totalizing pretensions of philosophy). On the contrary, what attracts Derrida to literature is not its corrosive, anti-Platonic recalcitrance, but the ways in which literature comprises its own alternative form of "totalization": literature for Derrida is quite literally that which "allows one to say everything, in every way."

Second, we note that Derrida's conception of literature (like Foucault's) is a distinctly modern and Western one, tied to the political rise of European democracies in the nineteenth century. More than that, "literature" for Derrida very specifically signifies Western European avant-garde writing in the mode of aesthetic high modernism: "Let's make this clear," Derrida replies to Attridge with a kind of uncharacteristic candor: "What we call literature (not belles-lettres or poetry) implies that license is given to the writer to say everything he wants to or everything he can, while remaining shielded, safe from all censorship, be it religious or political" (37). When pressed to expand on his sense of literature, Derrida clarifies: "The name 'literature' is a very recent invention. . . . Greek or Latin poetry, non-European discursive works, do not, it seems to me, strictly speaking belong to literature. One can say that without reducing at all the respect or the admiration they are due" (40). So it turns out that literature, far from being everything or everywhere in Derrida, is in fact very specifically confined in his work to describing the Western European avant-garde project of aesthetic modernist writing over the past 150 years or so, one that specifically tries to "say everything" in a form that rivals, rather than merely undermines or abandons, the philosophical inclination toward totalization.

10. Here I follow in the footsteps of Ngai's fine book *Ugly Feelings*, which also uses Andrews's work for an illustrative deal closer. In the closing pages of her book, she calls *Shut Up* "insistently ugly. Indeed, most readers would agree that no contemporary American poet has continued the modernist avant-garde's project of decoupling art from beauty . . . as consistently or aggressively as Andrews" (2007, 348). I'm less interested in the work's aesthetic beauty or ugliness than I am in its diagnostic power, the kind of force it deploys and/or asks—maybe even forces—its reader to redeploy. In fact, I tend to think of Andrews's work in the terms that Deleuze talks about Proust's (which is far from "ugly"): "The poet learns what is essential is outside of thought, in what forces us to think. The leitmotif of *Time Regained* is the word *force*: impressions that force us to look, encounters that force us to interpret, expressions that force us to think" (2004, 95).

CODA

1. As Amiri Baraka writes, for example: "The New Criticism, with its stress on literature as self-contained artifact, was actually part of the McCarthyism and reaction of the '50s. . . . *Formalists*, for whom form is principal or form is everything, generally uphold bourgeois aesthetics. We get offered nothing, really, except subjectivism, elitism, solipsism: the world-erasing super 'I' over everything" (1980, 12).

2. This idea was developed in Harpham's talk at Penn State, "How American Invented the Humanities," September 2010.

3. Or even if *you* somehow can twist free (live off the grid, opt out), it's a privatized escape, further suturing that logic that sees value only in individual accomplishments: recall Margaret Thatcher's handy guide to neoliberalism: "There is no such thing as society. There are individual men and women, and there are families. And no government can do anything except through people, and people must look to themselves first."

4. See, for example, Ebert's *The Task of Cultural Critique*, where she argues that deconstruction is a form of capitalist imperialism (2009, ix–xvi).

5. This periodizing "totalization," where you don't get to choose or reject axiomatic social power, is and has been a common critique of both Jameson's and Foucault's work. Such critiques tend to have a kind of signature effect, as they recycle the well-worn "postmodern" insistence on fragmentation and multiple interpretation (the hermeneutics of suspicion—attention to the quirkiness of the local and the individual, over any claim to collectivity) as the content of their critiques. See, for example, McHale's "What Was Postmodernism?" (2007): "There is no a priori reason to assume that 'postmodernism' means the same thing from one domain to the next, that it is one and the same everywhere. This is because, even if it is driven by the (presumably uniform) 'cultural logic' of a historical moment, cultural change is also driven by the internal dynamics of specific fields, differing from field to field."

6. A 2010 blog post outlining this idea got me denounced as a tool for the man, "evil," and (the height of confusion) it was insinuated that the idea smacked of Nazism—by philosophy professors no less, who should at least know that National Socialists in Germany were no boosters for unfettered international finance capitalism, which in their paranoid fantasies was part of the global Jewish conspiracy. See "Stanley Fish Doesn't Know What He's Talking About," October 12, 2010, http://www.newappsblog.com/2010/10/stanley-fish-doesnt-know-what-hes-talking-about.html#more.

7. See "Robot Teachers Invade South Korean Classrooms," CNN–Tech, http://www.cnn.com/2010/TECH/innovation/10/22/south.korea.robot.teachers/.

8. Sarah Gardner, "The Next Generation's Job Market," American Public Media, http://marketplace.publicradio.org/display/web/2010/10/26/pm-the-next-generations-job-market/.

Works Cited

Adorno, Theodor W. 1974. *Minima Moralia: Reflections from a Damaged Life.* Translated by E. F. N. Jephcott. New York: Verso.

———. 1993. *Hegel: Three Studies.* Translated by Shierry Weber Nicholsen. Cambridge, MA: MIT Press.

———. 1994. *The Stars Down to Earth.* Edited by Steven Crook. London: Routledge.

———. 1998. *Critical Models: Interventions and Catchwords.* Translated by Henry W. Pickford. New York: Columbia University Press.

Adorno, Theodor, and Max Horkheimer. 1993. *Dialectic of Enlightenment.* Translated by John Cumming. New York: Continuum.

Althusser, Louis. 1971. "Ideology and Ideological State Apparatuses." In *Lenin and Philosophy*, translated by Ben Brewster, 127–86. New York: Monthly Review Press.

Andrews, Bruce. 1992. *I Don't Have Any Paper, so Shut Up; or, Social Romanticism.* Los Angeles: Sun and Moon.

antin, david. 1993. *what it means to be avant-garde.* New York: New Directions.

Aronowitz, Stanley. 2001. *The Knowledge Factory: Dismantling the Corporate University and Creating True Higher Learning.* Boston: Beacon.

Badiou, Alain. 1994. "Being by Numbers—Interview with Lauren Sedofsky." *ArtForum* (October). http://www.findarticles.com/p/articles/mi_m0268/is_n2_v33/ai_16315394.

———. 1999. *Manifesto for Philosophy.* Translated by Norman Madarasz. Albany: SUNY Press.

Bangs, Lester. 2002. *Mainlines, Bloodfeasts, and Bad Taste: A Lester Bangs Reader.* Edited by John Morthland. New York: Anchor Books.

Baraka, Amiri. 1963. *Blues People: Negro Music in White America.* New York: William Morrow.

———. 1980. "Afro-American Literature and Class Struggle." *Black American Literature Forum* 14.1:5–14.

Basinger, Julianne. 2004. "Proving Presidential Worth: Federal Scrutiny and

Faculty Resentment Accompany Increases in Top Executives' Pay." *Chronicle of Higher Education*, November 19. http://chronicle.com/section/Home/5.

Baudrillard, Jean. 2005. "Continental Drift: Questions for Jean Baudrillard." *New York Times Magazine*, November 20.

Beck, Ulrich. 1992. *Risk Society*. London: Sage.

Bensaïd, Daniel. 2004. "Alain Badiou and the Miracle of the Event." In *Think Again: Alain Badiou and the Future of Philosophy*, edited by Peter Hallward, 94–105. London: Continuum.

Bernstein, Charles. 1993. *A Poetics*. Cambridge, MA: Harvard University Press.

Bérubé, Michael. 2006. *What's Liberal about the Liberal Arts?* New York: Norton.

Bérubé, Michael, and Cary Nelson. 1995. *Higher Education under Fire: Politics, Economics, and the Crisis of the Humanities*. New York: Routledge.

Borradori, Giovanna. 2004. *Philosophy in a Time of Terror: Dialogues with Jürgen Habermas and Jacques Derrida*. Chicago: University of Chicago Press.

Bourdieu, Pierre. 1989. "Social Space and Symbolic Power." *Sociological Theory* 7.1:14–25.

Bousquet, Marc. 2009. *How the University Works*. New York: NYU Press.

Bousquet, Marc, Tony Scott, and Leo Parascondola. 2004. *Tenured Bosses and Disposable Teachers: Writing Instruction in the Managed University*. Carbondale: Southern Illinois University Press.

Briadotti, Rosi. 2005. "A Critical Cartography of Feminist Post-Postmodernism." *Australian Feminist Studies* 20.47:1–15.

Brooks, David. 2007. "The Segmented Society." *New York Times*, November 20. http://www.nytimes.com/2007/11/20/opinion/20brooks.html.

Brown, Richard Harvey, and Remi Clignet. 2000. "Democracy and Capitalism in the Academy: The Commercialization of American Higher Education." In *Knowledge and Power in Higher Education*, edited by Richard Harvey Brown and J. Daniel Schubert, 17–48. New York: Columbia. Teachers College Press.

Burgan, Mary. 2006. *Whatever Happened to the Faculty?* Baltimore: Johns Hopkins University Press.

Burke, Kenneth. 1973. "Literature as Equipment for Living." In *The Philosophy of Literary Form*, 293–304. Berkeley: University of California Press.

Burrough, Bryan, and John Helyar. 1991. *Barbarians at the Gate: The Fall of RJR Nabisco*. New York: Harper and Row.

Burroughs, William. 1987. *The Western Lands*. New York: Penguin.

Butler, Judith. 1993. *Bodies That Matter*. New York: Routledge.

Byrne, Richard. 2006. "Being M. Badiou: The French Philosopher Brings His

Ideas to America, Creating a Buzz." *Chronicle of Higher Education*, March 24. http://chronicle.com/section/Home/5.

Chatterjee, Kalyan, and Robert C Marshall. 2005. "Lifelong Employment Contracts in Academia." http://econ.la.psu.edu/papers/ChatterjeeMarshall.pdf.

Christgau, Robert. 1991. "Classic Rock." *Details*. http://www.robertchristgau.com/xg/music/60s-det.php.

Cooper, Marc. 1997. "America's House of Cards." In *Crapped Out*, edited by Jennifer Vogel, 28–39. Monroe, ME: Common Courage.

Cooper, Melinda. 2008. *Life as Surplus: Biotechnology and Capitalism in the Neoliberal Era*. Seattle: University of Washington Press.

Culler, Jonathan. 1976. "Beyond Interpretation: The Prospects of Contemporary Criticism." *Comparative Literature* 28.3:244–56.

———. 1982. *On Deconstruction*. Ithaca, NY: Cornell University Press.

———. 2006. *The Literary in Theory*. Stanford, CA: Stanford University Press.

Datskovsky, Miriam. 2008. "Stairway Surprise." *Condé Nast Portfolio*, July. http://www.portfolio.com/culture-lifestyle/culture-inc/arts/2008/06/16/Stairway-to-Heavens-Revenues.

Davidson, Cathy. 2000. "Them vs. Us (and Which One of 'Them' Is Me?)." *ADE Bulletin* 125.3. http://www.mla.org/adefl_bulletin_d_ade_125_3.pdf.

Davis, Angela. 2000. *The Prison-Industrial Complex*. San Francisco: AK Press.

Deleuze, Gilles. 1987. "Nomad Thought." Translated by David B. Allison. In *The New Nietzsche: Contemporary Styles of Interpretation*, edited by David B. Allison, 142–49. Cambridge, MA: MIT Press.

———. 1988. *Foucault*. Translated by Sean Hand. Minneapolis: University of Minnesota Press.

———. 1989. *Cinema 2: The Time Image*. Translated by Hugh Tomlinson. Minneapolis: University of Minnesota Press.

———. 1995. *Negotiations, 1972–1990*. Translated by Martin Joughin. New York: Columbia University Press.

———. 1997. *Essays Critical and Clinical*. Translated by Daniel W. Smith and Michael A. Greco. Minneapolis: University of Minnesota Press.

———. 2004. *Proust and Signs*. Translated by Richard Howard. Minneapolis: University of Minnesota Press.

Deleuze, Gilles, and Félix Guattari. 1983. *Anti-Oedipus: Capitalism and Schizophrenia, Volume 1*. Translated by Robert Hurley et al. Minneapolis: University of Minnesota Press.

———. 1987. *A Thousand Plateaus: Capitalism and Schizophrenia, Volume 2*. Translated by Brian Massumi. Minneapolis: University of Minnesota Press.

DeLillo, Don. 1985. *White Noise*. New York: Vintage.

———. 1991. *Mao II.* New York: Vintage.

de Man, Paul. 1973. "Semiology and Rhetoric." *Diacritics* 3.3:27–33.

Densmore, John. 2002. "Riders on the Storm." *The Nation,* June 20. http://www.thenation.com/doc/20020708/densmore.

Derrida, Jacques. 1982. "Signature Event Context." In *Margins of Philosophy,* translated by Alan Bass, 307–30. Chicago: University of Chicago Press.

———. 1990a. "Force of Law: The 'Mystical Foundation of Authority.'" *Cardozo Law Review* 11.5–6:919–1045.

———. 1990b. "Some Statements and Truisms." Translated by Anne Tomiche. In *The States of "Theory,"* edited by David Carroll, 63–94. New York: Columbia University Press.

———. 1991. *Acts of Literature.* Edited by Derek Attridge. New York: Routledge.

———. 1993. "Circumfession." In *Jacques Derrida,* translated by Geoff Bennington, 3–315. Chicago: University of Chicago Press.

———. 1994. *Specters of Marx.* Translated by Peggy Kamuf. New York: Routledge.

———. 2005. *Rogues: Two Essays on Reason.* Translated by Pascale-Anne Brault and Michael Naas. Stanford, CA: Stanford University Press.

Dettmar, Kevin J. H. 2005. *Is Rock Dead?* London: Routledge.

Dollimore, Jonathan. 1984. *Radical Tragedy: Religion, Ideology, and Power in the Drama of Shakespeare and His Contemporaries.* Chicago: University of Chicago Press.

Donoghue, Frank. 2007. *The Last Professors: The Corporate University and the Fate of the Humanities.* New York: Fordham University Press.

Dostoyevsky, Fyodor. 1977. *The Gambler.* Translated by Andrew R. MacAndrew. New York: W. W. Norton.

Doyle, Richard. 1996. *On Beyond Living: Rhetorical Transformations of the Life Sciences.* Stanford, CA: Stanford University Press.

Eakin, Emily. 2001. "What Is the Next Big Idea? The Buzz Is Growing." *New York Times,* July 7.

———. 2004. "The Theory of Everything, R.I.P." *New York Times,* October 17.

Ebert, Teresa. 2009. *The Task of Cultural Critique.* Champaign: University of Illinois Press. Fish, Stanley. 1995. *Professional Correctness: Literary Studies and Political Change.* Oxford: Clarendon Press.

Fogg, Piper. 2004. "Another Kind of Tenure Case." *Chronicle of Higher Education,* March 19. http://chronicle.com/section/Home/5.

Foucault, Michel. 1972. *The Archaeology of Knowledge.* Translated by A. M. Sheridan Smith. New York: Pantheon.

———. 1973. *The Order of Things*. Translated by Alan Sheridan. New York: Vintage.

———. 1976. *Histoire de la sexualité 1*. Paris: Gallimard.

———. 1978. *The History of Sexuality, Volume 1*. Translated by Robert Hurley. New York: Vintage.

———. 1979. *Discipline and Punish*. Translated by Alan Sheridan. New York: Vintage.

———. 1980. *Power/Knowledge*. Edited by Colin Gordon. Translated by Colin Gordon et al. New York: Pantheon.

———. 1996. *Foucault Live: Interviews*. New York: Semiotext(e).

———. 1998. "Life: Experience and Science." In *Essential Works of Foucault, Volume II*, edited by Paul Rabinow, 465–78. New York: New Press.

———. 2003a. "Lives of Infamous Men." In *The Essential Foucault*, edited by N. Rose and P. Rabinow, 279–93. New York: New Press.

———. 2003b. "The Subject and Power." In *The Essential Foucault*, edited by N. Rose and P. Rabinow, 126–44. New York: New Press.

———. 2010. *The Birth of Biopolitics*. Translated by Graham Burchell. New York: Picador.

Frank, Thomas. 2001. *One Market under God: Extreme Capitalism, Market Populism, and the End of Economic Democracy*. New York: Anchor.

Frere-Jones, Sasha. 2007. "A Paler Shade of White: How Indie Rock Lost Its Soul." *New Yorker*, October 22. http://www.newyorker.com/arts/critics/musical/2007/10/22/071022crmu_music_frerejones.

Frith, Simon. 1998. *Performing Rites: On the Value of Popular Music*. Cambridge, MA: Harvard University Press.

Frith, Simon, with Will Straw and John Street, eds. 2001. *The Cambridge Companion to Pop and Rock*. Cambridge: Cambridge University Press.

Gates, Henry Louis. 1988. *The Signifying Monkey: A Theory of African-American Literary Criticism*. Oxford: Oxford University Press.

Goldsmith, Kenneth. 2001. "After Language Poetry." UbuWeb. http://www.ubu.com/papers/oei/goldsmith.html.

———. 2004. "Being Boring." Electronic Poetry Center. http://epc.buffalo.edu/authors/goldsmith/goldsmith_boring.html.

———. 2005. *The Weather*. Los Angeles: Make Now Press. http://epc.buffalo.edu/authors/goldsmith/.

———. 2007. *Traffic*. Los Angeles: Make Now Press. http://epc.buffalo.edu/authors/goldsmith/.

———. 2008. *Sports*. Los Angeles: Make Now Press. http://epc.buffalo.edu/authors/goldsmith/.

———. 2009. "Flarf Is Dionysus. Conceptual Writing Is Apollo. An Introduction to the 21st Century's Most Controversial Poetry Movements."
Poetry (July/August). http://www.poetryfoundation.org/journal/article.
html?id=237176.

Gordon, David. 1996. *Fat and Mean: The Corporate Squeeze of Working Americans and the Myth of Managerial "Downsizing."* New York: Free Press.

Goux, Jean-Joseph. 1990. *Symbolic Economies: After Marx and Freud*. Translated
by Jennifer Curtiss Gage. Ithaca, NY: Cornell University Press.

Grossberg, Lawrence. 1997. *Dancing in Spite of Myself: Essays on Popular Culture*.
Durham, NC: Duke University Press.

———. 1998. *Bringing It All Back Home: Essays on Cultural Studies*. Durham,
NC: Duke University Press.

———. 2002. "Reflections of a Disappointed Popular Music Scholar." In *Rock
Over the Edge*, edited by Roger Beebee, Denise Fulbrook, and Ben Saunders,
25–59. Durham, NC: Duke University Press.

Hallward, Peter. 2005. "The Politics of Prescription." *South Atlantic Quarterly*
104.4:769–89.

Hamman, Trent. 2009. "Neoliberalism, Governmentality, and Ethics." *Foucault
Studies* 6:37–59.

Harari, Josue. 1979. *Textual Strategies: Perspectives in Post-Structuralist Criticism*.
Ithaca, NY: Cornell University Press.

Hardt, Michael, and Antonio Negri. 2000. *Empire*. Cambridge, MA: Harvard
University Press.

Hebdige, Dick. 1981. *Subculture: The Meaning of Style*. New York: Routledge.

Hegel, G. W. F. 1977. *Phenomenology of Spirit*. Translated by A.V. Miller. Oxford: Oxford University Press.

Henwood, Doug. 1998. *Wall Street: How It Works, and for Whom*. New York:
Verso.

Hitchens, Christopher. 2005. "Transgressing the Boundaries." *New York Times
Book Review*, May 22.

Hoffman, Frank W. 2008. *Chronology of American Popular Music, 1900–2000*.
New York: Routledge.

Howard, Jennifer. 2005. "The Fragmentation of Literary Theory." *Chronicle of
Higher Education*, December 16. http://chronicle.com/section/Home/5.

Ingram, Richard T. 1999. "Faculty Angst and the Search for a Common Enemy." *Chronicle of Higher Education*, May 14. http://chronicle.com/section/
Home/5.

Jameson, Fredric. 1961. *Sartre: Origins of a Style*. New Haven, CT: Yale University Press.

———. 1971. *Marxism and Form.* Princeton: Princeton University Press.

———. 1972. *The Prison-House of Language.* Princeton: Princeton University Press.

———. 1981. *The Political Unconscious.* Ithaca, NY: Cornell University Press.

———. 1984. "Periodizing the 60s." In *The 60s without Apology,* edited by Sohnya Sayres et al., 178–209. Minneapolis: University of Minnesota Press.

———. 1990. *Late Marxism: Adorno.* London: Verso.

———. 1991. *Postmodernism; or, The Cultural Logic of Late Capitalism.* Durham, NC: Duke University Press. Originally published in *New Left Review* 146 (1984): 53–92.

———. 1997a. "Culture and Finance Capital." *Critical Inquiry* 24:246–65.

———. 1997b. "Marxism and Dualism in Deleuze." *South Atlantic Quarterly* 96:393–416.

———. 2009. *Valences of the Dialectic.* London: Verso.

———. 2011. *Representing Capital.* London: Verso.

Jay, Martin. 1984. *Adorno.* Cambridge, MA: Harvard University Press.

Jensen, Michael C. 2000. *A Theory of the Firm.* Cambridge, MA: Harvard University Press.

Johnson, Benjamin, Patrick Kavanagh, and Kevin Mattson, eds. 2003. *Steal This University: The Rise of the Corporate University and the Academic Labor Movement.* New York: Routledge.

Kandell, Jonathan. 2004. "Jacques Derrida, Abstruse Theorist, Dies in Paris at 74." *New York Times,* October 10.

Kaplan, Steven Neil. 1998. "We Are All Henry Kravis Now." *Capital Ideas* 1.2. http://www.chicagobooth.edu/capideas/win98/kaplan.htm.

Keightley, Keir. 2004. "Long Play: Adult-Oriented Popular Music and the Temporal Logics of the Post-War Sound Recording Industry in the USA." *Media, Culture, and Society* 26.3:375–91.

Kheshti, Roshanak. 2008. "Musical Miscegenation and the Logic of Rock and Roll: Homosocial Desire and Racial Productivity in 'A Paler Shade of White.'" *American Quarterly* 60.4:1037–53.

Kirby, David. 2004. "Theory in Chaos." *Christian Science Monitor,* January 27.

Krug, Steve. 2005. *Don't Make Me Think: A Common Sense Approach to Web Usability.* New York: New Riders Press.

Lambert, Gregg. 2002. *The Non-Philosophy of Gilles Deleuze.* London: Athlone.

Laurence, David. 2002. "The Latest Forecast." *ADE Bulletin* 131:14–19.

Lipsitz, George. 2007. *Footsteps in the Dark: Hidden Histories of Popular Music.* Minneapolis: University of Minnesota Press.

Lloyd, Carol. 1997. "I Was Michel Foucault's Love Slave." Salon.com, February.

Malabou, Catherine. 2007. "The End of Writing? Grammatology and Plasticity." *The European Legacy* 12.4:431–41.

———. 2009. *Plasticity at the Dusk of Writing: Dialectic, Destruction, Deconstruction.* Translated by Carolyn Shred. New York: Columbia University Press.

Marcus, Greil. 1990. *Lipstick Traces: A Secret History of the 20th Century.* Cambridge, MA: Harvard University Press.

Martin, Randy, ed. 1998. *Chalk Lines: The Politics of Work in the Managed University.* Durham, NC: Duke University Press.

———. 2002. *The Financialization of Daily Life.* Philadelphia: Temple University Press.

Marx, Karl. 1894. *Capital, Volume 3.* http://www.marxists.org/archive/marx/
works/1894-c3/index.htm.

Massumi, Brian. 1992. *A User's Guide to "Capitalism and Schizophrenia."* Cambridge, MA: MIT Press.

Maysles, Albert, David Maysles, and Charlotte Zwerwin. 1970. *Gimme Shelter.*
Los Angeles: Maysles Films and Cinema 5 Distributing.

McHale, Brian. 2007. "What Was Postmodernism?" Electronic Book Review,
December 20. http://www.electronicbookreview.com/thread/fictionspresent/
tense.

"Median Salaries of College Administrators by Job Category and Type of Institution, 2004–5." 2005. *Chronicle of Higher Education*, March 4. http://chroni-
cle.com/section/Home/5.

Mehdi, Semati. 2008. *Media, Culture, and Society in Iran: Living with Globalization and the Islamic State.* New York: Routledge.

Metcalf, Stephen. 2005. "The Death of Literary Theory." Slate.com, November
17.

Miller, J. Hillis. 1979. "The Critic as Host." In *Deconstruction and Criticism*, edited by Harold Bloom et al., 217–54. New York: Seabury Press.

———. 1987. *The Ethics of Reading.* New York: Columbia University Press.

Miyoshi, Masao. 2000a. "Ivory Tower in Escrow." *boundary 2* 27.1:7–50.

———. 2000b. "The University and the 'Global' Economy: The Cases of the
United States and Japan." *South Atlantic Quarterly* 99.4:669–96.

Moore, Allan. 2002. "Authenticity as Authentication." *Popular Music* 21.1:209–
23.

Murphy, Timothy. 1997. *Wising Up the Marks: The Amodern William Burroughs.*
Berkeley: University of California Press.

Natale, Samuel M., Anthony F. Libertella, and Geoff Hayward. 2001. *Higher
Education in Crisis: The Corporate Eclipse of the University.* Binghamton, NY:
Global.

National Education Association. 1998–2003. *Update* 4.3–4, 7.4, 9.2, 9.4. http://www.nea.org/home/34258.htm.

Nealon, Christopher. 2009. "Reading on the Left." *Representations* 108:22–50.

Nealon, Jeffrey T. 1993. *Double Reading: Postmodernism after Deconstruction.* Ithaca, NY: Cornell University Press.

———. 1998. *Alterity Politics: Ethics and Performative Subjectivity.* Durham, NC: Duke University Press.

———. 2008. *Foucault beyond Foucault: Power and Its Intensifications since 1984.* Stanford, CA: Stanford University Press.

Negri, Antonio. 1996. *Marxism beyond Marxism,* edited by Saree Makdisi et al. New York: Routledge.

———. 1999. "The Specter's Smile." In *Ghostly Demarcations: A Symposium on Jacques Derrida's* Specters of Marx, edited by Michael Sprinker, 5–16. London: Verso.

Nelson, Cary, ed. 1997. *Will Teach for Food: Academic Labor in Crisis.* Minneapolis: University of Minnesota Press.

———. 2010. *No University Is an Island.* New York: NYU Press.

Nelson, Cary, and Stephen Watt. 2004. *Office Hours: Activism and Change in the Academy.* New York: Routledge.

Ngai, Sianne. 2007. *Ugly Feelings.* Cambridge, MA: Harvard University Press.

Nietzsche, Friedrich. 1967. *"On the Genealogy of Morals" and "Ecce Homo."* Translated by Walter Kaufmann and R. J. Hollingdale. New York: Vintage.

———. 1974. *The Gay Science.* Translated by Walter Kaufmann. New York: Vintage.

———. 1982. *Daybreak: Thoughts on the Prejudices of Morality.* Translated by R. J. Hollingdale. Cambridge: Cambridge University Press.

———. 1989. "On Truth and Lying in an Extra-Moral Sense." In *Friedrich Nietzsche on Rhetoric and Language,* edited and translated by Sander L. Gilman, Carole Blair, and David J. Parent, 246–57. New York: Oxford University Press.

Noble, David. 1997–2001. "Digital Diploma Mills, Parts I–V." http://communication.ucsd.edu/dl/.

Nussbaum, Martha. 2010. *Not for Profit: Why Democracy Needs the Humanities.* Princeton: Princeton University Press.

Obama, Barack. 2008. CNBC Interview, June 10. http://thepage.time.com/obama-interview-on-cnbc/.

Parenti, Christian. 2000. *Lockdown America.* London: Verso.

Peters, Tom. 1988. *In Search of Excellence: Lessons from America's Best-Run Companies.* New York: Warner.

Pynchon, Thomas. 1972. *Gravity's Rainbow*. New York: Vintage.

Readings, Bill. 1996. *The University in Ruins*. Cambridge, MA: Harvard University Press.

Reich, Robert. 1992. *The Work of Nations: Preparing Ourselves for 21st Century Capitalism*. New York: Vintage.

Reynolds, Simon. 2011. *Retromania: Pop Culture's Addiction to Its Own Past*. London: Faber and Faber.

Rose, Gillian. 1978. *The Melancholy Science: An Introduction to the Thought of Theodor Adorno*. London: Macmillan.

Rose, Nikolas. 2006. *The Politics of Life Itself: Biomedicine, Power, and Subjectivity in the Twenty-First Century*. Princeton: Princeton University Press.

Shumway, David R. 2007. "Authenticity: Modernity, Stardom, and Rock & Roll." *Modernism/Modernity* 14.3:527–33.

Siebers, Tobin. 1993. *Cold War Criticism and the Politics of Skepticism*. Oxford: Oxford University Press.

Simmel, Georg. 1978. *The Philosophy of Money*. Edited by David Frisby. Translated by Tom Bottomore and David Frisby. London: Routledge.

Slaughter, Sheila, and Larry Leslie. 1997. *Academic Capitalism: Politics, Policies, and the Entrepreneurial University*. Baltimore: Johns Hopkins University Press.

Slaughter, Sheila, and Gary Rhodes. 2004. *Academic Capitalism and the New Economy: Market, State, and Higher Education*. Baltimore: Johns Hopkins University Press.

Smallwood, Scott. 2004. "2 Professors at U. of Southern Mississippi Settle for Pay without Jobs." *Chronicle of Higher Education*, May 14. http://chronicle.com/section/Home/5.

———. 2005. "Faculty Salaries Rose 2.8%, but Failed to Keep Pace with Inflation for the First Time in 8 Years." *Chronicle of Higher Education*, April 22. http://chronicle.com/section/Home/5.

Smith, Dinitia. 2004. "Cultural Theorists, Start Your Epitaphs." *New York Times*, January 3.

Solomon, Deborah. 2005. "Continental Drift: Questions for Jean Baudrillard." *New York Times Magazine*, November 20.

Spicer, Jack. 2008. *My Vocabulary Did This to Me: The Collected Poetry of Jack Spicer*. Edited by Peter Gizzi and Kevin Killian. Middletown, CT: Wesleyan University Press.

Strange, Susan. 1997. *Casino Capitalism*. Manchester, UK: Manchester University Press.

Thompson, Hunter. 1998. *Fear and Loathing in Las Vegas*. New York: Vintage.

Tighe, Thomas. 2003. *Who's in Charge of America's Research Universities?* Albany: SUNY Press.

Tompkins, Jane, ed. 1980. *Reader-Response Criticism: From Formalism to Post-Structuralism*. Baltimore: Johns Hopkins University Press.

Turner, Tom. 1996. *City as Landscape: A Post-Postmodern View of Design and Planning*. London: Taylor and Francis.

Venturi, Robert. 1977. *Learning from Las Vegas*. Cambridge, MA: MIT Press.

Virno, Paulo. 2004. *A Grammar of the Multitude*. Translated by Isabella Bertoletti et al. New York: Semiotext(e).

Ward, Paula Reed. 2004. "Curtains for PSU Theatre Teacher?" *Pittsburgh Post-Gazette*, February 24.

Washburn, Jennifer. 2005. *University, Inc.: The Corporate Corruption of American Higher Education*. New York: Basic.

Watkins, Evan. 1989. *Work Time: English Departments and the Circulation of Cultural Value*. Stanford, CA: Stanford University Press.

———. 2009. *Class Degrees: Vocational Education, Work, and Class Formation in the US*. New York: Fordham University Press.

Wegner, Philip. 2009. *Life between Two Deaths, 1989–2001: US Culture in the Long Nineties*. Durham, NC: Duke University Press.

Welles, Orson. 1973. *F for Fake*. Paris: Janus Films.

White, Geoffry, and Flannery C. Hauck, eds. 2000. *Campus, Inc.: Corporate Power in the Ivory Tower*. Amherst, NY: Prometheus.

Williams, Christina. 2001. "Does It Really Matter? Young People and Popular Music." *Popular Music* 20.2:223–42.

Williams, Jeffrey, ed. 2001. "Academostars." *Minnesota Review* 52–54.

Williams, Raymond. 1980. *Problems in Materialism and Culture*. London: New Left Books.

Williams, William Carlos. 1923. "The Red Wheelbarrow." http://writing.upenn.edu/~afilreis/88/wcw-red-wheel.html.

Wilson, Carl. 2007. "The Trouble with Indie Rock. It's Not Just Race. It's Class." Slate. com, October 18. http://www.slate.com/id/2176187/.

World Economic Forum. *Annual Report, 2010–11*. http://www.weforum.org/reports.

Zizek, Slavoj. 1993. *Tarrying with the Negative: Kant, Hegel and the Critique of Ideology*. Durham, NC: Duke University Press.

———. 2003. *Organs without Bodies: Deleuze and Consequences*. New York: Routledge.

Index